Culturally Responsive Reading

Teaching Literature for Social Justice

Durthy A. Washington

Foreword by Carolyn Denard

TEACHERS COLLEGE PRESS

TEACHERS COLLEGE | COLUMBIA UNIVERSITY
NEW YORK AND LONDON

Published by Teachers College Press,® 1234 Amsterdam Avenue, New York, NY 10027

Copyright © 2023 by Teachers College, Columbia University

Front cover image by paseven / iStock by Getty Images.

Library of Congress Cataloging-in-Publication Data
Names: Washington, Durthy, author. I Denard, Carolyn C., writer of foreword.
Title: Culturally responsive reading : teaching literature for social justice / Durthy A.
    Washington ; foreword by Carolyn Denard.
Description: New York, NY : Teachers College Press, [2023] I Includes
    bibliographical references and index. I Summary: "This book presents the
    LIST Paradigm to help educators 'unlock' literature with four keys to culture:
    Language, Identity, Space, and Time. The text includes teaching strategies,
    classroom examples, and texts by writers of color"—Provided by publisher.
Identifiers: LCCN 2022038415 (print) I LCCN 2022038416 (ebook) I
    ISBN 9780807768280 (paperback ; acid-free paper) I ISBN 9780807768297
    (hardcover) I ISBN 9780807781692 (ebook)
Subjects: LCSH: Literature—Study and teaching (Higher) I Literature—Study and
    teaching (Secondary) I Culturally relevant pedagogy. I Social justice and education.
Classification: LCC PN59 .W37 2023 (print) I LCC PN59 (ebook) I
    DDC 807.1—dc23/eng/20221024
LC record available at https://lccn.loc.gov/2022038415
LC ebook record available at https://lccn.loc.gov/2022038416

ISBN 978-0-8077-6828-0 (paper)
ISBN 978-0-8077-6829-7 (hardcover)
ISBN 978-0-8077-8169-2 (ebook)

One writes out of one thing only—one's own experience . . . This is the only concern of the artist, to recreate out of the disorder of life that order which is art.

—James Baldwin

One writes out of one thing only: one's own experience as understood and ordered through one's knowledge of self, culture, and literature.

—Ralph Ellison

For Alyssa and Kotomi

Contents

**PART II: EXPLORING THE LIST PARADIGM:
FOUR "KEYS TO CULTURE"**

PART III: EXPLORING THE LIST PARADIGM: UNLOCKING THE TEXT

Foreword

With the inclusion of multi-ethnic literature in high school and college class-rooms, beginning in the late 1970s, there has been a growing realization on the part of teachers and scholars who taught these works, that the traditional ways of analyzing literature—critical methods deeply rooted in Eurocentric literary and cultural paradigms—would need to change. Since the inclusion of these new works, the challenge for teachers has become how to provide concrete ways to give critical integrity to the reading and analysis of works which emanate artistically and culturally from different expressive spaces than the Eurocentric origins of the works that had been traditionally taught in literature classrooms. How could they, in other words, teach their students to read these new works in ways that were culturally responsive?

In this new work, *Culturally Responsive Reading: Teaching Literature for Social Justice*, Durthy A. Washington offers a critical paradigm to address this challenge. As she points out in her introduction,

> Today's students generally have few problems locating books by writers of color. But since they receive little guidance on how to approach these texts, they may feel frustrated upon realizing that the guidelines they learned to access and ana-lyze the works of Ernest Hemingway fall short when applied to the works of Ernest Gaines. To help students bridge this gap, I developed the LIST Paradigm.

Washington's LIST Paradigm is comprised of four components: Language, Identity, Space, and Time. Each component includes a core, focus question that guides the analysis: (1) "How does the author contextualize linguistic signs and symbols?"; (2) "Who are these people and what do they want?"; (3) "How do characters negotiate the text's physical, psychological, and cultural landscapes?"; and (4) "How does the author manipulate time?" These questions provide a guided way for students to analyze key components of any literary text with cultural and artistic integrity, and they help teachers, as Washington argues "bridge the gap between the conventional study of litera-ture, and the new multi-cultural literature that is now being taught."

Washington has used the LIST Paradigm successfully in her teaching dur-ing her 16-year career as a professor at the U.S. Air Force Academy, and she has written articles and presented the LIST Paradigm at many teacher workshops around the country to help other teachers understand and implement its strategies in their classrooms. In the summer of 2003 and in 2005, Washington presented the Paradigm at the Toni Morrison Society's NEH-sponsored workshop for high school teachers called "Language Matters" in Washington, D.C., and Cincinnati, Ohio respectively. In each of these workshops, she led 20 teachers from across the country in developing lesson plans for teaching *Song of Solomon* and *Beloved* according to guidelines of the LIST Paradigm, guidelines that they could later use when developing plans to teach other minority ethnic writers as well.

As Washington has developed the LIST Paradigm over the years, she has continued to expand the works that have been the focus of her analysis to include different genres and the works of younger contemporary writers from different cultural backgrounds. The list of multicultural works that she uses in her classes not only includes the fiction works we know by Morrison, Gaines, Walker, Wright, Hurston, Baldwin, and Ellison, but it has been expanded to include poetry, nonfiction essays, memoir, and the fictional works of other writers like Edwidge Danticat, Junot Díaz, Ruth Ozeki, Charles Yu, Ocean Vuong, Viet Thanh Nguyen, and others. The LIST Paradigm will be especially helpful with this new generation of post-colonial writers whose commitments to the nuances of their culture in language and world view are even more intentional than minority ethnic writers who preceded them.

This volume will be a useful critical and pedagogical resource for teachers who are teaching these new writers in their classes. Each chapter has an introduction to and sample analyses of each component of the LIST Paradigm and a set of significant questions to guide class discussions. The volume also contains an invaluable set of supplemental resources for teachers: literary history, definitions of terms, a reader's guide, a bibliography, author biographies, and an appendix with questions for further analysis.

There is still much work that needs to be done in our efforts to teach in culturally responsive ways. Washington's book, outlining her new LIST Paradigm, provides an important foundation, especially for secondary teachers, to develop the strategies needed to help students read and analyze literature by writers from different cultural backgrounds. Our task now as teachers, scholars, and students of multicultural and post-colonial literature is to use these culturally responsive strategies in our approach to the new literature being added to the canon and to build on the contribution that scholars like Washington are making to create a systematic pedagogy that respects the cultural and artistic underpinnings of these new works.

Carolyn Denard
Atlanta, Georgia
November 2022

Acknowledgments

My deepest gratitude to the people without whom this book would still be "a dream deferred": Emily Spangler, my acquisitions editor at Teachers College Press, who believed in my project; Heather Jordan, my copyeditor, who saw me through countless drafts and revisions; and my Number One Son, Curtis Jevon, who inspired me and kept me moving forward.

I would also like to thank my parents and siblings, who made it possible for me to be where I am today.

Preface

"Why Are We Reading This?"

THE *TAR BABY* INCIDENT

Shortly after I started my first semester (spring 1999) with the Department of English and Fine Arts at the U.S. Air Force Academy, the course director for one of our "core" courses—"English 211: Literature and Intermediate Composition"—received an email from a cadet who objected to the inclusion of Toni Morrison's *Tar Baby* in the course syllabus. He couldn't "see a plot" to the story, dismissed it as "a romance novel," and found some of the sex scenes and language "very offensive." He arrogantly concluded that "we should not be reading [this book] because it has no literary value."

The course director, Major Tom Krise, who soon became a valued mentor and role model, did not dismiss the cadet's comments or chastise him for his ignorance. Instead, he responded with an eloquent, two-page email that he shared with all English 211 instructors. After disabusing the cadet of his misguided notions and introducing him to Toni Morrison, he went on to address the centrality of *Tar Baby* in the course and zeroed in on the cadet's resistance to reading it:

> The theme of English 211 this year is "Race and Identity" and is designed to get students to think seriously about how race contributes to our sense of identity and the social problems that engenders. *Tar Baby* is one of the best texts in the course for exploring these important issues.
>
> I am glad that you find some of the language in *Tar Baby* to be offensive. That suggests that our efforts to eradicate sexist, racist, and other hateful speech from our institution are being successful. But the idea of refusing to read (or see, as in art or film) anything that might offend you is the pathway to willful ignorance, not culture and education. I would hope that you are offended by the human sacrifice in the *Iliad*, the murdering of POWs in Shakespeare's *Henry V*, the unjustified torching of a town in the film *Glory*, or the abuse of power in Nabokov's *Lolita*. And I wouldn't be surprised if you were offended by the sexual language of the Old Testament's "Song of Solomon." But that doesn't mean that I also hope that you won't read or see these works. We the People expect our commissioned officers to be well educated—you can't hope to be so if you refuse

to read or appreciate works of the human imagination that challenge your sense
of propriety and value . . .

If you'd like to chat in person about any or all of this, I'd be happy to set up
an EI [Extra Instruction] appointment with you. (Krise, 1999)

Over the years, I shared this email with my own cadets on several occa-
sions as my selections for course texts were also challenged by students who
failed to see the "relevance" of reading works by writers of color, and who
became especially indignant if I included more than one text by a Black writer.
I cite it here because it illustrates two key issues concerning the teaching of
multicultural texts: (1) that these texts are often dismissed or discounted as
"less than" texts by White authors (such as Faulkner and Hemingway); and
(2) that because of their limited exposure to multicultural literature in high
school, students often enter college already predisposed to view works by
writers of color as irrelevant to their formal education. What's more, they
presumably feel entitled not only to challenge the reading of these texts in the
classroom, but also to question their place in the Western literary canon, ex-
hibiting an audacity in their ignorance that they would undoubtedly hesitate
to articulate regarding a "classic" Eurocentric text.

Unfortunately, our current educational system rarely includes works by
writers of color in the core curriculum, where works by writers of color are
often tolerated by being included in anthologies as "supplemental readings"
while the majority of readings focus on Western texts. Consequently, students
surmise that these works are not "relevant" to their education or worthy of
their attention. This approach is especially demeaning to students of color,
who conclude that writers of color have contributed nothing substantial to the
Western literary canon. As Gloria Naylor (1995) points out:

> We do not have to say to our children, "You are nothing." We don't have to
> stand up in an auditorium, or on a parade ground, and blatantly shout out to
> them, "You have nothing to give." We have done this much more effectively,
> through silence, through what they do *not* see, through what is *not* there when
> we parade before them what we declare is worthy. It is a very effective message.
> (pp. 172–173)

Naylor's observation reminds me of a defining moment in my academic
life: searching for a Black literature class at San Diego State University in the
fall of 1972. As I studied the course catalog, my pulse quickened when I came
across a class titled "Black Humor." Not sure what to expect—Redd Foxx
and Richard Pryor?—I was surprised to discover, on the first day of class, that
I had enrolled in a course on the works of Kurt Vonnegut Jr.

Today's students generally have few problems locating books by writers
of color. But since they receive little guidance on how to approach these texts,
they may feel frustrated upon realizing that the guidelines they learned to

access and analyze the works of Ernest Hemingway fall short when applied to the works of Ernest Gaines. To help students bridge this gap, I developed the LIST Paradigm.

THE LIST PARADIGM: A GUIDED APPROACH TO TEACHING LITERATURE

The LIST Paradigm is a culturally responsive approach to reading (or teaching) literature that helps readers unlock the power of literature with four keys to culture: Language, Identity, Space, and Time. In essence, it prompts readers to *access* and *analyze* a text by *asking significant questions* designed to foster close reading and critical thinking. In its approach to critical reading, it combines aspects of *literary analysis* (exploring the elements of fiction, such as plot, setting, character, and point of view) and *literary criticism* (exploring works from various perspectives, such as historical, psychological, and archetypal).

By incorporating race, culture, and identity into the conventional study of literature, the LIST Paradigm bridges the gap between conventional literary analysis and cultural studies by encouraging readers to explore unique elements of multicultural literature often dismissed or discounted by "mainstream" scholars and critics. The LIST Paradigm encourages readers to move beyond conventional literary analysis and forge personal connections with a text.

Drawing on James Baldwin's observation that "The purpose of all art is to lay bare the questions which have been hidden by the answers," the LIST Paradigm focuses on four significant questions:

> *Language*: "How does the author contextualize linguistic signs and signals?"
> *Identity*: "Who are these people and what do they want?"
> *Space*: "How do characters negotiate the text's physical, psychological, and cultural landscapes?"
> *Time*: "How does the author manipulate time?"

Each question leads to a series of progressively more specific questions concerning each LIST component. Consequently, the LIST Paradigm guides students through the reading process by providing them with a series of significant questions designed to help them "unlock" a text while encouraging them to formulate their own questions.

In short, the LIST Paradigm provides a guided, culturally responsive approach to reading virtually any text.

Over the years, I have used the LIST Paradigm as the basis of numerous presentations at meetings of professional organizations such as the College Reading and Learning Association, the American Literature Association, and the National Association of African American Literature. I have also used it to teach graduate and undergraduate courses at several colleges and universities, including Colorado College and the U.S. Air Force Academy. In addition, I have published articles in academic texts and professional journals that illustrate how the LIST Paradigm can be used to teach works such as Ernest Gaines's *A Lesson Before Dying* and Toni Morrison's *Beloved* and *Song of Solomon*.

During my 16 years at the Air Force Academy (1999 to 2015), I used the LIST Paradigm to teach a broad range of texts. In addition to Jonathan Swift's *Gulliver's Travels*, Toni Morrison's *Song of Solomon*, and Chinua Achebe's *Things Fall Apart*—which, according to the criteria of most academic institutions, would be categorized as "mainstream," "minority," and "other"—I have used it to teach John Okada's *No-No Boy*, Ralph Ellison's *Invisible Man*, Ernest Gaines's *A Lesson Before Dying*, Franz Kafka's *The Metamorphosis*, Leo Tolstoy's *The Death of Ivan Ilych*, and N. Scott Momaday's *House Made of Dawn*. I have also used it as a framework for teaching the works of Gary Soto, Alice Walker, Sandra Cisneros, Leslie Marmon Silko, Ann Petry, Amy Tan, and Sherman Alexie. I have even used it to teach Shakespeare's *Macbeth* and *Othello*, for I soon discovered that—regardless of the various genres and categories we create to compartmentalize literature—any work that can withstand the scrutiny of active, inquisitive readers and the probing analyses of students, scholars, and critics can be taught effectively by instructors willing to do the work required to help students succeed.

Over the years, I have used the LIST Paradigm to teach a diverse range of students, such as the following.

Teaching Select Audiences

In the summer of 2003 and 2005, I served as a Visiting Scholar for the Language Matters Teaching Initiative, a series of professional development workshops for secondary school language arts teachers. The workshops, held at various locations across the United States, focus primarily on the challenges of teaching Toni Morrison's works to high school students. Sponsored by the Toni Morrison Society and funded by the National Endowment for the Humanities (NEH), the workshops are offered in conjunction with the Society's Biennial Conference.

In 2003, my workshop focused on *Song of Solomon*; in 2005, it focused on *Beloved*. In both instances, I knew that my audience and I shared a passion for Morrison's works. I was confident that they had read the novels in preparation for the workshop and that they were already familiar with Morrison's oeuvre and her status as a literary icon. This freed me to concentrate solely on the selected texts.

For *Song of Solomon*, each participant had a copy of my *Cliffs Notes* on the novel prior to the workshop. This enabled us to immediately forge connections among critical reading, literary criticism, and scholarly interpretations of literary works. Since I was aware that many teachers still view *Cliffs Notes* as "cheat sheets" for students who see them as an alternative to reading the novels, I discussed the process of creating the Notes, pointing out that while they do include plot summaries, character descriptions, and discussions of key themes, symbols, and images, they also include extensive research, discussion questions, and bibliographies designed to engage students and encourage them to conduct their own research.

For *Beloved*, we began with a discussion of the novel as a contemporary slave narrative, modeled after Harriet Jacobs's *Incidents in the Life of a Slave Girl*, that explores the interior life of an enslaved African woman, struggling to cope with the traumatic memories of slavery as well as her profound guilt over having killed her infant daughter to save her from slavery. We then forged connections between Sethe, Morrison's protagonist, and Margaret Garner, a woman who, in fact, did kill two of her children (Harris et. al., 1974). (Her story is told in a newspaper clipping included in *The Black Book*, a source Morrison cites as her inspiration for the novel.) Unlike Sethe, Garner was tried for her crimes and found guilty of destruction of property.

In both workshops, I introduced participants to the LIST Paradigm through two handouts I had prepared to guide their reading. (Versions of the LIST "Reader's Guide" are provided in **Appendix A.1**, created specifically for the selected novel, and Appendix B, "Defining Elements of Morrison's Fiction.") And in both cases, I received overwhelmingly positive feedback, with many participants stating that they would definitely use the LIST Paradigm in teaching their classes. Moreover, each workshop led to a published critical essay, which enabled me to contribute to the ever-expanding field of Morrison scholarship (see Washington, 2007, 2015).

Teaching Across Disciplines

In 2008, I taught a colloquium, "Teaching Multicultural Texts: Exploring the LIST Paradigm," as part of a series of summer programs at Colorado College. Designed for experienced teachers enrolled in the Master of Arts in Teaching program, the intensive, 1-week faculty development seminar consisted of 10 hours of training (5 days per week, 2 hours per day). To prepare students for the course and introduce them to the LIST Paradigm, I provided them with a copy of my critical essay, "Teaching Ernest Gaines's *A Lesson Before Dying*," which they were to read prior to our first meeting. The class consisted of eight students (1 male, 7 female), each of whom was currently engaged in teaching classes at various levels (elementary school, middle school, and high school) in several disciplines (English/Language Arts, geography, world history, American history, and social studies).

My goals for the class were straightforward: to encourage students to use the LIST Paradigm as a framework for teaching a text appropriate for their class. Since several students mentioned they had specific texts they were required to teach, I felt compelled to expand my guidelines to include works of nonfiction as well as novels and short stories. In addition to works such as Rudolfo Anaya's *Bless Me, Ultima*; Frank Waters's *The Man Who Killed the Deer*; Christopher Paul Curtis's *The Watsons Go to Birmingham*; and Piri Thomas's *Amigo Brothers*, selected texts included Elie Wiesel's *Night* and Jeanne Wakatsuki Houston's *Farewell to Manzanar*.

My structure was guided by our time frame: Day 1 consisted of class introductions, a course overview, an introduction to the LIST Paradigm, and a discussion of the essay. Days 2 through 4 consisted of discussions of the four LIST components (Language, Identity, Space, and Time), supplemented by selected readings. Day 5 was reserved for presentations, during which students shared some highlights from their course papers.

As I listened to each student's presentation, I was encouraged by their engagement and enthusiasm. Moreover, I was delighted to discover that, although I had designed the LIST Paradigm with high school and college-level English teachers in mind, it worked equally well for elementary and middle-school teachers across disciplines.

Teaching Community

As a former English professor, I particularly enjoy the opportunity to teach literature workshops and classes through two local Colorado Springs organizations: the Pikes Peak Library District's Adult Reading Program and the PILLAR Institute for Lifelong Learning, an organization consisting primarily of active senior citizens. The classes—brief 2-hour offerings I develop and present periodically throughout the year—not only provide me with an opportunity to share my passion for literature with adult learners, an engaging, inquisitive audience whose questions and insights never cease to surprise; they also remind me to stay focused on my personal mission to liberate literature from the confines of academia and make it accessible to general readers. What's more, they inspire me to keep writing, since the classes often lead to essays and articles.

In fall 2017, the library asked me to offer a course on "the classics." Given my focus on reading works by writers of color, I hesitated. But then I realized I could explore "the classics" while maintaining my personal commitment to multicultural literature by focusing on two key points: (1) our limited definition of "classics," which ignores the fact that every culture has its classics; and (2) the fact that reading "the classics" can help us understand and appreciate contemporary literary fiction. I created a class titled "Reading in Reverse: Connecting With 'the Classics.'" To illustrate the process, I began by introducing Viet Thanh Nguyen's *The Sympathizer* as a contemporary postmodern text that, through numerous references and allusions to "the classics," builds on and expands the literary landscape of "the Western canon." Consequently, we explored how Nguyen—by connecting with classics like Ralph Ellison's *Invisible Man*, T. S. Eliot's *The Waste Land*, and Joseph Conrad's *Heart of Darkness*—transforms dated definitions of classic literature.

We began our discussion by exploring various definitions of "classics" (classic cars, classic Coke, classic rock). Moving on to literature, we explored quotes from various writers ranging from Mark Twain ("A classic is something that everybody wants to have read and nobody wants to read") to Italo Calvino ("A classic is a book that has never finished saying what it has to say"). We then went on to explore how the works of Ellison, Eliot, and Conrad met the definition of "classic" literature and how all three works influenced Nguyen's novel, which provides a Vietnamese perspective of the Vietnam war. To facilitate discussion, I introduced participants to the LIST Paradigm through a handout I had created specifically for the novel. Based on the overwhelmingly positive response, which included an invitation to serve as facilitator for the library's book discussion group on *The Sympathizer* (see Chapter 3), I was convinced that the LIST Paradigm could be a useful tool for general readers as well as specialized audiences.

CREATING THE LIST PARADIGM

I created the LIST Paradigm in response to two eye-opening experiences during the mid-1990s that illustrated the pervasive—and potentially dangerous—misunderstandings and misconceptions surrounding the concept of culture that still persists in the teaching of literature, which often excludes works by writers of color or leads to egregious misreadings of their works.

The first was a diversity training seminar presented by the Colorado Equal Opportunity/Affirmative Action Coalition, Inc. Apparently uncomfortable with the topic of racial and ethnic diversity, the facilitator decided to open his presentation by discussing "Diversity at the Personal Level." To illustrate this concept, he displayed a graphic of two concentric circles. The smaller, innermost circle contained the single word "people." The larger, outermost circle (which resembled a makeshift pie chart) consisted of 16 segments, each depicting an aspect of "personal diversity," such as age, gender, race/nationality, social class, and sexual orientation. One of the segments was labeled "culture," implying not only that culture is a characteristic equivalent to age or gender, but also that it is a separate and distinctive personality trait, rather than an all-encompassing concept that shapes and influences every aspect of our lives. I'm sure that, at some point, he addressed racial and ethnic diversity, but by that time, I had long since tuned out.

The second was a summer course for "at risk" high school students I taught while an adjunct instructor at the University of Colorado Colorado Springs (UCCS). I was not surprised to find that my class consisted primarily of Black and Latino students. Aware of the research surrounding the disproportionate labeling of "minority" students—who are rarely exposed to the works of writers from their own cultures—I resolved to remedy the situation. Scanning my bookshelves, I selected several works by some of my favorite African American writers including James Baldwin, Langston Hughes, Toni Morrison, Alice Walker, and Ernest Gaines. When I reviewed my rather sparse collection of Latino writers, I turned to a colleague for recommendations. As a result, my syllabus also included works by Rudolfo Anaya, Sandra Cisneros, Gary Soto, Julia Alvarez, and Jimmy Santiago Baca. And although the course presented some unique challenges, when students started to linger after class instead of dashing for the door at the first sound of the bell, I felt that I had made a small but significant impact on their lives.

Given such egregious distortions and misconceptions of culture and diversity in the macrocosm of society at large, it is not surprising that they persist in the microcosm of the classroom. Consequently, teachers who find themselves caught in the crossfire of "the canon wars" may decide that teaching "the classics" is ultimately safer—and far less stressful—than the alternative: taking proactive steps to develop a multicultural curriculum.

Based on countless conversations with instructors from various institutions seeking effective strategies for teaching multicultural texts—loosely defined as works by women and writers of color who have been historically excluded from the Western canon—I became convinced that much of the reluctance to teach these texts stems not from an unwillingness to explore unfamiliar territory, but rather from feelings of frustration that some of the best, time-tested methods for teaching Western Eurocentric literature simply do not "work" for non-Western texts.

Pedagogy: Applying the LIST Paradigm

Culturally Responsive Reading provides a practical approach to reading these texts through the LIST Paradigm. Depending on course content and instructional objectives, teachers may view the LIST Paradigm from a variety of perspectives: as a teaching strategy that promotes active reading and critical thinking, as a concept map for analyzing the diverse aspects of culture, or as a tool for advocating Paulo Freire's philosophy of "education as the practice of freedom." They may also use it to explore some of the critical questions that must be addressed by anyone involved in the teaching of literature:

- How can we, as teachers, make multicultural texts more accessible to our students?
- How can we avoid the egregious error of misreading multicultural texts by approaching them through the lens of Western Eurocentric culture?
- How can we develop an inclusive multicultural curriculum that bridges the gap between "mainstream" and "minority" literatures?

Having addressed these issues, we are infinitely better prepared to enter the classroom and answer that inevitable question, "Why are we reading this?" We are also more likely to realize that the teaching of works by writers of color—not unlike the teaching of "mainstream" texts—demands an awareness of the cultural context that shaped the work, an awareness that, in turn, allows us to explore literature through the author's (and the reader's) "ethnic lens" rather than through the distorted lens of monocultural monocles. This paradigm shift is critical if we are to move from a culturally relevant approach to literature, which presumes that a selected text can "represent" an entire cultural or ethnic group, to a culturally responsive approach, which emphasizes diversity within cultures.

Rather than advocating a restrictive, formulaic approach to the study of literature (such as the linear approach provided by the Freytag Pyramid, which traces a work's narrative arc from inciting action to resolution), the LIST Paradigm encourages the study of literature from multiple perspectives. Drawing on the research and scholarship of eminent educators and cultural critics such as James Banks, Geneva Gay, bell hooks, Robert Stepto, and Henry Louis Gates Jr., *Culturally Responsive Reading* advocates a redesign of our educational system from "teaching to conform" to "teaching to transform" and presents the LIST Paradigm as a dynamic, culturally responsive framework for achieving this objective. In short, this text offers practical strategies for making nontraditional texts more accessible to students by expanding and transcending the boundaries of the Western literary canon.

Early approaches to teaching non-Western texts often focused on separating "ethnic" literatures into four disparate groups: African American, Native American, Mexican American, and Asian American, an approach employed by John R. Maitino and David R. Peck's *Teaching American Ethnic Literatures*. And while such an approach is certainly valid and highlights four broad groups that have been historically excluded from the Western canon, it fails to identify more specific groups within each category, such as Afro-Caribbean writers from countries such as Haiti and the Dominican Republic; writers who identify with their Chinese, Japanese, or Vietnamese roots; Hawaiian and Pacific Islanders; or Latinx writers from countries other than Mexico. Rather than privileging the writer's cultural identity, the LIST Paradigm focuses first and foremost on the writer's works. Consequently, although it foregrounds cultural elements, they do not overshadow the text as a literary work of art.

Developing a Diverse Curriculum

Several texts have addressed the need to develop a more diverse curriculum not only by including more texts by multicultural writers, but also by recognizing and respecting the diversity of our students. (Examples include Birkenstein & Hauhart, 2017; Borsheim-Black & Sarigianides, 2019; Gay, 2018; Howard, 2016; and Watson et al.; 2018). But while each of these texts offers insightful ideas for transforming the literature classroom, none provides specific guidelines for approaching virtually any text (poem, short story, novel, or play) through the lens of culture.

In his insightful essay "Globalizing Literary Study," Edward Said (2001) explores the shift in literary study over the past several decades:

> For scholars and teachers of my generation who were educated in what was an essentially Eurocentric mode, the landscape and topography of literary study have . . . been altered dramatically and irreversibly. Literary study now operates with different aims and goals. . . . scholars of the new generation are much more attuned to the non-European, genderized, decolonized, and decentered energies and currents of our time. (p. 65)

Said's essay vehemently rejects the cultural arrogance of British imperialists who claimed that "a single shelf of a good European library [is] worth the whole native literature of India and Arabia" (Jeffrey, 2017, p. 23).

In *Required Reading: Why Our American Classics Matter Now*, Andrew Delbanco (1997) takes a more inclusive approach to reading and teaching "the classics." Recognizing that the phrase is not reserved exclusively for Western Eurocentric texts, he includes two African American classics—Zora Neale Hurston's *Their Eyes Were Watching God* and Richard Wright's *Native Son*—on his list of "required reading." In doing so, he also acknowledges an often-overlooked fact: Each culture has its own classics that are revered by its people and that are not modeled on "the classics" revered by the West.

In his essay "MFA vs. POC" (People of Color), Junot Díaz expresses a similar concern, lamenting the fact that his MFA program at Cornell during the early 1990s had almost no people of color. As Díaz (2018b) points out:

> From what I saw the plurality of students and faculty had been educated exclusively in the tradition of writers like William Gaddis, Francine Prose, or Alice Munro—and not at all in the traditions of Toni Morrison, Cherríe Moraga, Maxine Hong Kingston, Arundhati Roy, Edwidge Danticat, Alice Walker, or Jamaica Kincaid. In my workshop the default subject position of reading and writing—of Literature with a capital L—was White, straight, and male. . . . Simply put, I was a person of color in a workshop whose theory of reality did not include my most fundamental experiences as a person of color—that did not, in other words, include *me*. (pp. 165–166)

Determined to remedy this situation, Díaz went on to cofound VONA (Voices of Our Nation Arts Foundation), which endeavors to support writers of color.

Clearly, despite the current focus on diversity and multiculturalism, much work remains to be done to bring the works of writers of color into the mainstream of literary study.

Introduction

Culturally Responsive Reading:
What It Is and Why It Matters

Despite renewed emphasis on diversity training, multiculturalism, and culturally responsive teaching over the past several decades, the conventional approach to reading and teaching literature still centers predominantly on a Western paradigm based on "classic" Eurocentric texts such as Homer's *Odyssey*, Shakespeare's plays, and the Bible. But reading multicultural literature—especially works by writers of color—through the lens of Western Eurocentric culture often distorts these texts and leads to egregious misreadings. In short, works by non-Western writers tend to be judged by two criteria: (1) how closely the work resembles that of Western writers, and (2) how well it "represents" the writer's culture. Neither approach honors the unique rhetorical devices non-Western writers bring to their works in terms of language, imagery, and symbolism.

To address this issue, I propose a paradigm shift to *culturally responsive reading:* Close, critical reading that foregrounds a work's cultural context, engages students emotionally and intellectually, and challenges them to expand their worldview and their frame of reference for reading and analyzing literature. It acknowledges and honors the culture that shaped a text and highlights the author's distinctive linguistic and rhetorical devices. Culturally responsive reading recognizes that every culture has its own narrative tradition of oral and written classics that inform its contemporary literature and rejects the notion that Western Eurocentric "classics" provide models and touchstones for non-Western texts. It seeks to expose cultural myths, reveal racist and culturally biased language, dismantle stereotypes, and prevent the egregious misreading of works by writers of color through the distorted lens of white supremacy. Ultimately, culturally responsive reading invites students to explore the intertextuality of literature, discover the power of telling their own stories, and think more deeply and compassionately about the world. Culturally responsive reading can significantly enhance our reading experience and transform our relationship to the study of literature.

1

Reflecting on her own writing, Nobel laureate Toni Morrison (1984) states:

> I don't like to find my books condemned as bad or praised as good, when that condemnation or praise is based on criteria from other paradigms. I would much prefer that they were dismissed or embraced based on the success of their accomplishment within the culture out of which I write. (p. 342)

In her seminal essay, "Unspeakable Things Unspoken: The Afro-American Presence in American Literature," Morrison notes that "classic" Western texts, from Greek tragedies to Melville's *Moby-Dick*, reflect the culture that created them. Morrison (1990) then cites four arguments traditionally used to denigrate "third world art":

> (1) There is no Afro-American (or third world) art; (2) it exists but is inferior; (3) it exists and is superior when it measures up to the "universal" criteria of Western art; (4) it is not so much "art" as ore—rich ore—that requires a Western or Eurocentric smith to refine it from its "natural" state into an aesthetically complex form. (p. 206)

The "unspeakable things," of course, are race and racism. Insisting that "Cultures . . . seek meaning in the language and images available to them" (1990, p. 208), Morrison proceeds to dismantle the four arguments by describing the process she used to create her first five novels: *The Bluest Eye* (1970/1994a), *Sula* (1973), *Song of Solomon* (1977), *Tar Baby* (1981), and *Beloved* (1987/2004). In essence, she demonstrates that while her works focus on the experiences of Black characters and draw primarily on the richness of African and African American culture and literature, they also acknowledge their undeniable links to Western Eurocentric culture. This stance is perhaps most evident in *Song of Solomon*, which incorporates biblical imagery, Greek myths, and European fairy tales in a novel rooted in Black culture and history.

Morrison recognizes the powerful impact of culture on the creative process and the critical link between culture and literature. In this respect, her philosophy echoes that of Ralph Ellison (1994), who declares, "One writes out of one thing only: one's own experience as understood and ordered through one's knowledge of self, culture, and literature" (p. 57).

Culturally responsive reading recognizes the importance of a writer's worldview (*Weltanschauung*). For example, Ellison's worldview as a Black man shaped by segregation and Jim Crow differs dramatically from Morrison's worldview as a Black woman shaped by the Civil Rights and Black Arts/Black Power Movements. To take a more extreme example, although both William Faulkner and Richard Wright are Southern writers from Mississippi, Wright's depiction of "the South" bears little resemblance to Faulkner's.

But what is culture? How does it impact our reading experience? And what are the "other paradigms" to which Morrison refers?

As discussed in Chapter 1, definitions of culture have changed dramatically over time. But regardless of how we choose to define it, we continually come back to three fundamental "truths": (1) culture is rooted in the beliefs and values held by a people, (2) language is the basis of culture, and (3) culture shapes our perceptions of reality. Once we acknowledge these truths, we can begin to forge meaningful connections between culture and literature. We can also start to explore some similarities and differences between multicultural literatures and Western Eurocentric texts. And we can address some differences between reading literature through the lens of Western Eurocentric culture—distorted by racism, colonialism, and white supremacy—and reading it through the lens of the culture that created it.

"MOVING OUT BEYOND YOURSELF": COPING WITH CULTURE SHOCK

In her 2000 essay, "Moving Out Beyond Yourself," Natalie Goldberg, a Jewish American writer, describes her frustrations with struggling to grasp the unique vision and narrative structure of Leslie Marmon Silko's *Ceremony* (1977). The novel tells the story of Tayo, a mixed-race Indian and World War II veteran suffering from PTSD who returns to his Navajo community a broken man. Having exhausted the limits of Western medicine, Tayo's only hope for recovery is a traditional ceremony performed by a local healer. With its numerous flashbacks, its circular narrative structure, and its emphasis on oral tradition (such as songs, chants, and prayers), the novel clearly reflects the worldview of the Navajo people. Goldberg (2000) writes,

> My mind couldn't grasp this. I was used to novels formed by white culture and the way they saw the world. I was comfortable with that: the story was set up, you entered and were carried along down the book. This was stretching my brain—I was afraid it would snap. (p. 112)

Goldberg's culture shock reflects the experience of countless readers raised on Western "classics." But she recognizes that her frustration stems from her ignorance of Native American culture and literature, as well as her failure to grasp the unique vision and narrative structure of Silko's novel. And she admits that she is not mentally or emotionally prepared to enter Silko's world. But several weeks later, she returns to the novel and approaches it from a fresh perspective. This time, she finds herself engaged in the narrative and able to connect with both the novel and its author.

Unlike Goldberg, few readers who encounter works that challenge their preconceived notions of literature will take time to process their reactions and find new ways to enter a text. Instead, they are more likely to dismiss the work as too complex or to attempt to read it through the lens of Western culture.

DEFINING "AMERICAN" LITERATURE:
READING WESTERN "CLASSICS"

But where do these preconceptions originate? What are the "novels formed by White culture"? And what are the "other paradigms" to which Morrison refers? To address these questions, we must turn to a text that virtually every American student has encountered in the classroom: Mark Twain's *The Adventures of Huckleberry Finn.*

Published in 1885, Twain's novel tells the story of Huck Finn, a 12-year-old White boy from rural Mississippi who runs away from home to escape the violence and restrictions of his family and community. Along the way, he meets the enslaved African, "Nigger Jim," and decides to help him escape. Together, the two embark on a journey down the Mighty Mississippi, seeking freedom and independence.

Since we accept Twain as an *American* author, we tend to overlook that he is a White, Southern writer born and raised in Missouri, writing through the lens of White, Southern culture. On the other hand, we find it difficult to accept Ralph Ellison and Toni Morrison as simply American authors. As Morrison (1992) points out, "American means white, and Africanist people struggle to make the term applicable to themselves with ethnicity and hyphen after hyphen after hyphen" (p. 47).

In her analysis of *Huckleberry Finn*, Morrison (1999) reveals that "fear and alarm are what I remember most about my first encounter with [the novel]," which she describes as "deeply disturbing" (p. 385). I experienced a similar sensation on my first encounter with the novel. So did my siblings. So did my son. Undoubtedly, for students of color, much of the "fear and alarm" stems from the word "nigger" sprinkled liberally throughout the text. Clearly, Twain recognized repetition as an effective rhetorical device. Yet one wonders what compelled him to repeat the racial slur 219 times in the space of 320 pages (Schutz, 2011).

But Morrison (1992) focuses on an issue that resonates at a deeper level; as she points out:

> Two things strike us in this novel: the apparently limitless store of love and com-passion the black man has for his white friend and white masters; and his as-sumption that the whites are indeed what they say they are, superior and adult. This representation of Jim as the visible other can be read as the yearning of whites for forgiveness and love, but the yearning is made possible only when it is understood that Jim has recognized his inferiority (not as slave, but as black) and despises it. (p. 56)

In short, *Huckleberry Finn* illustrates the "other paradigms" that per-petuate the "Myth of White Supremacy" through characteristics such as the following:

- The reading audience is presumed to be White.
- Unless noted otherwise, characters are assumed to be White.
- The beliefs and values of "classic" Western literature are presented as "universal."
- The culture of White, Eurocentric Americans is presented as the "default" culture.

But *Huckleberry Finn* does not stand alone in its racist depictions of African Americans. We must also consider the profound impact of two other "classics": Joseph Conrad's *Heart of Darkness*, which established the image of Africa as the "Dark Continent" and its inhabitants as wild Black savages, and Margaret Mitchell's *Gone With the Wind*, which created a nostalgia for the antebellum South, when Whites ruled over massive plantations and their Black slaves toiled in the fields. *Heart of Darkness* invariably appears on the required reading lists of liberal arts students, while *Gone With the Wind*, first published in 1936, ranks second only to the Bible among American readers (Harris Poll, 2014).

EXPLORING POSTCOLONIAL LITERATURE: TELLING OUR OWN STORIES

To counter the devastating impact of racism and make their voices heard, writers of color began to create their own unique narratives. But writers are readers. So it stands to reason that novice writers seek models to emulate as they create their first works.

In her 2018 essay, "The Danger of the Single Story" (the basis of her 2009 TED Talk), Nigerian author Chimamanda Ngozi Adichie, deeply influenced by her reading of British literature, ruefully recalls writing the kinds of stories she was reading:

> All my characters were white and blue-eyed, they played in the snow, they ate apples, and they talked a lot about the weather, how lovely it was that the sun had come out. Now, this despite the fact that I lived in Nigeria . . . We didn't have snow, we ate mangoes, and we never talked about the weather because there was no need to. (p. 216)

Adichie concludes that her experience demonstrates "how impressionable and vulnerable we are in the face of a story, particularly as children." She notes that later in her career, "because of writers like Chinua Achebe and Camara Laye, I went through a mental shift in my perception of literature. I realized that people like me, girls with skin the color of chocolate, whose kinky hair could not form ponytails, could also exist in literature." Consequently, Adichie (2018) notes, "I started to write about things I recognized" (p. 216).

ACHIEVING AGENCY: REJECTING "THE WHITE CRITERION"

Adichie's story illustrates the chasm created by stories steeped in the "Myth of White Supremacy" (see Chapter 1).

It also illustrates the process of "miseducation" often suffered by children of color, as documented in Carter G. Woodson's classic text *The Mis-Education of the Negro* (1933), in which he asserts that the American educational system is designed to reinforce the theory of Black inferiority, a theme echoed more than 3 decades later by James Baldwin in his oft-quoted essay, "A Talk to Teachers." Moreover, it speaks to the poet Clarence Major's (1968) pronouncement in "A Black Criterion" concerning the role of the Black artist/poet:

> The black poet confronted with western culture and civilization must isolate and define himself in as bold a relief as he can. He must chop away at the white criterion and destroy its hold on his black mind because seeing the world through white eyes from a black soul causes death. (p. 37)

Although Major's statement may seem overly dramatic, we would do well to note that "the white criterion" of Western European "classics" portrayed as models that set the standard for "quality" literature still persists. For 20th-century literature, it consisted of White male writers such as William Faulkner, Ernest Hemingway, and F. Scott Fitzgerald. In the 21st century, the white criterion for postmodern literature, especially short stories, consists primarily of the "Dynamic Duo" of George Saunders and the late David Foster Wallace. Consequently, writers as diverse as Junot Díaz, Charles Yu, and Nana Kwame Adjei-Brenyah, who run the gamut from "comic book realism" to Afrofuturism, are often judged by standards purportedly set by Saunders and Wallace. Readers who encounter texts that fail to meet their preconceived notions may simply dismiss them or, as illustrated in the following pages, attempt to read them through the lens of Western Eurocentric culture.

MISREADING MULTICULTURAL TEXTS

Invisible Man (Ralph Ellison)

Invisible Man explores the life of a Black man in White America who believes himself to be invisible "because people refuse to see me" (Ellison, 1952/1995b, p. 3). The Invisible Man, who serves as both narrator and protagonist, escapes from his life in the rural South (Greenwood, South Carolina) to the urban North (Harlem, New York) during the Great Migration, after being expelled from a prestigious Black college that bears a striking resemblance to Booker T. Washington's Tuskegee Institute. Determined to shed his Southern "country" roots, he sets out to create a new identity and shares the story of his journey "from purpose to passion to perception."

To fully appreciate this novel, we must understand its literary and historical allusions, its surrealistic vision, and its exploration of inverted reality. With its focus on the hero's journey, we can read *Invisible Man* as a quest narrative in the tradition of Homer's *Odyssey*. And with its emphasis on the narrator's journey from innocence to experience, we can also read it as a coming-of-age novel, or *bildungsroman*. But with its focus on folklore and Black vernacular, coupled with its movement from "down South" to "up North" (which emulates the narrative structure of the traditional slave narrative); its emphasis on "signifying" (a subversive form of wordplay rooted in African culture); its use of sermonic language; its exploration of "the underground man"; and its use of code-switching (which Ellison refers to as "reverse English"), *Invisible Man* is clearly an African American text.

Since the protagonist ultimately returns to his underground hideout, some critics have described the novel as essentially a story of defeat. But Ellison (1952/1995b) denounces this egregious misreading. As he points out:

> The final act of *Invisible Man* is not that of a concealment in darkness in the Anglo-Saxon connotation of the word, . . . [the protagonist's retreat] . . . into a coal cellar, a source of heat, light, and power . . . is a process of rising to an understanding of the human condition. (p. 57)

Ellison underscores the fact that the protagonist's internal landscape, rather than his physical environment, defines his sense of freedom and identity, for as the narrator finally realizes, "When I discover who I am, I'll be free" (p. 243).

"Sonny's Blues" (James Baldwin)

"Sonny's Blues" (Baldwin, 1995) tells the story of two brothers raised in the Harlem ghetto: the unnamed narrator, a high school algebra teacher, and his young brother Sonny, a struggling musician addicted to heroin. The beauty and power of "Sonny's Blues" lies in its portrayal of the power of Black music—especially jazz, gospel, and blues—to redeem and transform the lives of ordinary people. According to Ralph Ellison (1994), the blues "at once express both the agony of life and the possibility of conquering it through sheer toughness of spirit. They fall short of tragedy only in that they provide no solution, offer no scapegoat but the self" (p. 94).

It is a travesty, therefore, that in his critical essay, "A Question of Identity," Marcus Klein discounts the motif of music at the heart of Baldwin's story, choosing instead to read it as a story about race that focuses on Sonny's older brother. According to Klein (1986), "the music is unimportant. Any message of reconciliation would have worked as well" (p. 33).

What makes this blatant misreading of Baldwin's story even more troubling is that it appears in *James Baldwin: Modern Critical Views*, compiled and edited by the venerable Harold Bloom.

Beloved (Toni Morrison)

Beloved tells the story of Sethe, an escaped slave who kills her beloved 2-year-old daughter to save her from being returned to slavery. Years later, the spirit of her dead child returns to haunt her. But the editors of *The Reading Group Book* (Laskin & Hughes, 1995) wonder, "Did she need the ghost device here? Opinions may be sharply divided" (p. 122).

Since *Beloved* symbolizes the ghost of slavery that still haunts us today, yes, she *did* need "the ghost device." Without recognizing this aspect of the novel—and without identifying *Beloved* as a contemporary version of the classic slave narrative that explores the interior lives of enslaved Africans—we cannot understand and appreciate Morrison's novel.

But let's look at two more recent examples of misreading.

The Brief Wondrous Life of Oscar Wao (Junot Díaz)

Junot Díaz's 2007 Pulitzer prize-winning novel, *The Brief Wondrous Life of Oscar Wao*, focuses on an innovative reframing of the Dominican American immigrant narrative that casts its characters as comic book heroes and villains, an approach some critics describe as "comic book realism." Throughout the novel, Díaz uses extensive footnotes to interrupt the narrative and comment on significant events. For example, in the novel's opening pages, when the narrator first introduces us to "Our then dictator for life Rafael Leonidas Trujillo Molina," a footnote explains:

> For those of you who missed your mandatory two seconds of Dominican history: Trujillo, one of the twentieth century's most infamous dictators, ruled the Dominican Republic between 1930 and 1961 with an implacable ruthless brutality. (Díaz, 2007a, p. 2)

Several critics claimed that Díaz's use of footnotes was influenced by David Foster Wallace. However, David Mura (2018) points out that

> The use of footnotes was influenced by Patrick Chamoiseau's *Texaco*, a novel set in Martinique. . . . That Díaz would have been influenced by a fellow Caribbean writer is quite understandable, especially given Chamoiseau's focus on Creole

linguistics and cultural practices and the shared themes of political repression, colonialism, and racism in both works. (p. 76)

Further evidence of Díaz's connections with fellow Caribbean authors is his choice of an excerpt from "The Schooner *Flight*," a poem by West Indian Nobel laureate Derek Walcott, as an epigraph for *Oscar Wao*.

The Sympathizer (Viet Thanh Nguyen)

Viet Thanh Nguyen's 2015 Pulitzer prize-winning novel *The Sympathizer* explores American culture and history through the eyes of a Vietnamese refugee living in the United States. The unnamed narrator, a Communist sympathizer—alternately referred to as "the man of two minds" and "the bastard"—escapes from Vietnam after the fall of Saigon. Still loyal to his Vietnamese roots, he serves as a double agent who reports to "the commandant" on his new life in the United States.

A key component of the novel's narrative structure centers on the protagonist's recurring visions and nightmares about a man with a "third eye," a victim of assassination with a bullet hole in the center of his forehead. A culturally responsive reading of *The Sympathizer* would acknowledge the centrality of Buddhism in Vietnamese culture. Given this context, it would suggest that "the third eye" alludes to the sixth chakra in Buddhism, located in the center of the forehead and believed to provide spiritual insight. But a book club guide to the novel, clearly determined to situate the text within the Western literary canon, contends that "the third eye" alludes to "the eyes of Dr. T. J. Eckleburg in [F. Scott Fitzgerald's] *The Great Gatsby*" (Cope, 2016, p. 55).

But placing too much emphasis on culture can be equally dangerous.

In his classic essay on teaching African American literature, noted scholar and critic Robert Stepto laments the practice of focusing on "survey" versus "tradition." To illustrate, he describes a typical survey course that includes the poetry of Langston Hughes. But instead of focusing on Hughes's distinctive use of language, the instructor uses the poet's work as a segue for discussing Harlem, the Harlem Renaissance, and the life of Langston Hughes. Stepto (1979) concludes that in such instances, "Afro-American history and social science are being taught while Afro-American language, literature, and literacy are not" (p. 46).

Writing nearly 4 decades later, contemporary author Laila Lalami, best known for her novel *The Other Americans*, supports Stepto's argument. As Lalami (2018) points out:

There is a tendency, among certain critics, to treat writing by white writers as literature and writing by writers of color as ethnology. A lot of space is devoted to the scrupulous tallying of cultural detail and relatively little to literary choices made by the author. (p. 75)

A traditional approach to reading literature often prompts students to learn the language of literature (symbol, metaphor, imagery, irony); explore the reading process (prereading, reading, reflection); and study the elements of fiction (plot, setting, theme, characters, point of view). A culturally responsive approach would also consider elements such as the following:

- The author's cultural identity and worldview
- The text's cultural and historical context
- The text's narrative structure
- The author's distinctive use of language
- The text's connections to our lives

With its emphasis on four components of culture—Language, Identity, Space, and Time—the LIST Paradigm offers an ideal framework for exploring these elements.

CHALLENGING CENSORSHIP

In the current political climate marked by mass shootings, police brutality, and violence against people of color, one of the biggest threats to writers of color is censorship.

Over the past 2 decades, censorship has increased dramatically, targeting primarily works by writers of color and those geared toward the LGBTQ+ community. In 2021, nine states passed legislation banning educators from discussing topics considered to be under the umbrella of critical race theory. And from September 2020 to September 2021, recorded attempts to ban school library books rose by 67% ("Did You Know?," 2022, p. 12). Texts repeatedly banned include Richard Wright's *Native Son*, Alice Walker's *The Color Purple*, and Toni Morrison's *The Bluest Eye*, which appeared on the American Library Association's Top 10 Most Challenged Books in 2006, 2013, 2014, 2020, and 2021.

According to Dana A. Williams, president of the Toni Morrison Society and dean of the Graduate School at Howard University, efforts to ban Morrison's books are not only about their content, but also about Morrison herself. As Williams points out (as cited in Waxman, 2022):

[Following] any advance by Black people, you will see some stirrings around banning a Toni Morrison book. After the Black Lives Matter movement, after the 1619 project, after the election of Barack Obama, any major moment in history where you see progress of people of color—Black people in particular—backlash will follow . . . Morrison books tend to be targeted because she is unrelenting in her belief that the very particular experiences of Black people are incredibly universal. Blackness is the center of the universe for her and for her readers, or for her imagined reader. And that is inappropriate or inadequate or unreasonable or unimaginable for some people. (Waxman, 2022, para. 11)

By providing students with a guided approach to reading such as the LIST Paradigm, teachers can help them explore complex texts and gain a deeper appreciation for multicultural literatures.

PART I

THE LIST PARADIGM: A GUIDE TO CULTURALLY RESPONSIVE READING

[Culture is] a dynamic system of social values, cognitive codes, behavioral standards, worldviews, and beliefs used to give order and meaning to our own lives as well as the lives of others.

—Richard Delgado

Culture, like any other social or biological organism, is multidimensional and constantly changing. It must be so to remain vital and functional for those who create it and for those it serves.

—Geneva Gay

Culture is by definition the observation of an outsider.

—Anil Ramdas

CHAPTER 1

Culture in the Classroom

Introducing the LIST Paradigm

By incorporating race, culture, and identity into the conventional study of literature, the LIST Paradigm helps students access literary works and analyze them from multiple perspectives. Moreover, it prompts them to examine the process of *knowledge construction*, one of the five dimensions of multicultural education established by Dr. James A. Banks (1998), which focuses on promoting critical thinking by helping students "to understand, investigate, and determine the implicit cultural assumptions and frames of reference and perspectives" of various disciplines (para. 4).

By encouraging students to consider unique aspects of literature—especially works by writers of color—the LIST Paradigm prompts them to cultivate an awareness of language, literary style, and narrative structure that can dramatically enhance their reading experience.

In this respect, the LIST Paradigm aligns with the stance expressed in Donald E. Hall's 2001 *Literary and Cultural Theory*, that

> An analysis of race, ethnicity, and/or post-coloniality can enrich any critical reading, or . . . provide an exciting central focus in analyzing a literary or other cultural text. (p. 265)

As Hall points out, an understanding of "post-coloniality" or postcolonialism is central to critical reading. But what, exactly, is postcolonialism? Grounded in the works of Henry Louis Gates, Jr. (*"Race," Writing, and Difference*, 1986), Bill Ashcroft (*The Empire Writes Back*, 1989), and Edward Said (*Culture and Imperialism*, 1993), postcolonial criticism emerged as a distinctive field in the 1990s, focused primarily on foregrounding individual cultures and dismantling the claim that all great literature can be judged by a "universal" standard.

Consequently, a postcolonial reading of *The Tempest* would focus on Caliban not as a deformed, uncivilized "creature," but as a human being (specifically a West Indian) who is denied his humanity according to European standards (Ashcroft et al., 2002, p. 187).

Closely related to the field of postcolonialism is the field of cultural studies, which focuses on similarities and differences between cultures based on their beliefs and values. For example, a comparison between Mexican American and Anglo American culture might highlight the Mexican American's emphasis on cooperation, family identity, and stress as a normal part of life, as opposed to the Anglo American's emphasis on competition, individuality, and resistance to stress ("Comparison," n.d.).

Critics of multiculturalism contend that discussions of race and culture in the classroom compromise the concept of the classroom as a safe, supportive learning environment. But if we take a closer look at this argument, we realize that the classroom is the *ideal* place for such discussions, since students will invariably encounter these issues, often in a less nurturing and supportive space.

TEACHING AT THE ACADEMY

To open our discussion of culture in my classes at the U.S. Air Force Academy, I often began with Ralph Ellison's (1994) assertion that "[One writes] out of one thing only: one's own experience as understood through one's knowledge of self, culture, and literature" (p. 110). I then asked several students to share their definitions of "culture." While some defined culture in terms of our appreciation of the arts (i.e., visiting museums and art galleries), others viewed it in terms of traditional dress, music, or food. Invariably, a White student (often enamored of Black hip-hop culture) bemoaned the "fact" that "White people have no culture." This generally led us to broader explorations of "culture" and "civilization" in Western society, including the belief that "Black people have no culture."

I then encouraged cadets to think about their early childhood experiences: What was your favorite food? Your favorite story? Who told you that story? What does it mean to you today? I asked them to try to identify initial moments of cultural awareness. This generally led us to acknowledge that, as children, we are oblivious to culture, simply accepting our family traditions as "the way things are." Our awareness of "culture" begins only when we step outside the circle of family, a process that often begins with the first day of school.

Of course, a defining element of culture is race. For people of color, racism is often one of the first things we encounter as we enter the world at large. In his classic poem "Incident," Harlem Renaissance poet Countee Cullen depicts the moment of racial awareness through the eyes of a Black child whose joyful experience of exploring a new city is shattered when a White boy calls him "nigger." Clearly, the poem rejects the comforting notion of the nursery rhyme most of us learned as children: "Sticks and stones may break my bones, / But names will never hurt me."

We also note that culture manifests through language. For example, we agree that "R2D2," "Jedi lightsaber," and "Death Star" hold meaning only for those familiar with Star Wars culture. Following this line of reasoning leads us to consider characteristics that define American (U.S.) culture, Black culture, Asian culture, academic culture, prison culture, LGBTQ+ culture, and cyberculture, as well as those that define the culture of violence, the culture of fear, and the culture of silence. At this point, the discussion naturally gravitates toward Academy culture, where midterm exams are "GRs" (Graded Reviews), class leaders are "Section Marchers," guidelines for cadet etiquette are provided by "ROEs" (Rules of Engagement), and I, as instructor, have the dubious distinction of being "Commander of the Classroom."

EXPLORING CULTURAL MYTHS

To continue our exploration of culture, we discuss the power of myths. Generally defined as "creation stories," myths are often employed to explain the unknown. But according to Joy Connolly (2005), former Distinguished Professor of Classics at New York University and current president of the American Council of Learned Societies:

> Myths are networks of stories and images by which systems of oppression and violence are made to seem inevitable and beyond the reach of rational criticism or change. Repetitious and exemplary, myth makes the ideas that ground culture seem natural and fixed: heroism is linked with war, women with the private domain, the unfamiliar with the savage. Myth becomes an expression of social power, and its study serves to justify and explain the dominant order. But myth is also an enabler of the imagination, a way to transcend habits of prejudice and domination.

We then explored the impact of several cultural myths that shape American society: (a) the Hamitic Myth, (b) the Myth of White Supremacy, (c) the Myth of the American Dream (Horatio Alger), (d) the Myth of the Frontier, and (e) the Myth of "the Other."

The Hamitic Myth (Genesis 9:25–27)

Often cited by Christians to justify "the peculiar institution" of slavery, the Hamitic Myth alleges that the descendants of Canaan (Noah's grandson), allegedly a dark-skinned people, have been cursed to serve as "the lowest of slaves" to their brothers. According to the biblical story, the prophet Noah was lying naked and drunk in his tent. His son, Ham, entered the tent and saw his father naked. Upon waking, Noah was so furious with Ham that he cursed him and his offspring. As a result, Ham's son Canaan and all of Canaan's descendants were destined to be slaves.

In *The Bluest Eye*, which challenges various cultural myths, including the myth of White female beauty and the myth of the perfect family, Toni Morrison alludes to the Hamitic Myth when Maureen Peal asks Pecola if she has ever seen her father naked, suggesting that this might be the reason she has been cursed to suffer rape and alienation.

The Myth of White Supremacy

Unlike the global myths championed in Joseph Campbell's 1972 *The Hero With a Thousand Faces*, which compels us to recognize the similarities between myths from diverse cultures that embody universal truths about the human experience—our search for meaning, our need for love and community, our fear of death—the Myth of White Supremacy seeks to supplant global myths and redefine "universal values" as those values revered by White Eurocentric culture. Alleging that Whites are inherently superior to Blacks, the myth is often traced to Thomas Jefferson's "Notes on the State of Virginia" (1785/2004), in which he declared:

> I advance it, therefore, as a suspicion only, that the blacks, whether originally a distinct race, or made distinct by time and circumstances, are inferior to the whites in the endowments both of body and mind. (pp. 551–556)

Jefferson's declaration was reinforced by the Dred Scott decision (1857) in which the Supreme Court declared that blacks were "so far inferior that they had no rights which a white man was bound to respect." Despite the abolition of slavery in 1863, the Myth of White Supremacy led to the formation of the Ku Klux Klan and the establishment of Black Codes and Jim Crow laws, all determined to limit the rights of former slaves.

In *A Lesson Before Dying*, Grant Wiggins, Jefferson's former teacher, realizes that Jefferson, a young death row inmate, has internalized the Myth of White Supremacy when he passively accepts the defense attorney's depiction of him as a "hog." To help Jefferson free his mind and regain his human dignity, Grant seizes the situation as a teaching moment:

> Do you know what a myth is, Jefferson? . . . A myth is an old lie that people believe in. White people believe they're better than anyone else on earth—and that's a myth. The last thing they ever want is to see a black man stand, and think, and show that common humanity that is in us all. It would destroy their myth. (Gaines, 1993a, p. 192)

Knowing that we need our myths to make sense of the world, Grant gives Jefferson a new myth to replace the "old lie." Citing the example of Mr. Farrell, a local artist, using "any little piece of scrap wood" to make a slingshot handle, Grant tells Jefferson, "[T]hat's all we are . . . a piece of drifting wood, until we—each one of us, individually—decide to become something else" (Gaines, 1993a, p. 193).

Toni Morrison refers to the process of dismantling the Myth of White Supremacy as "dusting off the myth." In discussing her novel *Tar Baby*, she points out that the "Tar Baby" story (published by White folklorist Joel Chandler Harris) "used to frighten me." She also notes that "tar baby" is "a name, like nigger, that white people [used to call] black girls." She continues:

Tar seemed to me to be an odd thing to be in a Western story, and I found that there is a tar lady in African mythology. I started thinking about tar. At one time, a tar pit was a holy place . . . because tar was used to build things. It came naturally out of the earth; it held together things like Moses's little boat and the pyramids. For me, the tar baby came to mean the black woman who can hold things together. The story was a point of departure to history and prophecy. That's what I mean by dusting off the myth, looking closely at it to see what it might conceal. (LeClair, 1981/1994, p. 122)

The Myth of the American Dream

Also known as the Horatio Alger myth, the myth of the American Dream alleges that anyone can achieve the American Dream of success—a house, a car, money—if only he is willing to "pull himself up by his bootstraps." But as countless people trapped in the vicious cycle of poverty have pointed out, this feat is literally impossible for those who have no boots.

The novel most often used to introduce the myth of the American Dream is F. Scott Fitzgerald's *The Great Gatsby*. The story of the immigrant Jay Gatz, who transforms himself into the Great Gatsby and appears to achieve his dream of wealth, power, and success only to lose everything in the end, is often cited as a cautionary tale for those who would sacrifice everything to obtain the trappings of success.

A counterpart to the Gatsby story might be Toni Morrison's *Jazz*, which tells the story of a young couple, Joe and Violet Trace, who come to New York in search of their American Dream. Unable to blend in by simply changing their name, theirs is a different struggle, with a decidedly different ending.

Other texts that explore the American Dream from a Black perspective include Lorraine Hansberry's play *A Raisin in the Sun* and August Wilson's *The Piano Lesson*.

The Myth of the Frontier (Manifest Destiny)

The Myth of the Frontier is rooted in the concept of *Manifest Destiny*, a phrase coined in 1845, which contends that

the United States is destined by God . . . to expand its dominion and spread democracy and capitalism across the entire North American continent. The philosophy drove 19th-century U.S. territorial expansion and was used to justify the forced removal of Native Americans and other groups from their homes. (History.com, 2010, para. 1)

In July 2022, the continuing devastation suffered by Indigenous people as a result of this philosophy, which, in essence, deemed all non-Christians "savages," was revealed when Pope Francis visited Canada to apologize to Indigenous people for the Catholic Church's role in the oppression, mistreatment, and cultural genocide of their ancestors, which included government-funded schools that were part of a policy meant to destroy Indigenous cultures and languages. As reported, the genocide was sanctioned by the Papal Doctrine of Discovery from the 15th century, which gave blessing to European colonizers to seize land that was not inhabited by Christians (Yousif, 2002).

To counter this destructive myth, the works of Native American authors such as N. Scott Momaday, Leslie Marmon Silko, Joy Harjo, and Tommy Orange often explore the concept of *ecocriticism*, a form of nature writing that focuses on environmental concerns and sees humans as a part of nature, rather than as superior beings entitled to dominate it.

The Myth of "the Other"

The Myth of "the Other" contends that there is an essential difference between members of a dominant group and those outside that group, who are perceived as inferior. In his landmark 1979 text, *Orientalism*, Arab American author and cultural critic Edward Said (1935–2003) attributes this perception to "Orientalism," a worldview created and perpetuated by Eurocentric Western culture, which represents people from "the East" (Asia, North Africa, and the Middle East) as inferior to people from "the West." In an article titled "Islam through Western Eyes," Said (1980) summarizes this worldview as follows:

> So far as the United States seems to be concerned, it is only a slight overstatement to say that Moslems and Arabs are essentially seen as either oil suppliers or potential terrorists. Very little of the detail, the human density, the passion of Arab-Moslem life has entered the awareness of even those people whose profession it is to report the Arab world. What we have, instead, is a series of crude, essentialized caricatures of the Islamic world, presented in such a way as to make that world vulnerable to military aggression. (para. 11)

In her 2017 book, *The Origin of Others*, Toni Morrison supports Said's argument by illustrating how "the Other" is represented in Western literature.

EXPLORING DEFINITIONS OF "CULTURE"

Eventually, we reached a consensus concerning a general definition of culture as the *beliefs and values* of a people, passed on to succeeding generations, that shapes our worldview. We also found ourselves gravitating toward the definition of culture proposed by South American journalist Anil Ramdas (1998):

> Culture in the broadest sense of the term is actually nothing more than a collection of styles, from the smallest ways of doing things to the grandest ways of life. Culture is an aggregate of knowledge, which means that *lived* culture . . . is a

practical impossibility. When you live inside it, you do not see a culture but only a chaos of styles . . . Culture is by definition the observation of an outsider. (p. 523)

Of course, Ramdas's definition of culture is a far cry from the definitions proffered by 19th- and 20th-century scholars and critics such as Matthew Arnold (1822–1888) and T. S. Eliot (1888–1965). According to Arnold (2001), best known for his "touchstone method" of judging the worth or value of a literary work:

Culture . . . is a study of perfection. It seeks to . . . make the best which has been thought and known in the world current everywhere; to make all men live in an atmosphere of sweetness and light. [To identify the "best" poetry, a reader must] have always in one's mind lines and expressions of the great masters, and . . . apply them as a touchstone to other poetry. (p. 3)

Contemplating "the Culture Wars"

In exploring the teaching of literature, much debate centers on "the culture wars" between two opposing camps: "the monoculturalists" and "the multiculturalists." The monoculturalists, represented by E. D. Hirsch (*Cultural Literacy*), Allan Bloom (*The Closing of the American Mind*), and Harold Bloom (*The Western Canon: The Books and School of the Ages*) argue for a return to the "Great Books" tradition of Western "classics." The multiculturalists, represented by Henry Louis Gates Jr. (*Loose Canons: Notes on the Culture Wars*), James Banks (*Multicultural Education*), and Geneva Gay (*Culturally Responsive Teaching*), argue for an expanded canon that includes the works of women and writers of color.

Over the years, the antagonism between the two camps appears to have lost some of its intensity, as the conversation has shifted from *which texts to teach* to *how to teach a diverse range of texts*. This perspective is perhaps best articulated by Toni Morrison, who, despite her focus on Black history and culture, recognizes that culture's connection to the Western literary canon. As Morrison (1993) points out:

I've always thought the public schools needed to study the best literature. I always taught *Oedipus Rex* to all kinds of what they used to call remedial or development classes. The reason those kids are in those classes is that they're bored to death, so you can't give them boring things. You have to give them the best there is to engage them. (p. 392)

Alice Walker concurs. Confessing her initial love for the works of Flannery O'Connor, Walker (1983) recalls:

For several years, while I searched for, found, and studied black women writers, I deliberately shut O'Connor out, feeling almost ashamed that she had reached me first . . . [But then] I realized that . . . I would never be satisfied with a segregated literature. I would have to read Zora Hurston *and* Flannery O'Connor, Nella Larsen *and* Carson McCullers, Jean Toomer *and* William Faulkner, before I could begin to feel well read at all. (p. 42)

TEACHING VALUES

In her classic essay, "How Can Values Be Taught in the University?," Morrison (2005) asserts that "explicitly or implicitly, the university has always taught . . . values" (p. 1). Referring to her own experience as a teacher, she points out:

What I think and do is already inscribed on my teaching, my work. . . . We teach values by having them. (p. 3)

Amy Tan, in responding to reviews of *The Joy Luck Club*, notes the fallacy concerning writers "representing" their culture. As Tan (1996) points out:

I am not an expert on China, Chinese culture, mah jong, the psychology of mothers and daughters, generation gaps, immigration, illegal aliens, assimilation, acculturation, racial tension, Tiananmen Square, the Most Favored Nation trade agreements, human rights, Pacific Rim economics, the purported one million missing baby girls of China, the future of Hong Kong after 1997, or, I am sorry to say, Chinese cooking. Certainly I have personal opinions on many of these topics, but by no means do my sentiments and my world of make-believe make me an expert.

So I am alarmed when reviewers and educators assume that my very personal, specific, and fictional stories are meant to be representative, down to the nth detail not just of Chinese Americans but, sometimes, of all Asian culture. (para. 9)

Rudolfo Anaya, one of the founders of Chicano literature, concurs. As Anaya (1999) observes in the introduction to *Bless Me, Ultima*, "a novel is not written to *explain* a culture, it creates its own" (p. xiii).

Once students have a basic understanding of culture, they are prepared to explore the four components of culture that comprise the LIST Paradigm: Language, Identity, Space, and Time.

INTRODUCING THE LIST PARADIGM

As noted in the Preface, the LIST Paradigm is a culturally responsive approach to reading (or teaching) literature that prompts readers to *access* and *analyze* a text by *asking significant questions* designed to foster close reading and critical thinking. By combining aspects of *literary analysis* (exploring the elements of fiction, such as plot, setting, character, and point of view) and *literary criticism* (exploring works from multiple perspectives, such as histori-cal, psychological, and archetypal), the LIST Paradigm helps readers unlock the power of literature with four keys to culture—Language, Identity, Space, and Time—by focusing on four significant questions:

> **Language:** "How does the author contextualize linguistic signs and symbols?"
> **Identity:** "Who are these people and what do they want?"
> **Space:** "How do characters negotiate the text's physical, psychological, and cultural landscapes?"
> **Time:** "How does the author manipulate time?"

Each question leads to a series of progressively more specific questions concerning each LIST component. And each component is introduced by a working definition that challenges readers to expand the definition based on their own experiences. Consequently, the LIST Paradigm guides students through the reading process by providing them with a series of questions they can apply to virtually any text while encouraging them to formulate their own questions. Although the four components are discussed separately, they are, of course, interrelated (e.g., language reveals identity, which is, in turn, influenced by space and time).

LITERARY ANALYSIS

An "Introduction to Literature" course invariably begins with an introduc-tion to the elements of fiction: plot, setting, theme, character, and point of view. How well students can identify these elements within a selected text and understand how they work together to advance the narrative will largely determine their success in analyzing a text and in understanding how writers use rhetorical devices such as diction, syntax, and imagery to create a unique reading experience. As illustrated in the following paragraphs, approaching a text through the lens of culture expands the process of literary analysis and enhances the reading experience.

In its approach to literary analysis, the LIST Paradigm emulates the *social reform* approach to teaching, summarized as follows:

> Class discussion is focused less on how knowledge has been created, and more by whom and for what purposes. Texts are interrogated for what is said and what is not said; what is included and what is excluded; who is represented and who is omitted from the dominant discourses within a field of study or practice. Students are encouraged to take a critical stance to give them power to take social action to improve their own lives; critical deconstruction, though central to this view, is not an end in itself. (Pratt & Collins, 2000, para. 5)

In preparing students to read Toni Morrison's 1977 *Song of Solomon*, I begin by pointing out that the powerful myths of one culture, which form the foundation of its moral and religious values, are often trivialized and reduced to simple folktales or superstitions by cultures with different beliefs and values. Depending on one's perspective, we can view the Bible as either a divinely inspired spiritual and historical text or as a collection of myths and stories that attempt to explain the mystery of creation. With this in mind, we read "The People Could Fly," an African American folktale that tells the story of enslaved Africans who escape slavery by flying back to Africa (Hamilton, 1985). Within the context of this folktale, we explore the concept of magical realism, the power of imagination to transform reality, and the plight of a displaced people longing for home. We also read excerpts from "Song of Solomon" in the Old Testament, noting that "Song of Solomon" can be interpreted as either a series of love poems portraying the relationship between King Solomon and his beloved, the Queen of Sheba, or as a commentary on the relationship between Christ and the church. We also use this text to explore the power of language, noting the sensual nature imagery as well as the description of Solomon's "beloved," who, depending on the translation of the Bible, is described as either "Black, *but* beautiful" or "Black *and* beautiful." Finally, we note that Morrison's novel reimagines the African American folktale and, through several key characters, exploits its motif of flight.

Some readers may point out that we automatically take these steps in preparing students to read a text. After all, in teaching Greek mythology, don't we begin by providing some background on Greek and Roman culture? In teaching Shakespeare, don't we begin with a discussion of Shakespeare's language, the Globe Theatre, and the absence of female actors on the Shakespearean stage? In teaching Faulkner, don't we begin by exploring Faulkner's life in Oxford, Mississippi, citing it as the model for his fictional community of Yoknapatawpha County? My response is an unqualified "Yes, but. . . ." *Yes*, we generally do take these steps. *But* most students enter our classrooms already predisposed to learn about Greek mythology, Shakespeare's plays, and Faulkner's novels because they consider these texts to be an integral component of their formal education. They may even be intrinsically motivated to read *Hamlet* or *Macbeth* not only because they have been previously exposed to these works and therefore consider them "worthy" of study, but because they believe that quoting Shakespeare will make them look smart and sophisticated. Since students generally have no such preconceived notions about Morrison or other writers of color, encouraging them to explore both Western and non-Western texts through the lens of culture will compel them to view all literature as "multicultural," since each text invariably reflects its cultural origins. By focusing on the four components of the LIST Paradigm, students will have an opportunity to reflect on the infinite ways culture manifests in literature, both implicitly and explicitly, and how recognizing various aspects of culture can profoundly enhance the reading experience.

LITERARY CRITICISM

Because of its seemingly complex subject matter, teachers may be reluctant to address literary criticism in an introductory literature course. But being exposed to comments that challenge an author's work can stimulate students' critical thinking and compel them to formulate their own questions concerning a text.

In his essay "Disliking Books at an Early Age," cultural critic Gerald Graff describes his introduction to literary criticism, citing it as a turning point in his approach to literary studies. Reflecting on his days as a student, Graff (1992) explains:

> Even when I had done the assigned reading, I was often tongue-tied and embar-rassed when called on. What was unclear to me was what I was supposed to *say* about literary works, and why. . . . What first made literature, history, and other intellectual pursuits seem attractive to me was exposure to critical debate. (p. 41)

Graff goes on to discuss his experience of reading *Huckleberry Finn*, noting that he became interested in the novel only after his instructor mentioned that critics had disagreed about the novel's ending. As he points out:

> Having the controversy over the ending in mind, I now had some issues *to watch out for* as I read, issues that reshaped the way I read the earlier chapters as well as the later ones and focused my attention. And having issues to watch out for made it possible not only to concentrate, as I had not been able to do earlier, but to put myself into the text—to read with a sense of personal engagement that I had not felt before. (p. 43)

LIST PARADIGM EXERCISES

To introduce the LIST Paradigm to my students, I provide them with the handout "Exploring the LIST Paradigm: A Reader's Guide" (**Appendix A.1**). I then guide them through the four components of the LIST Paradigm: Language, Identity, Space, and Time.

Exercise 1

After guiding students through this process, I give them a copy of Gary Soto's poem, "Mexicans Begin Jogging," which explores two explosive social and political issues—immigration and racial profiling—from a humorous perspec-tive. I ask them to read the poem twice: once to get a feel for the story, and again to focus on the poet's language by underlining or highlighting striking words and phrases. I then give them about 5 minutes to jot down initial re-sponses to the poem in their reading journals. Next, I give them an additional

5 minutes to share their responses with a partner. I then read the poem aloud and invite students to share their responses with the class (a process sometimes described as "Think, Pair, Share").

Once we have completed this initial analysis of the poem, I provide students with a copy of my LIST Paradigm Worksheet (**Appendix A.2**) and have them work in small groups to further discuss the poem and identify some of its key components in terms of Language, Identity, Space, and Time. To help generate discussion, I share with them Gary Soto's perspective on his work (as cited in Hoyt, 2011, para. 1): "As a writer, my duty is not to make people perfect, particularly Mexican Americans. I'm not a cheerleader. I'm one who provides portraits of people in the rush of life." I also ask them to consider the identity of the narrator, the poem's narrative setting, and how Soto's metaphor of jogging impacts the poem's overall tone. Once we reconvene, I invite students to share key points from their small-group discussions.

Exercise 2

To help students gain additional practice using the LIST Paradigm before we apply it to a longer work, I give them two copies of my LIST Paradigm Worksheet, one to use for their current writing assignment, and one to save and copy for future assignments. I then give them a list of poems and ask them to choose one, use the worksheet to guide their analysis, and write a short paper (350–500 words) responding to and analyzing their poem. (I often combine this lesson with a lesson on poetry explication.) Over the years, my list has included titles such as the following:

- "Immigrants in Our Own Land" (Jimmy Santiago Baca)
- "Black Hair" (Gary Soto)
- "Quinceañera" (Judith Ortiz Cofer)
- "Girl" (Jamaica Kincaid)
- "Eating Together" (Li-Young Lee)
- "We Are Many" (Pablo Neruda)
- "My Father Is a Simple Man" (Luis Omar Salinas)
- "Those Winter Sundays" (Robert Hayden)
- "Slam, Dunk, and Hook" (Yusef Komunyakaa)
- "Nikki-Rosa" (Nikki Giovanni)
- "won't you celebrate with me" (Lucille Clifton)
- "Phenomenal Woman" (Maya Angelou)
- "Miscegenation" (Natasha Trethewey)

Since these poems represent a broad range of themes explored by poets from diverse cultures, I have found them especially useful in engaging students emotionally and intellectually. Of course, teachers will want to provide their own list of recommended poems, depending on course content.

TEACHING THROUGH THE LENS OF CULTURE

As discussed in Chapter 3 ("Intertextuality: Everything Is Connected"), all texts are interconnected, reaching beyond time and space and across cultures. But in the traditional classroom, they are generally separated by genre and taught as independent, isolated entities. Moreover, the same standard texts are often used to teach key concepts and complex social issues. To illustrate, consider three topics invariably included in an "Introduction to Literature" course: Satire, the Sonnet, and Drama. As illustrated in the following paragraphs, approaching these topics through the lens of culture can lead to a more rewarding and inclusive learning experience for both students and teachers.

Satire

Satire—"a mode of writing that exposes the failings of individuals, institutions, or societies to ridicule and scorn"—is a critical concept for students to understand as informed members of society (Baldick, 2015, p. 322). In what has become known as "The Rushdie Affair," Salman Rushdie's novel *The Satanic Verses* was banned in 13 countries, including India, Iran, South Africa, and Pakistan, after Iran's religious leader, Ayatollah Khomeini, declared a *fatwa* (death sentence) against Rushdie and everyone associated with the publication of his book for allegedly blaspheming the prophet Mohammad. The *fatwa* forced Rushdie to go into hiding for nearly 12 years.

The devastating consequences of misreading satire were brought home with a vengeance on August 12, 2022, when Rushdie was stabbed multiple times as he was about to give a public lecture at the Chautauqua Institution in Chautauqua, New York, on the importance of freedom of speech for writers. Although he survived the attack, it left him blinded in one eye and unable to use one of his hands.

The standard text used to introduce satire is Jonathan Swift's 1729 essay, "A Modest Proposal," in which the narrator proposes that, to ease the burden of poverty among the Irish, they should consider eating their children. To bring the discussion into the modern era, students may be introduced to works such as Joseph Heller's *Catch-22* or Kurt Vonnegut's *Welcome to the Monkey House*.

To approach satire through the lens of culture, we might begin by asking students to consider the impact of media images and political cartoons on readers. For example, you might ask students to study the illustration of then-senator Barack Obama and his wife Michelle that appeared on the cover of the July 21, 2008, edition of *The New Yorker*. The cover depicts the Obamas giving each other a fist bump as they celebrate his nomination as the Democratic presidential candidate and envision their life in the White House. He is depicted as a flag-burning Muslim, while she is portrayed as a machine-gun-toting, Afro-wearing, 1960s-style radical. Although *The New Yorker* defended the illustration as satire, the Obama campaign, as well as millions of Americans, saw it as "tasteless and offensive."

Satire has long been popular among writers of color, who use it as a form of subversion and resistance to protest racism, violence, and other injustices. But these writers are conspicuously absent from college anthologies, which often choose to focus on less controversial authors. Some writers of color for whom satire is the weapon of choice are George S. Schuyler, Langston Hughes, Alice Childress, George C. Wolfe, and Charles Yu.

In his novel *Black No More*, Schuyler (1931/1999) satirizes the notion of Blacks trying to become White by bleaching their skin, straightening their hair, or changing their language. His novel introduces us to a breakthrough in modern science: "Negro announces remarkable discovery: Can change black to white in three days" (p. 9).

Although best known as "the poet laureate of Harlem," Langston Hughes was also a brilliant satirist. In his "Simple" stories, which first appeared in the Black newspaper *The Chicago Defender* in 1943, Hughes presents the stories in the form of dialogues between the uneducated but wise and sympathetic Jesse B. Semple (Simple), a Black "Everyman," and his college-educated friend, Boyd, who share their views on race and women over drinks at Harlem's Wishing Well Bar. Simple's commonsense approach to his problems and his folk wisdom earned the Simple stories a devoted following. Their popularity led to the publication of several volumes: *Simple Speaks His Mind* (1950), *Simple Takes a Wife* (1953), *Simple Stakes a Claim* (1957), and *Simple's Uncle Sam* (1965). Selections from the various volumes were published in 1961 as *The Best of Simple*.

In a discussion on Jim Crow laws, segregation, and violence against Blacks, Simple proposes a simple solution:

> If the government can set aside some spot for a elk *to be a elk* without being bothered, or a fish *to be a fish* without getting hooked, or a buffalo *to be a buffalo* without being shot down, there ought to be some place in this American country where a Negro can be a Negro without being Jim Crowed. (Hughes, 1995d, p. 61)

Hughes's Simple stories served as the inspiration for Alice Childress's 1986 *Like One of the Family*. Subtitled "Conversations from a Domestic's Life," *Family* consists of 62 "conversations" between Mildred, a Black domestic worker, and her friend Marge that highlight the complacency and condescension of Marge's White employers. Through these conversations, Childress debunks the myth, originated and perpetuated by White slave owners, that slaves (and later, Black domestic workers) were treated "like one of the family."

One of the best (and decidedly underrated) contemporary satirists is the playwright George C. Wolfe. In his highly controversial play *The Colored Museum* (1987), Wolfe imagines a time when racism has been eradicated and exists only as a series of "exhibits" in the Colored Museum. Instead of traditional acts and scenes, the play's narrative structure consists of a series of sketches that highlight various exhibits. For example, in the first exhibit, Miss Pat, a Black "stewardess" in "a hot pink mini-skirt," welcomes passengers aboard the "Celebrity Slaveship." As the Slaveship prepares for departure, Miss Pat reminds passengers to "wear [their] shackles at all times" (Wolfe, 1986, p. 1). Another exhibit, "Symbiosis," features two characters identified only as "Man" and "The Kid." Dressed in corporate attire and holding a Saks Fifth Avenue shopping bag, Man stands next to a large garbage can and methodically disposes of the contents of his bag—a pair of Converse All-Stars, an Afro-comb, a dashiki, an autographed picture of Stokely Carmichael—as The Kid looks on in horror. Near the end of the sketch, Man tells The Kid, "Being black is too emotionally taxing; therefore I will be black only on weekends and holidays" (Wolfe, 1986, p. 36).

In the play's most controversial sketch, "The Last Mama-on-the-Couch Play"—which features a character named Walter-Lee-Beau-Willie—Wolfe satirizes plays by Black women such as Lorraine Hansberry's *A Raisin in the Sun* and Ntozake Shange's *For Colored Girls Who Have Considered Suicide When the Rainbow Is Enuf*, which feature domineering "Big Mama" characters and portray Black men in less-than-heroic roles.

In his 2020 National Book Award–winning novel *Interior Chinatown*, Charles Yu presents a scathing indictment of Asian and Asian American stereotypes, as portrayed in films and on television. As he reveals in an interview with Trevor Noah (2020), despite the success of films such as *The Joy Luck Club* and *Crazy Rich Asians*, there is still a decided lack of on-screen representation for Asian Americans. Yu also criticized the "model minority" stereotype—the math whiz, the musical prodigy—which he describes as a means of promoting divisiveness in the Asian American community, since it perpetuates the mindset, "If he can make it, so can you."

In the novel, presented in the form of a screenplay, Yu tells the story of Willis Wu, an actor often called upon to play background roles such as "Generic Asian Man," "Delivery Guy," "Disgraced Son," or "Silent Henchman." But Wu dreams of being "Kung Fu Guy," the most respected role any Asian actor can hope to achieve.

As he reveals at the beginning of the novel:

Ever since you were a boy, you've dreamt of being Kung Fu Guy.
You are not Kung Fu Guy.
You are currently Background Oriental Male, but you've been practicing.
Maybe tomorrow will be the day. (Yu, 2020, p. 3)

Set in an anonymous Chinatown, most of the novel's action takes place in the Golden Palace, a Chinese restaurant that serves as the setting for a TV police series titled *Black and White*, modeled after *Law and Order*, which is in perpetual production. Consequently, "interior Chinatown" not only refers to the show's physical setting; it also represents the racialized space occupied by the Asian characters and their interior landscape.

As the novel opens, Wu reminisces about his elderly parents, who played virtually the same roles he is now being offered. We also gain insight into his childhood memories of watching Bruce Lee movies, which inspired him to become an actor. (Of course, the ultimate irony of Lee's career is that before he became a legendary superstar, he was denied the lead role in the 1972 TV series *Kung Fu*, a role that went to White actor David Carradine.) But Yu, who works as a Hollywood scriptwriter, doesn't limit his focus to films. As he traces the history of his protagonist and envisions his future, he also compels us to consider that we all live life according to the scripts we have been given. And although much of the novel is presented as a comedy, as we watch Wu consistently pursue roles he will never obtain, Yu also offers a historical view of the violence and racism perpetuated against Asian Americans and the struggles of immigrants from various countries to assimilate into American culture by incorporating historical documents tracing U.S. immigration policies into his narrative. Critics who described the novel as "rollicking fun" and "hilarious" obviously missed the message. Clearly, teaching satire through the lens of culture can dramatically enhance the learning experience and provide students with a broader context for exploring the genre.

The Sonnet

Introducing the sonnet, a 14-line lyric poem that often celebrates love and the beauty of nature, invariably means focusing on the works of Shakespeare, Milton, Wordsworth, Keats, and Elizabeth Barrett Browning.

But African American poets often employed the sonnet form to address issues such as racism, violence, and death. During the Harlem Renaissance, the sonnet was conceived as *an invitation to converse*, "a space from which a single voice launched an appeal to an implied audience in an attempt to elicit a reply or reaction" rather than a mere imitation of the European sonnet (Francini, 2003, p. 1).

Black scholars and critics cite four criteria that define the African American sonnet: (a) lyrical language, (b) historical perspective, (c) indirection, and (d) signifyin(g).

One of the most famous African American sonnets is Claude McKay's "If We Must Die," included in his 1922 poetry collection *Harlem Shadows*, which protests the horrific treatment of Black soldiers returning to the States in the aftermath of World War I.

The poem's opening line, "If we must die, let it not be like hogs" (McKay, 2020, p. 238) evokes images of the "protest novel" epitomized by Richard Wright's *Native Son*. During World War II, Winston Churchill allegedly recited "If We Must Die" in a speech, without knowing or acknowledging its author. The poem became famous once more during the 1971 uprising in New York's

Attica Correctional Facility when a copy was discovered in possession of one of the inmates.

Other African American poets who employed the sonnet as a form of protest are Paul Laurence Dunbar, Countee Cullen, and Gwendolyn Brooks.

Contemporary sonnet cycles—a series of sonnets linked to a common theme—include Marilyn Nelson's *A Wreath for Emmett Till* and Natasha Trethewey's *Native Guard*, which honors the role of Black soldiers during the Civil War.

As illustrated, exploring sonnets through the lens of culture can dramatically enhance students' learning experiences and provide them with a broader perspective for examining these works.

Drama

To approach drama through the lens of culture, instructors might focus on teaching the plays of August Wilson in addition to Shakespeare, Sophocles, Henrik Ibsen, and Arthur Miller.

In May 2019, I taught a course titled "The Plays of August Wilson" for PILLAR, a local Colorado Springs nonprofit that provides lifelong learning opportunities for seniors. Since I realized the futility of attempting to discuss all of Wilson's plays in two hours, I decided to focus on his two Pulitzer Prize–winning plays—*Fences* (1986) and *The Piano Lesson* (1990)—as well as his "signature" play, *Joe Turner's Come and Gone* (1988). To give participants a cultural context for the playwright and his works, I provided them with handouts highlighting the life of August Wilson (1945–2005), summaries of the 10 plays that comprise his "century cycle" depicting African American life during the 20th century (1904 to 1997). (The plays are sometimes referred to as his "Pittsburgh cycle," since all except one—*Ma Rainey's Black Bottom* [1985]—are set in Pittsburgh's Hill District, aka "the Hill.")

To introduce August Wilson, I note his biracial (Black/White), bicultural (German/American) heritage and his childhood growing up on "the Hill." I point out that he was greatly influenced by blues singers such as Ma Rainey, Bessie Smith, and Buddy Bolden, who figures prominently in *Joe Turner's Come and Gone*. I also note that Wilson, a former poet, dropped out of high school at age 15 after being accused of plagiarism by his teacher, continuing his education by reading in the library. As he recalls, "I discovered the Negro section of the Carnegie Library when I was fourteen years old and on my way home from playing basketball. There were about thirty books in that section. This began my growing awareness of being black" (Carroll, 1995, p. 250).

I also highlight the key theme threaded throughout his plays: the ability of Black people to survive racism and violence through family, community, and the healing power of Black music, a theme also prevalent in the works of Langston Hughes ("Jazzonia"), Toni Morrison (*Song of Solomon*), and James Baldwin ("Sonny's Blues").

Defining elements of Wilson's plays include his use of Black vernacular to record the language of ordinary people and his determination to document the culture and history of Black America through stories. Citing James Baldwin's call for "a profound articulation of the black tradition" (Bryer & Hartig, 2006, p. 105), Wilson explains:

> The suffering is only a part of black history. What I want to do is place the culture of black America on stage, to demonstrate that it has the ability to offer sustenance, so that when you leave your parents' house, you are not in the world alone. You have something that is yours, you have a ground to stand on . . . and . . . a way of proceeding in the world that has been developed by your ancestors. (Bryer & Hartig, 2006, p. 104)

Commenting further, he contends:

> I think my plays are a testament to the resiliency of the human spirit. And that no matter what, we are still here, the culture is still alive, it is vital, and it is as vibrant and zestful as ever. (p. 105)

Another defining element of Wilson's plays—for which he is often criticized—is his emphasis on "loud talking": Characters deliver loud (and lengthy) dramatic monologues. Wilson describes this tactic as "an unconscious rebellion against the notion that blacks do not have anything important to say" (Bryer & Hartig, 2006, p. 104).

To link August Wilson to the lineage of contemporary American playwrights, I point out that Lloyd Richards (1919–2006), who directed Lorraine Hansberry's *A Raisin in the Sun*, "discovered" Wilson and directed six of his plays. I also point out that, like Arthur Miller (*Death of a Salesman*), Wilson focuses on the common man as a tragic hero.

Fences. Set in 1957, the play spans four generations and tells the story of Troy Maxson and his family: Rose, his wife of 18 years; Cory, their 15-year-old son; Lyons, Troy's oldest son by a former marriage; Raynell, Troy's daughter by his mistress, Alberta; Gabriel, Troy's brother, a disabled World War II veteran; and Jim Bono, Troy's friend. We then watch a brief video clip of the 2016 film starring Denzel Washington and Viola Davis. To open our discussion, we contemplate Jim Bono's comment: "Some people build fences to keep people out . . . and other people build fences to keep people in" (Wilson, 1986, p. 61).

The Piano Lesson. I note that the play's title was inspired by a painting, *The Piano Lesson,* by Romare Bearden (1911–1988), a postmodern artist best known for his expansive murals depicting everyday scenes from African American life. I also note that, like *A Raisin in the Sun, The Piano Lesson* centers on the conflicting themes of honoring history and legacy versus the more practical quest for money and survival. Set in 1936, it focuses on two siblings—Berniece

Charles and Boy Willie—who clash over the fate of their prized family heirloom: an ornately carved piano. While Berniece wants to keep the piano, which symbolizes the struggles of their ancestors, Boy Willie wants to sell it to buy a tract of land their ancestors worked on as slaves. To open our discussion, we contemplate the pros and cons of the siblings' arguments. We also watch a video clip of the 1995 CBS film starring Charles S. Dutton and Alfre Woodard.

Joe Turner's Come and Gone. I point out that the play's title comes from the blues song "Joe Turner's Come and Gone," which warns black people about Joe Turner, a White man who embodied the convict leasing system that kidnapped black men during the Great Migration, imprisoned them, and used them as free labor (Shannon, 2016, p. 34). The title also alludes to Joe Turner the blues musician. Set in 1911, the play explores the healing power of Black music through the story of Herald Loomis, who returns to "the Hill" searching for his wife and daughter after spending 7 years on Joe Turner's chain gang. Unable to reconnect with his family and community, Loomis remains lost until Bynum Walker, a local healer, helps him find his song. To explore the impact of the play for the 21st century, we discuss the convict leasing system as a legacy of slavery that still haunts us today.

Given its rootedness in Black culture, this course proved to be a challenge, given that my audience was predominantly White. However, I was delighted to discover that several students signed up for my subsequent course, "*Ma Rainey's Black Bottom*: A Viewer's Guide," which I taught to coincide with the release of the 2020 film starring Chadwick Boseman and Viola Davis.

Three excellent resources for teaching the plays of August Wilson are Christopher Bigsby's *The Cambridge Companion to August Wilson*; Sandra G. Shannon's *August Wilson's Pittsburgh Cycle: Critical Perspectives on the Plays*; and Sandra G. Shannon and Sandra L. Richards's *Approaches to Teaching the Plays of August Wilson.*

Planning a curriculum that highlights works by writers of color vastly expands the range of texts available to students; moreover, it encourages teachers to disrupt the practice of adding these works as "supplementary readings."

As bell hooks (1994) points out in *Teaching to Transgress: Education as the Practice of Freedom* (her homage to Paulo Freire's 1970 *Pedagogy of the Oppressed*): "When we, as educators, allow our pedagogy to be radically changed by our recognition of a multicultural world, we can give students the education they desire and deserve" (p. 44).

There is no agony like bearing an untold story inside you.

—Zora Neale Hurston

A story is a formula for extracting meaning from chaos, a handful of water we scoop up to recall an ocean.

—John Edgar Wideman

We must learn to become the protagonists in our own stories.

—Rudolfo Anaya

Who lives, who dies, who tells your story?

—Lin-Manuel Miranda, *Hamilton*

Telling Our Stories

Exploring the Power of Narrative

"We tell ourselves stories in order to live." Joan Didion's observation is often cited to illustrate the power of stories. But in the ELA classroom, stories by writers of color are often omitted or distorted to fit into the literary landscape still dominated by White writers and Western Eurocentric texts.

In the preface to his essay collection, *The Man Made of Words*, N. Scott Momaday (1998), the first Native American to win the Pulitzer Prize for his novel *House Made of Dawn*, reflects on the power of stories:

> Stories are true to our common experience; they are statements which concern the human condition. To the extent that the human condition involves moral considerations, stories are true in that they are established squarely upon belief. In the oral tradition stories are told not merely to entertain or to instruct; they are told to be believed. Stories are not subject to the imposition of such questions as true or false, fact or fiction. Stories are realities lived and believed. They are true. (p. 3)

In the opening pages of *Ceremony*, Leslie Marmon Silko (1977) echoes Momaday's philosophy: "[Stories] . . . aren't just entertainment / Don't be fooled. / They are all we have, you see, all we have to fight off / illness and death" (p. 2).

Unfortunately, many of the stories we encounter through various news media are stories of mass shootings, police brutality, and other forms of violence, targeted primarily toward people of color. Our initial reaction to such stories is often fear, rage, and an overwhelming sense of grief, loss, and helplessness. Attempting to address such traumatic issues in the classroom can be challenging, since we are, in essence, asking students to deal with complex feelings and emotions they may not know how to process or articulate. But addressing the issues through literature can help students establish a sense of distance from the immediacy of the horrors, process their emotions, feel compassion for the victims, and develop survival strategies and coping mechanisms that can help them gain a sense of control over their own lives. Moreover, approaching stories of violence through fiction can encourage students to explore feelings and emotions they might otherwise feel compelled to suppress.

Each year, countless students are introduced to Ralph Ellison's *Invisible Man* through anthologies, which invariably focus on the "Battle Royal" (Chapter 1), a brutal rite of passage for Black youth into a violent, chaotic world that symbolizes the social and political power struggle depicted throughout the novel. By participating in a boxing match with "no rounds [and] no bells at three-minute intervals" (1952/1995b, p. 23), the narrator learns that life is a struggle for survival, yet he still believes that, like Booker T. Washington, he can achieve success through "education and industry." But this chapter also introduces the imagery of people as dolls and puppets. For example, the narrator compares the naked blonde's yellow hair to that of "a circus kewpie doll" (p. 19). Later, a blow to the narrator's head causes his right eye to pop "like a jack-in-the-box" (p. 25). In short, the narrator's depiction of people as dolls or puppets emphasizes their powerlessness and lack of control over their own bodies. This imagery resurfaces in Chapter 20, when the narrator, searching for the charismatic youth leader, Tod Clifton, is shocked to find him selling dancing paper Sambo dolls on a Harlem street corner and watches him being shot down by a White policeman.

Tod Clifton's death has a profound impact on the narrator. For the first time, he becomes emotionally involved with the fate of another human being as he wrestles with his conscience, wondering if there was something he could have said or done to prevent this tragedy. As he recalls his feelings of humiliation and disgust at seeing Brother Clifton selling the Sambo dolls, he also reflects on the love, respect, and admiration he felt for his friend, which prompts him to plan a lavish funeral for Clifton, at which he delivers a powerful eulogy:

> His name was Clifton and they shot him down. His name was Clifton and he was tall and some folks thought him handsome . . . His name was Clifton and he was black and they shot him. Isn't that enough to tell? Isn't it all you need to know? . . . Here are the facts. He was standing and he fell. He fell and he kneeled. He kneeled and he bled. He bled and he died . . . That's all . . . It's an old story . . . Aren't you tired of such stories? Aren't you sick of the blood? . . . His name was Clifton, Tod Clifton, he was unarmed and his death was as senseless as his life was futile . . . His name was Tod Clifton and he was full of illusions. He thought he was a man when he was only Tod Clifton. (pp. 455–457)

In reflecting on this passage, it would be difficult for students not to subconsciously insert the names of other victims of violence and police brutality—Trayvon Martin, Oscar Grant, Eric Garner, Tamir Rice, Breonna Taylor, George Floyd—and to forge connections between their deaths and the death of Tod Clifton. At this point, teachers can intervene and encourage students to view such tragedies from a broader perspective, as part of the human experience that encompasses love and loss, as well as life and death. More importantly, they can point out that we can choose how to respond in such situations by either retaliating with more violence or, like the narrator, honoring the victim's death by celebrating their life.

In his Kafkaesque story "The Finkelstein 5" (included in his 2018 dystopian short story collection *Friday Black*), Nana Kwame Adjei-Brenyah also addresses violence against Black Americans. Approaching his subject matter through the lens of Afrofuturism, Adjei-Brenyah explores several key themes that resonate throughout the narrative: racial profiling, police brutality, the corrupt U.S. judicial system, and the murder of Black children by White vigilantes.

The story opens with a chilling scene:

> Fela, the headless girl, walked toward Emmanuel. Her neck jagged with red savagery. She was silent, but he could feel her waiting for him to do something, anything.
> Then his phone rang, and he woke up. (2018, p. 1)

We soon discover that Emmanuel's nightmare—like that of Gregor Samsa in Franz Kafka's *The Metamorphosis*, who wakes to find himself transformed into a "monstrous vermin" (p. 3)—is not a dream; it is, in fact, a vision rooted in reality:

> [A]fter twenty-eight minutes of deliberation, a jury of his peers had acquitted George Wilson Dunn of any wrongdoings whatsoever. He had been indicted for allegedly using a chain saw to hack off the heads of five black children outside the Finkelstein Library in Valley Ridge, South Carolina. The court had ruled that because the children were basically loitering and not actually inside the library reading . . . it was reasonable that Dunn had felt threatened by these five black young people and, thus, he was well within his rights when he protected himself, his library-loaned DVDs, and his children by going into the back of his Ford F-150 and retrieving his Hawtech PRO eighteen-inch 48cc chain saw. (p. 2)

Adjei-Brenyah, a former student of George Saunders, draws on numerous texts and tropes to craft his narrative, merging scenes and images from *The Texas Chainsaw Massacre* with allusions to the films of Jordan Peele (*Get Out, Us, Nope*) in which racism emerges as the ultimate horror. He also signifies on the "Say Their Name" movement launched by Black Lives Matter to commemorate the victims of racial violence. (To avenge the deaths of the Finkelstein 5, a Black vigilante group vows to kill a White person for each Black life taken. To empower their group, they create the ritual of "naming," in which members chant the name of one of the Black children as they attack their White victims.)

But although the narrative centers on the Finkelstein 5, it also tells the story of Emmanuel "Manny" Gyan, a Black, middle-class teenager whose life revolves around school, friends, and family until it is violently disrupted by the murders, which draws him into a vortex of violence he is unable to escape.

Surprisingly, Adjei-Brenyah brings both humor and pathos to his story of murder and revenge. (Throughout the narrative, Emmanuel, whose name means "God is with us," repeatedly adjusts his "level of blackness" on a scale from 1 to 10 by changing his wardrobe.) And despite its inevitable tragic ending, the story gives us a glimpse of hope for a new beginning.

DEFINING "STORY"

In his classic work *Aspects of the Novel*, E. M. Forster (1955) contends that "Story . . . can have only one merit: that of making the audience want to know what happens next" (p. 27). Forster differentiates between *story* and *plot*, noting that while story focuses on time sequence or *what happened* ("The king died and then the queen died"), plot focuses on causality or *why it happened* ("The king died, and then the queen died *of grief*") (p. 86).

In a *Flash Fiction* piece titled "Stories," John Edgar Wideman (2006) tells the story of a man walking down the street in the rain, eating a banana. He then poses a series of questions about the man: "Where is he coming from?"; "Where is he going?"; "Why is he eating a banana?"; "How hard is the rain falling?" Gradually, he moves on to larger questions: "Who is asking all these questions?"; "Who is supposed to answer them?"; "Why?"; "Does it matter?" His point, of course, is that a single event or incident can lead to countless stories, depending on the storyteller's selective attention to specific details. His questions also illustrate the process of "interrogating the text" (see Chapter 4). Interestingly, Wideman uses periods instead of question marks throughout the story, a stylistic choice that adds another level of irony and ambiguity.

In Tim O'Brien's *The Things They Carried*, his bestselling short-story cycle about the Vietnam War, O'Brien (1998) reflects on the nature of stories, as the author/narrator observes that:

> [T]he war occurred half a lifetime ago, and yet the remembering makes it now. And sometimes remembering will lead to a story, which makes it forever. That's what stories are for. Stories are for joining the past to the future. Stories are for those late hours in the night when you can't remember how you got from where you were to where you are. Stories are for eternity, when memory is erased, when there is nothing to remember except the story. (p. 38)

A 2008 study on the power of stories and storytelling reported in *Scientific American Mind* revealed some intriguing facts:

- Storytelling is a human universal, and common themes appear in tales throughout history and all over the world.
- These characteristics of stories, and our natural affinity toward them, reveal clues about our evolutionary history and the roots of emotion and empathy in the mind.
- By studying narrative's power to influence beliefs, researchers are discovering how we analyze information and accept new ideas. (Hsu, 2008, p. 48)

BIBLIOTHERAPY

As suggested in the *Scientific American Mind* study, stories can offer readers a lifeline that helps them cope with the chaos of life. In their handbook *Biblio/ Poetry Therapy: The Interactive Process*, Arleen Hynes and Mary Hynes-Berry (2012), two renowned psychotherapists, discuss the healing power of literature. As they point out:

> The recognition that literature can be a healing tool is as old as Aristotle's discussion of catharsis. In bibliotherapy an individual reads or listens to a work of literature specifically for its therapeutic value. . . . to promote greater self-knowledge, to renew the spirit, and, in general, to aid in the healing process. (p. iii)

Bibliotherapy—the prescribing of fiction for life's ailments—emerged as a viable alternative treatment for wounded soldiers in hospital libraries during World War I. The term was coined in 1916 by American essayist Samuel Crothers (1857–1927), who drew on his research of the ancient Greeks, who portrayed the library as "the house of healing for the soul," and of early European psychiatric institutions, in which libraries played a central role. Today, bibliotherapy is accepted as an innovative treatment for mental or psychological disorders that has been endorsed by advocates of narrative medicine such as the Healing Story Alliance, a special interest group of the National Storytelling Network. It has also been promoted as a cure for depression and for various physical and emotional problems.

MINDFUL READING

Related to the healing power of stories is *mindful reading*, a type of deep, reflective reading that involves thinking about what we read in order to forge personal connections with a text on an emotional, an intellectual, and a spiritual level. Mindful reading compels us to shift our perspective to literature by approaching a *secular* text (poem, short story, novel) with the kind of disciplined focus and passionate attention we might bring to a *sacred* text (the Bible, the Qur'an, the Heart Sutra, the Tao Te Ching). It involves rereading a text to focus on specific passages and being fully immersed in the reading experience. In short, mindful reading enables us to experience a state of mindfulness (clarity of mind) generally associated with prayer or meditation.

Of course, asking students to engage in mindful reading requires us to give them enough time to reflect on a text and remind them to slow down, rather than merely striving to "get through" a text.

TYPES OF STORIES

Myths, legends, parables, fables, folktales, fairy tales, allegories, anecdotes—stories reflect the human desire to communicate, to preserve the past, and to imagine the future.

"For sale: baby shoes, never worn." Hemingway's famous six-word story is often cited as an example of extreme brevity in storytelling. In fact, with our current emphasis on "sound bytes" and text messages, and our reportedly decreasing attention span, interest in the six-word story has resurfaced. The journal *Narrative* features the blog yoursixwordstory, which invites readers to submit their stories. Seemingly inspired by the trend, the editors of *SMITH Magazine*, an online forum for storytelling, launched the six-word memoir, a form celebrated in their book *Not Quite What I Was Planning: Six-Word Memoirs by Writers Famous and Obscure* (Fershleiser & Smith, 2008).

The six-word story format has also been employed to explore issues of race, ethnicity, and identity. In 2010, journalist Michelle Norris, a *Washington Post* columnist, set out to explore "the hidden conversation" on race in America. As part of her research, she conducted hundreds of interviews, asking people to share their stories. She then asked them to condense their stories into six-word phrases. The project gained momentum via social media and became known as the Race Card Project, involving thousands of individuals eager to share their "racial narratives."

Other popular short story forms include the iStory (150 words maximum), tweets as stories (140 characters maximum), and flash fiction (750 words maximum). Although touted as a new genre, flash fiction can arguably be traced to Yasunari Kawabata's Palm-of-the-Hand stories, popular in Japan during the 1920s, limited to two facing pages of text.

Clearly, stories "aren't just for entertainment." As Salman Rushdie points out:

> We need, all of us, whatever our background, to constantly examine the stories inside which we live. We all live in stories, so called grand narratives. Nation is

a story. Family is a story. Religion is a story. Community is a story . . . And it seems to me that a definition of any living vibrant society is that you constantly question those stories. That you constantly argue about the stories. In fact the arguing never stops. The argument itself is freedom. . . . When you can't retell for yourself the stories of your life then you live in a prison . . . Somebody else controls the story. (Rushdie, 2006, audio recording).

We read to know that we are not alone.

—C. S. Lewis

Books are the poor man's cinema.

—Junot Díaz

Usually when we . . . read something new, we just compare it
to our own ideas. If it is the same, we accept it and say that it is
correct. If it is not, we say it is incorrect. In either case, we learn
nothing.

—Thich Nhat Hanh

CHAPTER 3

Readers, Reading, and the Reading Process

On March 10, 2018, I participated in my local library's Human Library program. An international program created in Copenhagen, Denmark, in 2000, it uses a library analogy of lending people rather than books to reduce prejudice and dismantle stereotypes by encouraging participants to share their stories with strangers they would not ordinarily encounter.

Our first task was to decide on a personal story to share with our readers and choose a title for our book. I am a biracial (Black/White), bicultural (German/American) woman, and the story I wanted to share was what it felt like growing up as a *Mischling* (the Nazi classification for Germans of mixed race) in conservative Colorado Springs during the 1950s. Since most readers would not recognize "Mischling," I chose "Afro-German," a term coined by poet/warrior Audre Lorde. Shelved among titles such as "Felon," "Sexual Abuse Survivor," and "Transgender," my book focused on a single theme threaded throughout my story: When I learned a new name to call myself and began to identify with other Afro-Germans such as Boris Kodjoe, May Opitz, and Hans Massaquoi, I was finally able let go of my crippling inferiority complex rooted in guilt, shame, and fear and embrace both sides of my cultural heritage. (I learned recently that my condition has been defined by "mixed-blood" Native Americans as "cultural schizophrenia.")

Sharing my "book" through one-on-one conversations with "readers" renewed my appreciation for reading as both a means of creating community and an intimate process of communication between two people engaged in the common endeavor of decoding a text.

But reading is a complex process that involves much more than simply decoding a text.

In *Falling Into Theory: Conflicting Views on Reading Literature*, David H. Richter explores three aspects of reading: Why We Read, What We Read, and How We Read. I have adapted his three-part structure to examine some critical issues concerning readers, reading, and the reading process.

WHY WE READ

In his posthumously published Greenwich Village memoir *Kafka Was the Rage*, renowned book critic and *New York Times* columnist Anatole Broyard (1993) describes the passion he and his friends shared for reading:

> We didn't simply read books; we became them. We took them into ourselves and made them our histories. . . . Books were to us what drugs were to young men in the sixties. They showed us what was possible. (p. 30)

Ultimately, this is the kind of reading experience we desire for our students: that they will be changed by their encounter with a text. Unfortunately, few teachers ever witness such a passion for reading. But knowing it exists and anticipating that magical moment is enough to keep most of us dedicated to our profession. Using the LIST Paradigm to guide students through the reading process can bring us one step closer to that ideal.

Of course, our reasons for reading depend primarily on what we hope to gain from a text.

WHAT WE READ

Amazon. Goodreads. *Publishers Weekly. The New York Times* Best Seller List. Pulitzer Prize–winning novels. Nobel Laureates. *100 Books to Read Before You Die. 10 Books That Will Change Your Life . . .*

Meant to guide our reading while presenting us with a plethora of choices, book lists can be intimidating and overwhelming. So how do we choose the books on which to spend our hard-earned cash and precious time?

I've learned to trust the recommendations of my favorite authors and to read new authors who cite my literary heroes as their inspiration. So when Toni Morrison endorsed the works of Haitian American writer Edwidge Danticat, I sought out her novels and short stories, and when Morrison proclaimed Ta-Nehisi Coates as heir to the legacy of James Baldwin and declared Coates's *Between the World and Me* to be "required reading," I paid attention. Similarly, when I read that Ruth Ozeki was one of Junot Díaz's favorite novelists, I couldn't wait to read *A Tale for the Time Being*. And when Sherman Alexie praised Tommy Orange as "the new Native American voice of his generation," I sought out Orange's (2019b) debut novel, *There, There*. Moreover, when I learned that Vietnamese American writer Viet Thanh Nguyen so admired *Invisible Man* that he named his son Ellison, I knew I had to read *The Sympathizer*. (I also felt we had something in common since, during the 1960s, I so admired the music of Curtis Mayfield that I named my son Curtis.) So far, I have rarely been disappointed with my selections.

But what I read also depends on my mood. When I feel the world closing in on me, I turn to the poetry of Rita Dove, Maya Angelou, Lucille Clifton, Nikki Giovanni, and—a new favorite—Natasha Trethewey, whose poems about growing up biracial in rural Mississippi resonate with me on a profoundly personal level. Of course, for pure pleasure and to remind myself of the absurdities of life, I can always turn to Billy Collins.

So here's my best advice: scan the lists, but find a more reliable way to choose reading material that works for you.

Genre Fiction Versus Literary Fiction

In choosing what to read, we must begin by distinguishing between *genre fiction* (horror, romance, crime, science fiction, fantasy) and *literary fiction* (poetry, short stories, novels, and plays). In general, genre fiction focuses on plot versus character and highlights action, sex, and violence. It usually features a linear structure (a clear beginning, middle, and end), employs a single narrator, and uses direct, unambiguous language ("Here's what happened").

By contrast, literary fiction focuses on character versus plot. It may employ little external action, focusing instead on dialogue, internal monologue, or stream-of-consciousness. Literary fiction is also notable for its use of multiple narrators and points of view, its use of figurative language, and its reliance on subtext (ideas are implied, rather than articulated), an approach often attributed to Hemingway's "iceberg theory" of writing, in which meaning resides beneath the surface of the text. Literary fiction can also be identified by its diverse approach to narrative structures (see **Appendix C**).

However, over the past several decades, the lines between genre and literary fiction have become blurred, especially in the realm of science fiction and fantasy. Consequently, dystopian novels such as Margaret Atwood's *The Handmaid's Tale* and Kazuo Ishiguro's *Never Let Me Go* appeal to a broad range of readers.

A relatively new category of science fiction currently enjoying popular acclaim is Afrofuturism, Black science fiction described as "an intersection of imagination, technology, the future and liberation" (Womack, 2013, p. 9). However, as with many "new" literary genres, Afrofuturism appears to be a new name for a style of writing that dates back to at least the 1920s and W. E. B. Du Bois's short story "The Comet," which imagines a new world free of racism when a comet hits New York City, apparently killing everyone except a Black man and a White woman. Derrick Bell's "The Space Traders," published roughly 50 years later (included in his controversial text *Faces at the Bottom of the Well: The Permanence of Racism*), compels us to consider the impact of economic racism in his story about aliens who land on planet Earth and offer to share their resources with White America, in exchange for their Black citizens. And Henry Dumas's "Ark of Bones," which reverses the biblical myth of Noah's Ark, stands as a classic of Afrofuturism. But perhaps the most popular Afrofuturistic text today is Octavia Butler's *Parable of the Sower*, a dystopian novel set in the year 2024 when all of humanity's vices have led to the annihilation of civilized society.

In addition to Octavia Butler (1947–2006) and Henry Dumas (1934–1968), contemporary Afrofuturists include Samuel L. Delany as well as Nana Kwame Adjei-Brenyah (whose dystopian short story collection *Friday Black* was proclaimed as one of *New York Times*'s 100 Notable Books of 2018).

An excellent resource for Afrofuturism is Sheree R. Thomas's *Dark Matter: A Century of Speculative Fiction from the African Diaspora*.

The Classics

Readers interested in literary fiction often begin by exploring "the classics," a phrase generally used to describe texts revered as exemplary works of literature. Western classics include the Bible, Homer's *Odyssey*, and the plays of Shakespeare. Eastern classics include the Qu'ran, *The Ramayana*, *The Bhagavad Gita*, and *Arabian Nights*. African American classics include *Native Son*, *Invisible Man*, and *Their Eyes Were Watching God*.

In his essay, "What Is an African American Classic?," historian and cultural critic Henry Louis Gates Jr. (2018) defines a classic as

> a work somehow endlessly compelling, generation upon generation, a work whose author we don't have to look like to identify with, to feel at one with, as we find ourselves transported through the magic of a textual time machine; a work that refracts the image of ourselves that we project onto it, regardless of our ethnicity, our gender, our time, our place. (p. 145)

In *A Home Elsewhere: Reading African American Classics in the Age of Obama*, Robert B. Stepto, professor of English and African American Studies at Yale University, explores the power of African American classics in a series of essays inspired by the presidency of Barack Obama. As he explains in his introduction, he selected his texts—which include Frederick Douglass's *My Bondage and My Freedom* (1855), W. E. B. Du Bois's *The Souls of Black Folk* (1903), and Toni Morrison's *Song of Solomon* (1977)—because they address some of the same themes as Obama's memoir, *Dreams from My Father* (1995). Consequently, Stepto (2010) defines "classics" as works that reflect "age-old themes in African American literature," such as "how protagonists raise themselves, often without one or both parents; how black boys invent black manhood . . . ; [and] how protagonists seek and find a home elsewhere" (p. 5).

Modern/Postmodern Novels

Exemplified by Franz Kafka's *The Metamorphosis*, James Joyce's *Ulysses*, Ralph Ellison's *Invisible Man*, and Toni Morrison's *Beloved*, modern/

postmodern novels reject 19th-century traditions and conventions, such as realism and formal structures.

Unlike the classics, modern and postmodern novels do not follow a strict linear structure, nor do they have a definitive beginning, middle, and end. Defining elements include stream-of-consciousness, multiple narrators, internal monologue, and fragmentation, a seemingly disjointed narrative structure that often consists of fragments (bits and pieces of stories, anecdotes, and events) readers must assemble in order to obtain a coherent picture of the whole. As one critic points out, in the postmodern novel, "All that is solid melts into air" (Connolly, 2005).

Cultural Narratives

Within the context of American literature, cultural narratives (also referred to as immigrant narratives) tell the stories of people coming to America in search of a better life, struggling to adapt to American (U.S.) culture while striving to maintain their identities and resist "the cancer of assimilation." Given their focus on personal narrative and family history, cultural narratives may be viewed as a fusion of memoir and historical fiction. A classic example of the cultural narrative is Eva Hoffman's *Lost in Translation: Life in a New Language*.

Over the past several decades, cultural narratives such as Julia Alvarez's *Something to Declare*, Maxine Hong Kingston's *The Woman Warrior*, and Kip Fulbeck's "fictional autobiography" *Paper Bullets* have enjoyed a wide readership in the United States. Fictionalized versions of cultural narratives include Jhumpa Lahiri's *The Namesake*, Mohsin Hamid's *The Reluctant Fundamentalist*, and Chimamanda Ngozi Adichie's *Americanah*. An excellent resource to introduce these narratives in the classroom is Linda Watkins-Goffman's *Understanding Cultural Narratives: Exploring Identity and the Multicultural Experience*.

Graphic Novels

No, they're not comic books. Despite their nontraditional format, graphic novels often tackle some of the same complex themes as more traditional works. The classic example is Art Spiegelman's (1986) *Maus*, which represents Jews as mice and Germans as cats, and depicts Spiegelman interviewing his father about his experiences as a Polish Jew and Holocaust survivor. In 1992, *Maus*—which, over the years, has been variously classified as memoir, biography, history, fiction, and autobiography—became the first graphic novel to win a Pulitzer Prize.

Another classic example is Marjane Satrapi's graphic memoir *Persepolis*, which depicts Satrapi's childhood and adolescence in Iran and Austria during and after the 1979 Islamic Revolution in Iran. Originally published in French, it has been translated into numerous other languages, including English, Spanish, Portuguese, Italian, Greek, and Chinese.

An excellent guide to graphic novels is Russ Kick's *The Graphic Canon: The World's Great Literature as Comics and Visuals.*

Poetry

Students often resist reading poetry because they consider it "too difficult." In the introduction to his book *Poetry 180: A Turning Back to Poetry*, which supports his Library of Congress project, *Poetry 180: A Poem a Day for American High Schools*, former U.S. Poet Laureate Billy Collins (2003) summarizes their dilemma as "a frustrating syllogism":

> I understand English.
> This poem is written in English.
> I have no idea what this poem is saying.
>
> (p. xviii)

Collins explores this topic in his poem "Introduction to Poetry," in which he contrasts the poet/narrator's approach to teaching poetry to that of frustrated students who want to "torture [the poem] . . . to find out what it really means" (p. 3). A former English professor, he mourns the fact that "all too often . . . [high school] is the place where poetry goes to die" (p. xvii). To reverse this trend, Collins (2001) insists:

> Poetry can and should be an important part of our daily lives. Poems can inspire and make us think about what it means to be a member of the human race. By just spending a few minutes reading a poem each day, new worlds can be revealed. (para 1)

Collins (as cited in Meyer, 2011) attributes much of students' resistance to poetry to overinterpretation and an emphasis on revealing a poem's meaning:

> More interesting to me than what a poem means is how it travels. In the classroom, I like to substitute for the question, "What is the meaning of the poem?" other questions: "How does this poem go?" or "How does this poem travel through itself in search of its own ending?" (p. 525)

To emphasize the power of poetry in my classes, I adapted Collins's suggestion and generally start each class with a poem, often asking students to share their favorites. As illustrated throughout this text, I also use poems to introduce longer works. And I encourage students to experiment with activities such as writing a "found poem" based on their reading of a novel or short story.

To encourage reluctant readers—especially students of color—teachers will want to point out that for the past decade, U.S. Poet Laureates have been women and people of color, including Natasha Trethewey (2012–2014), Juan Felipe Herrera (2015–2017), Tracy K. Smith (2017–2019), and Joy Harjo (2019–2022).

Excellent anthologies published over the past 2 decades that feature a diverse range of poets include Kevin Young's *African American Poetry: 250 Years of Struggle and Song*; Carolyn Forché and Duncan Wu's *Poetry of Witness*; and Joy Harjo's *When the Light of the World Was Subdued, Our Songs Came Through: A Norton Anthology of Native Nations Poetry*.

Short Stories

As noted in Chapter 2, stories include a wide range of narratives, from myths and legends to six-word stories. But the traditional short story stands alone in its ability to capture a moment in time.

In 2016, Junot Díaz served as guest editor for *The Best American Short Stories*. In his introduction to the volume, Díaz (2016) offers a poignant and incisive description of the short story:

> Give a short story a dozen pages and it can break hearts bones vanities and cages. . . . Novels might be able to summon entire worlds, but few literary forms can match the story at putting a reader in touch with life's fleeting, inexorable rhythm. It's the one great benefit of the form's defining limitations.
>
> Stories, after all, are short, just like our human moments. . . . stories strike like life and end with its merciless abruptness as well . . . To me this form captures better than any other what it is to be human—the brevity of our moments, the cruel irrevocability when those times places and people we hold the most dear slip through our fingers. (pp. xiii–xiv)

In teaching the short story, teachers tend to lean toward the stories of George Saunders, Alice Munro, Tobias Wolff, and Raymond Carver. But those seeking to expand their repertoire of short stories will want to seek out short stories by writers of color, including Alice Walker, Toni Cade Bambara, John Edgar Wideman, James Alan McPherson, Sherman Alexie, Edwidge Danticat, Junot Díaz, and Jhumpa Lahiri.

HOW WE READ

With the advent of smartphones, tablets, and computers—not to mention ebooks, audiobooks, and podcasts—"reading" in the 21st century has taken on a whole new meaning. But whether we prefer print or electronic versions of books, how we read ultimately revolves around how we engage with a text and its author.

In envisioning their audience, writers tend to identify three types of read-ers: common, implied, and ideal. The *common reader* may pick up a book on impulse or in response to a friend's recommendation. Consequently, they have no grand expectations of the book, other than enjoying a pleasurable reading experience. The *implied reader* may wait impatiently for the next re-lease by their favorite author. They are familiar with the author's themes, top-ics, and writing style and have a more vested interest in their book purchases. According to Henry James, the *ideal reader* is "The one on whom nothing is lost." This is the reader who appreciates the power of language; recognizes symbols, images, and allusions; "gets" the author's innuendos, inside jokes, and double entendres; and relishes the reading experience as an opportunity to connect with great minds on an intellectual, an emotional, and a spiritual level. As literature teachers, it is our responsibility to develop "ideal" readers by guiding our students through the reading process, an approach to critical reading that consists of three stages: Pre-reading, Reading, and Reflection.

Pre-Reading

Pre-reading involves familiarizing ourselves with a text before reading it, such as noting the author's background; the date of publication; the significance of the title, epigraphs, acknowledgments, and dedications; and the work's division into sections and chapters. (One of my favorite dedications is Alice Walker's for *The Color Purple*: "To the Spirit: / Without whose assistance / Neither this book / Nor I / Would have been / Written.")

Once students have familiarized themselves with the text, they are better prepared to engage in the process of close, critical reading.

Reading

As noted earlier, reading is the process of decoding linguistic signs and sym-bols that forge conversations between author, narrator, and reader. This pro-cess can be further divided into three stages: surface reading, critical reading, and close reading.

- **Surface Reading.** Surface reading involves a first reading of the text to familiarize ourselves with the story and its characters. We might also note distinctive elements of the author's style, such as diction and syntax; recurring themes and motifs; and scenes and images we find especially striking. This initial reading should set the stage for a deeper analysis of the text.
- **Critical Reading.** Critical reading prompts readers to examine their assumptions, biases, and personal values in light of selected texts.

> In addition to paying close attention to the language of the text,
> as well as its tone and narrative structure, I encourage students to
> contemplate the author's message and worldview as they relate to the
> struggles experienced by people of color.

To introduce my students to the process of critical reading, I often lead them through a reading of Lorraine Hansberry's *A Raisin in the Sun*. The first drama by a Black woman to be produced on Broadway, the play tells the story of the Youngers, a Black family living in a tenement apartment in 1950s Chicago. When Lena (Mrs. Younger) receives a check for $10,000 as an insurance settlement following the death of her husband, the family disagrees over how to spend the money. The major conflict centers on a disagreement between Lena Younger and her son, Walter Lee. While Lena wants to use the money to buy a house in an all-White neighborhood, Walter Lee wants to invest in a liquor store, which he believes will create a brighter future for his family.

In *How to Read Literature Like a Professor*, Thomas C. Foster (2003), a professor of English at the University of Michigan, attempts to establish the "universality" of this classic play by presenting it as a reimagining of Goethe's *Faust*. He portrays Walter Lee as a modern-day Mephistopheles who narrowly escapes making a deal with the devil, the White man dispatched by the neighborhood "Welcoming Committee" to buy out the family's property claim. But although this approach is certainly valid, it fails to highlight features that distinguish the play as an African American text, such as the title (an homage to Langston Hughes's poem "Harlem"); Hansberry's "signifying" on the Myth of the American Dream, which, for countless Black Americans, remains "a dream deferred"; the setting of the play in Clybourne Park (a fictional version of Woodlawn, a predominantly Black neighborhood on Chicago's South Side); the numerous references to Africa and African culture; and the inclusion of an African character.

To introduce *A Raisin in the Sun*, I invariably begin with a reading of Langston Hughes's "Harlem," which sets the stage for the numerous themes explored throughout the play, such as the American Dream of home ownership, family, money, love, loyalty, culture and identity, racism, human dignity, redemption, and "White flight." We also read Nikki Giovanni's 1996 poem "Nikki-Rosa," which references Woodlawn and declares that "black love is black wealth" (p. 42). To highlight the family's horrific living conditions, we read "The Kitchenette" from Gwendolyn Brooks's *Maud Martha*. We might also watch a video clip from the 2008 film version of *A Raisin in the Sun* starring Phylicia Rashad and Sean Combs and listen to a recording of Nina Simone's "To Be Young, Gifted, and Black," an homage to Hansberry.

Were I to teach the text today, I would also consider pairing it either with Toni Morrison's *Jazz*, which offers another perspective of "a dream deferred," or with Bruce Norris's (2010) Pulitzer Prize–winning play, *Clybourne*

Park, which responds to and expands on the themes explored in *A Raisin in the Sun*.

- **Close Reading.** Close reading involves a conversation between author and reader in which the reader initiates the process of "interrogating the text" in order to "unpack" its themes, symbols, and images.

To help my students understand the process of close reading, I ask them to begin with a key passage from a selected text—a phrase, a sentence, or a paragraph—that puzzles or intrigues them. For example, in reading *The Brief Wondrous Life of Oscar Wao*, which focuses on a Dominican-American family's struggle to come to terms with their history and culture, we selected the statement, "It's never the changes we want that change everything," which serves as the opening sentence of Chapter 2, "Wildwood, 1982–1985" (Díaz, 2007a, p. 51). After a first reading of the chapter, we read it again, focusing our attention on the key passage, which begins our process of "interrogating the text."

What's going on here? Who is speaking to whom? And what are "the changes" the narrator refers to? As we continue our process of interrogation, we discover that the point of view has shifted from the primary narrator, Yunior (aka "The Watcher"), to Lola, Oscar's older sister. As Lola tells her story, we learn that "the changes" she refers to are the changes in her relationship with Beli, her mother, prompted by Beli's breast cancer.

But why breast cancer? We recall that, as a young woman, Beli gained her "superpowers" when she became sexually mature and that she has always been especially proud of her hair and her breasts. Because of breast cancer, she will lose both of these physical attributes that have been an integral part of her identity as a woman. How will this loss change her identity and self-image? By connecting with the text and reflecting on these questions, we eventually arrive at even more profound and significant questions: How do we define ourselves? What physical (and psychological) attributes shape our self-image? And what happens when we lose our sense of identity and are forced to adapt to difficult changes?

But why cancer? Following this line of inquiry compels us to consider broader issues concerning the text as a whole and, by extension, the world beyond the text as we realize that under the brutal dictatorship of Rafael Trujillo, violence has spread throughout the Dominican Republic like a cancer, ravaging the land and its people, much like Beli's cancer is ravaging her body.

Reflection

Reflection involves thinking about a text to determine not only how it aligns with or challenges our worldview, but how it contributes to our spiritual, emotional, and intellectual development.

For example, after reading Ernest Gaines's *A Lesson Before Dying*, I found myself reflecting on Reverend Mose Ambroses's remark to Grant Wiggins, who has returned to Louisiana after graduating from college in California: "You think you educated? . . . What did you learn about your own people?" (Gaines, 1993a, p. 214) To me, it captures the essence of the ongoing debate about the purpose of education and the roles and responsibilities of teachers. More specifically, it recalls James Baldwin's "A Talk to Teachers," in which he asserts that "Any Negro who is born in this country and undergoes the American educational system runs the risk of becoming schizophrenic" (Baldwin, 1985c, p. 326). Both Gaines and Baldwin argue that, to reach their students, teachers must first respect them as intelligent human beings capable of learning and then tailor their teaching strategies to meet their students' needs.

Similarly, after reading Ruth Ozeki's *A Tale for the Time Being*, I found myself reflecting on Japan's culture of suicide. As someone who is part Japanese and who lived in Japan for several years, Ozeki is not afraid to dismantle the stereotype of Japan as a nation of peace and tranquility where violence is almost unheard of to reveal the underlying stress in a society that manifests as excessive discipline and control. I also found myself recalling the mixed emotions I experienced nearly 3 decades ago when I learned that my son, who had chosen to major in Asian Studies at the University of Hawaii, would be moving to Japan, proclaimed as "the suicide capital of the world."

In short, reflection compels us to move beyond the page and forge connections with ideas and concepts outside the text that prompt us to consider what it means to be human.

"Only Connect"

E. M. Forster's sage advice about forging personal connections with a text is often passed on to students, who tend to view it as merely cryptic and confusing. But how *do* we connect with texts that, initially, seem completely beyond our realm of reality?

In the fall of 2019, I had an opportunity to explore this conundrum when I was asked to lead a book discussion on Viet Thanh Nguyen's *The Sympathizer* for my local library's Adult Reading Program. Before the meeting, the organizer warned me that the group included a retired Vietnam veteran who had expressed his resistance to the author's perspective of the war and who might present a problem. During our introductions, the veteran made it clear that he was there to challenge the text. But as it turned out, he was one of the few who had actually *read* the novel, and his questions and comments generated discussion and prompted others to engage with the text on a deeper level. In fact, his questions provided an opening for me to share my reading experience.

I began by validating his frustration. I then shared two personal stories I rarely share with close friends, let alone total strangers: On September 9,

1968, my ex-husband, a former Lance Corporal in the Marine Corps, was awarded the Purple Heart "for wounds received in action in Vietnam on 14 February 1968," just two months shy of his 21st birthday. On March 21, 1987, my youngest brother was shot and killed in San Diego, just shy of his 30th birthday, by a Vietnam veteran who claimed post-traumatic stress disorder (PTSD) as his defense.

After an awkward silence, I could sense a shift of energy in the room as people began to realize that our discussion had moved far beyond the novel. Moreover, I knew that for the veteran and me, our shared reading experience had had a profound impact on both of us and had enabled us to connect on a human level that transcended our obvious differences of race, class, and gender.

I had a similar experience decades earlier while writing the *Cliffs Notes* on Ernest Gaines's *A Lesson Before Dying*. As part of my research, I scheduled a telephone interview with Mr. Gaines, during which he generously shared his experience writing the novel and expressed his interest in my project. During the interview, he told me that an inmate at the Louisiana State Penitentiary at Angola had read the novel and reviewed it for *The Angolite*, the prison news magazine.

As soon as we concluded our conversation, I called Angola and requested a copy of the magazine, which I received within a few weeks. After reading the review, "To Kill a Hog," by Michael Glover, I called again to ask if I might correspond with Mr. Glover via mail. When the warden informed me that Mr. Glover had died "of natural causes," I felt overwhelmed by sadness. At first unable to identify my seemingly unwarranted emotional response, I soon realized that, through our shared experience of reading *A Lesson Before Dying*, I had forged a connection with the Angola inmate, even though we had never met.

Book Groups and Reading Guides

Oprah's Book Club, launched in the fall of 1996, sparked a veritable explosion of book discussion groups nationwide. Consequently, several book publishers now provide online book discussion guides for select novels. Some even include Reading Group Guides as part of the printed novel, encouraging readers to recommend it for their own book groups. Clearly capitalizing on this marketing trend, a plethora of books has appeared that purport to teach us how to become better readers. Recent titles include Thomas Foster's *How to Read Literature Like a Professor*; Francine Prose's *Reading Like a Writer*; James Woods's *How Fiction Works*; Jane Smiley's *Thirteen Ways of Looking at the Novel*; John Sutherland's *How to Read a Novel*; and Linda Christensen's *Reading, Writing, and Rising Up*. (Of course, the original "how to read" guide is Mortimer J. Adler and Charles Van Doren's *How to Read a Book*. First published in 1940, this "classic guide to intelligent reading," continually revised and updated, remains one of the most popular guides for general readers.)

But while these texts offer information designed to help readers access a text, none provides a basic introduction to the reading process, an essential component of literacy instruction. Instead, the authors tend to separate the *reading process* from the *reading experience*, assuming that, once provided with general directions, readers can create their own literary road maps. Moreover, as one might expect, the texts focus primarily on "the classics" and on contemporary Western texts by writers such as Philip Roth, Michael Crichton, Alice Munro, and Raymond Carver. But even when they include works by writers of color, they tend to view them through the lens of Western Eurocentric culture, which, as noted in the Introduction, can lead to egregious misreadings.

The clamor for "how to read" guides also led to the publication of several important works by writers of color, all of which address issues of social justice. Titles include Marita Golden's *The Word: Black Writers Talk About the Transformative Power of Reading and Writing*; Robert Stepto's *A Home Elsewhere: Reading African American Classics in the Age of Obama*; Stephanie Stokes Oliver's *Black Ink: Literary Legends on the Peril, Power, and Pleasure of Reading and Writing*; Kevin Young's *The Grey Album*; and Farah Jasmine Griffin's *Read Until You Understand: The Profound Wisdom of Black Life and Literature*. Instructors dedicated to providing a culturally responsive curriculum will want to explore these texts as well.

The proliferation of Reading Group Guides speaks to two undeniable truths: (1) despite the popularity of movies and video games, people still turn to books for escapism, entertainment, and intellectual stimulation; and (2) readers are hungry for guidance on how to approach new and unfamiliar works of literary fiction. But with so much emphasis on reading as a social event (often fueled by food and drink), we tend to forget that reading is, essentially, a solitary activity that demands focused attention, introspection, and reflection.

Clearly, an important goal of any introductory literature course is to create critical readers able to access and analyze a text from multiple perspectives. But before we address the concept of critical reading, let's review some basic tenets concerning reading and the reading process.

Reading is the process of decoding linguistic signs and symbols that forge conversations between author, narrator and reader. Consequently, it relies on our awareness of and attention to the nuances of language.

Reading is both a skill and an art. Consequently, it requires readers to master basic skills such as understanding the elements of fiction (plot, character, theme, setting, point of view) and the language of literature (symbol, metaphor, allusion, irony, etc.) in order to forge personal and emotional connections with the text. But it also expects readers to master the art of close, critical reading.

In the essay "Interpretive Communities and Literary Meaning," David H. Richter (2000) addresses this issue:

> Most of us learned to read so long ago that we have forgotten how complicated and confusing it must have been. . . . We have internalized and automatized the entire process so completely that, unless we are forced to reflect on it, it seems entirely natural: we "just read." But it isn't natural at all. . . . In college, . . . we quickly become aware that though we can "just read" newspapers and magazines and the fiction sold on drugstore paperback racks, [college literature requires] a "close reading" that is almost as difficult to master as reading and speech, with as many seemingly arbitrary rules. (p. 235)

Richter also points out that how we learn to read literary fiction, as well as where and when we first encounter a text, has a profound impact on how we approach new and unfamiliar texts.

Literary interpretation is a process only partly guided by the reader. Readers often attempt to impose their own interpretation on a work, based on their background and experience. But as Susan Sontag (1966) points out in her classic essay "Against Interpretation," this process, if taken to extremes, can lead to textual distortion by focusing on "what it means" rather than on "what it is" (p. 14).

Writing nearly 4 decades later, Mark Edmundson (2004) offers a kinder, gentler perspective on interpretation in *Why Read?* As he points out:

> [T]he art of interpretation is . . . the art of arriving at a version of the work that the author—as we imagine him, as we imagine her—would approve and be gratified by. The idea is not perfectly to reproduce the intention; [but] to bring the past into the present and to do so in a way that will make the writer's ghost nod in something like approval. (p. 53)

A Note on *Cliffs Notes*

As a former *Cliffs Notes* author, I grappled with the concept of interpretation while creating the *Notes* for Toni Morrison's *Song of Solomon.* I realized that in my new role, I was neither the scholar preparing a conference paper for my peers nor the teacher preparing a lecture for my students. I was a faceless writer addressing anonymous readers.

Eventually, I began to visualize potential readers as students in my virtual classroom. I started with Morrison's statement that *Song of Solomon* is about "a man who learns to fly and all that that means. But it's also about the ways in which we discover, all of us, who and what we are. And how important and truly exciting that journey is" (Burrelle's Transcript, 1996, p. 16).

For me, creating the *Cliffs Notes* for *Song of Solomon* (and, later, for Ernest Gaines's *A Lesson Before Dying,* Harriet Jacobs's *Incidents in the Life of a Slave Girl,* and Ralph Ellison's *Invisible Man*) was one of the most rewarding experiences of my academic career. I had 1 year to complete each *Note,* during which I immersed myself in the text and conducted the most intense research I had ever undertaken.

Consequently, when I began teaching at the Air Force Academy, I was devastated to discover that what I had approached as a scholarly research project designed to help students access complex texts was frowned upon by my colleagues, who viewed me as a traitor to academia. So my self-esteem received a much-needed boost when I stumbled upon a review of Harold Bloom's 1998 magnum opus—*Shakespeare: The Invention of the Human*—which stated that the tome "may be destined to become the grand Cliffs Notes for scholars" (Bloom, 1998, p. 3).

Resources for Literary Criticism

Students who feel pressured to "get through" a text will invariably seek shortcuts, sometimes turning to questionable sources such as Amazon reviews written by other students. For teachers reluctant to consider *Cliffs Notes* as a form of literary criticism, I suggest the following:

1. Give students more time to read (and reread) a text.
2. Provide students with reading guidelines, such as the LIST Paradigm.
3. Use Norton Critical Editions of selected works, which include critical essays that encourage students to read beyond the text.
4. Use annotated editions of selected texts.
5. Introduce students to contemporary literary critics such as Michiko Kakutani, Roland Barthes, Henry Louis Gates Jr., and Nellie McKay.
6. Introduce students to publications such as *The New York Times Book Review, World Literature Today,* and *Poets & Writers,* all of which carry articles, interviews, and reviews of new books by a broad range of writers.
7. Obtain a copy of *The Paris Review Interviews* for your classroom. This four-volume set—which includes interviews with prominent authors conducted between 1953 and 2008—offers amazing insights into "the writing life."
8. Introduce students to the *Writers at Work* series, in which writers discuss their influences and inspirations, as well as their creative process.
9. Encourage students to visit the websites of their favorite authors.
10. Encourage students to form their own book discussion groups.

An excellent resource for African American literary criticism is Hazel Arnett Ervin's *African American Literary Criticism, 1773 to 2000.*

Intertextuality: "Everything Is Connected"

Critical reading requires an awareness and appreciation of intertextuality, the notion that "everything is connected." One of the most important lessons we can teach our students is that literary works do not exist in isolation by introducing them to the concept of *intertextuality*, a term coined in 1966 by French critic Julia Kristeva.

Intertextuality holds that no text is truly "original," since it responds to or builds on previous texts. Consequently, we might envision literature as a continuous conversation between authors across space and time.

Viewed from the perspective of the African American literary tradition, we might imagine this interchange as an extended example of "call and response." We realize that James Baldwin's autobiography *Notes of a Native Son* responds to Richard Wright's novel *Native Son*, and that Wright's short story collection *Uncle Tom's Children* responds to Harriet Beecher Stowe's *Uncle Tom's Cabin*. Recognizing the connections between texts can enhance our reading experience and remind us of the timeless nature of stories across cultures.

To introduce my students to the concept of intertextuality, I often have them read short narrative poems before engaging with longer works that explore similar themes and motifs. For example, to introduce *Beloved*, which explores the complex roles of memory and imagination as devices that can help us cope with trauma and the arduous process of redemption, recovery, and healing, we read "The Lanyard," a seemingly simple poem by contemporary poet Billy Collins that explores a son's relationship with his mother, triggered by memories of a lanyard he made for her as a child. After introducing us to his story in the first stanza, the narrator begins the second stanza with the statement, "No cookie nibbled by a French novelist / could send one more suddenly into the past" (Collins, 2005, p. 45).

Why does Collins mention a "cookie nibbled by a French novelist" in a poem about a lanyard? Who is this French novelist? And what's the significance of this particular cookie? Of course, I don't expect my students to answer these questions, but I *do* expect them to ask the questions, which can "unlock" the poem—and, by extension, the novel—and enable them to understand and appreciate it on a deeper level.

As we explore these questions, we discover that the French novelist is Marcel Proust and that the cookie is the infamous madeleine. But what's the connection? As we dig deeper, we discover that Collins alludes to Proust's most famous work, *Remembrance of Things Past* (or *In Search of Lost Time*), to illuminate the power of seemingly small, insignificant things—a cookie, a lanyard—to serve as triggers for a deluge of memories. Specifically, he alludes to the moment when Proust's narrator is suddenly overwhelmed by childhood memories after tasting a madeleine dipped in lime-blossom tea (Proust, 2004, pp. 47–48).

Once students grasp this concept, they are better prepared to explore *Beloved*, a complex novel in which Sethe, a formerly enslaved African woman struggling to escape the past, finds her memory repeatedly triggered by seemingly random, insignificant things—a tree, a song, a pair of crystal earrings—that recall painful memories of slavery. (To help students internalize this lesson, I resort to a somewhat unorthodox teaching strategy: I buy two dozen madeleines—half plain, half chocolate-dipped—and bring them to our next class meeting.)

If we expand the term "text" to include other media such as films, musical compositions, and visual arts, we realize that both Lauryn Hill's album *The Miseducation of Lauryn Hill* and Zadie Smith's "The Miseducation of Irie Jones" (in *White Teeth*) respond to Carter G. Woodson's classic text, *The Mis-Education of the Negro*. Similarly, Marcel Camus's classic film *Black Orpheus* reimagines the Greek myth of Orpheus and Eurydice, and Spike Lee's film *Chi-Raq* (a "mash-up" of Chicago and Iraq) responds to Aristophanes's play *Lysistrata*.

Pairing Texts: Narratives and Counternarratives

Embedded in the concept of intertextuality is that of the *counternarrative*, a narrative that reverses or challenges a *master narrative* by shifting point of view from oppressor to oppressed. Examples include Jean Rhys's *Wide Sargasso Sea*—which offers a counternarrative to Charlotte Bronte's *Jane Eyre* by shifting the point of view from Jane to Mr. Rochester's first wife, "the mad woman in the attic"—and Margaret Walker's *Jubilee*, which provides a counternarrative to Margaret Mitchell's *Gone with the Wind*. Similarly, Langston Hughes's "I, Too," Nikki Giovanni's "Ego Tripping," and Sherman Alexie's "Song of Ourself" all provide counternarratives to Walt Whitman's "Song of Myself."

To introduce the concept of counternarratives to my students, I often begin with a contemporary text that responds to an earlier novel. Once students have completed a first reading of the text, I bring in materials such as author interviews and excerpts from the earlier text to demonstrate how an author responds to and expands on the works of a literary ancestor.

One of my most successful teaching experiences focused on Ernest Gaines's *A Lesson Before Dying*, which offers a counternarrative to Richard Wright's *Native Son*. Although both novels focus on the final days of a young Black man on Death Row and culminate in his execution, Wright's novel traces Bigger's inevitable path to death and destruction, whereas Gaines's offers us a vision of hope and redemption through Jefferson's transformation. (Ideally, students would read both novels.)

We began by comparing the two authors' worldviews. In his autobiography *Black Boy (American Hunger)*, Wright (1998a) laments, "When I brooded upon the cultural barrenness of black life, I wondered if clean, positive tenderness, love, honor, and the capacity to remember were native with man" (p. 261). He also admits that "In all my life—though surrounded by people—I had not had a single satisfying, sustained relationship with another human being and, not having had any, I did not miss it" (p. 261). But Gaines contends (1995a) that "Besides the conflict between the white and black, we also carry on a full life." He also points out that, "The major conflict in my work is when the black male attempts to go beyond the line that is drawn for him" (p. 5).

In comparing these two texts, teachers will want to focus on similarities such as the following: (a) historical context (Wright, the Robert Nixon case, 1938; Gaines, the Willie Francis case, 1947); (b) animal imagery (Bigger as "rat," Jefferson as "hog"); (c) religion (Reverend Hammond gives Bigger a wooden cross; Reverend Mose Ambrose offers Jefferson spiritual guidance); (d) nature imagery (Wright, snow and blizzards [hostile White society]); Gaines, trees, boulders, and cane fields [supportive Black community]; and (e) key themes (Wright, "You can't win"; Gaines, "You can be bigger than anyone.").

As illustrated in this chapter, a focused approach to reading and the reading process can lead to a more rewarding and enjoyable reading experience. Moreover, it can impress upon students the discipline, dedication, and intellectual rigor required for the study of literature.

The purpose of all art is to lay bare the questions which have been hidden by the answers.

—James Baldwin

Literature is the question minus the answer.

—Roland Barthes

CHAPTER 4

Interrogating the Text

Asking Significant Questions

Much like the study of philosophy—"the love of wisdom and pursuit of truth in all things"—the study of literature compels us to ask hard questions about our lives and our place in the universe. In short, an informed, critical reading of a literary text centers on *asking significant questions*: insightful, open-ended questions that not only help us delve more deeply into a text to unpack its language and discover the author's worldview, but also enable us to forge personal connections with a text in order to examine our own lives. Unfortunately, the conventional study of literature often encourages students to seek answers rather than ask questions. As Marjorie Garber (2012) points out in *The Use and Abuse of Literature:*

> Even when literature is read, taught, and studied, it is often interrogated for wisdom or moral lessons. The clumsy formulations I grew up with—what is the moral of the story? what is the hero's or heroine's tragic flaw?—still influence and flatten the questions people often ask about literary works, as if there were one answer, and a right answer, at that. The genius of literary study comes in asking questions, not in finding answers. (p. 14)

Fortunately, more recent pedagogy has shifted this perspective by acknowledging the power of "interrogating a text," a process that mirrors the Socratic method, designed to stimulate critical thinking by eliciting ideas and exposing underlying suppositions.

CONFLICTING VIEWS ON READING LITERATURE

In his classic text *Beyond the Culture Wars: How Teaching the Conflicts Can Revitalize Education* (a response to David H. Richter's *Falling Into Theory: Conflicting Views on Reading Literature*), Gerald Graff (1992) highlights some compelling questions to consider when reading a literary work:

> Why *study* literature, as opposed to just enjoying it in one's spare time? Which literature should be studied, and by what process should this be decided? From

what viewpoint should we read, given the variety of possible approaches to any text? Should we try to forget our ethnicity, gender, and sexual orientation when we read, or should we bring these factors into play, and if so how? Is the reading of literature inevitably political, or does it transcend politics? (p. v)

I believe that literature poses even more personal and powerful questions, such as the following:

- Who am I? Where do I belong?
- What does it mean to live an "authentic" life?
- What am I willing to sacrifice to pursue my dreams?
- Do I have the resilience to cope with inevitable loss?
- Am I prepared to face my own death?

Even so, we must decide which questions to ask. In their seminal text *Asking the Right Questions: A Guide to Critical Thinking*, Neil Browne and Stuart M. Keeley (2000) list 11 critical questions for instructors to consider, which can be adapted to their respective disciplines. (The questions form the outline for the text.)

1. What are the issue and the conclusion?
2. What are the reasons?
3. Which words or phrases are ambiguous?
4. What are the value conflicts and assumptions?
5. What are the descriptive assumptions?
6. Are there any fallacies in the reasoning?
7. How good is the evidence?
8. Are there rival causes?
9. Are the statistics deceptive?
10. What significant information is omitted?
11. What reasonable conclusions are possible?

Clearly, not all of these questions apply to literature, but those concerning ambiguous words and phrases, value conflicts and assumptions, and omitted information are key to literary analysis.

ENGAGING QUESTIONS FROM OTHER DISCIPLINES

Moving beyond the humanities to engage questions from other disciplines can yield rich rewards in terms of revitalizing our teaching of literature.

In *Questions of Character: Illuminating the Heart of Leadership Through Literature*, Joseph L. Badaracco Jr., Professor of Business Ethics at Harvard Business School, offers an innovative approach to reading literature. In his introduction, he describes teaching a leadership class for a group of executives in which he asked students to read Joseph Conrad's short story "The Secret Sharer." Since the story concerns a man on his first voyage as a ship's captain who allows a mysterious stranger to board his ship, Badaracco wanted to use it to generate discussion on leadership roles and responsibilities, but then wondered if he was wasting his students' valuable time by introducing fiction into a business course. To his surprise, his students became fully engaged with the story. Reflecting on the class, Badaracco (2006) wonders:

> What happened in the classroom that morning? Why did the discussion take off? Serendipity no doubt helped, as it does in any good class. The discussion also benefited from a trick: the executives had been induced to treat a work of fiction like a business school case study. This sleight of hand was important because many people associate literature with abstruse talk about Freudian imagery or deconstruction; case studies, on the other hand, are familiar tools for management education.
>
> But something more was going on. The captain's story resonated with the executives. None of them had commanded a merchant ship in Southeast Asia, but Conrad's fictional account of taking responsibility rang true. The story also raised several questions about leadership that the executives recognized as critical, and by pulling them in the story got the executives to think about these questions in personal terms. They moved back and forth, easily and naturally, between the challenges facing the captain and challenges in their own careers. Conrad's story worked as a remarkable mirror: by looking closely at the captain, the executives reflected on themselves as leaders. (pp. 2–3)

Because of the unexpected success of this class, Badaracco decided to change his approach to teaching leadership by "taking serious works of fiction, treating them as case studies, and examining them in depth" by posing questions such as the following:

- "Do I Have a Good Dream?" (Arthur Miller's *Death of a Salesman*)
- "How Flexible Is My Moral Code?" (Chinua Achebe's *Things Fall Apart*)
- "What Is Sound Reflection?" (Sophocles's *Antigone*) (pp. 2–3)

Drawing on Badaracco's example, teachers might include a study of historical documents—the Constitution, the Declaration of Independence, Jim Crow laws—in the literature curriculum. Similarly, they might encourage students to analyze letters and speeches by prominent historical figures from a literary perspective and to explore how historical events—slavery, segregation, immigration—are represented in contemporary fiction. Not only would such an approach enrich the study of literature, it would also help reduce the clamor over "teaching Critical Race Theory," a concept aimed at exposing racist precedents in our judicial system, taught within the context of legal studies—and introduce students to the legacy of racism in U.S. history.

"What If . . . ?"

One of the first—and most significant—questions fiction writers invariably pose for themselves is "What if"?

- *What if* a murdered child returns to the world as an adult to confront her killer?
- *What if* a ship's captain becomes obsessed with killing the white whale that bit off his leg?
- *What if* a man wakes up one morning to find himself transformed into a "monstrous vermin"?

In her short story "Nineteen Fifty-Five," Alice Walker compels us to consider the exploitation of Black musicians by White artists by posing an intriguing question: "What if Black musicians were actually compensated for their contributions to society?"

The narrative opens in 1955, a year marked by two significant events that launched the Civil Rights movement: the murder of Emmett Till in Money, Mississippi, and the arrest of Rosa Parks in Montgomery, Alabama. It tells the story of Gracie Mae Still, an aging former blues singer, whose life is suddenly disrupted when two southern White men—Traynor, a young singer, and his manager—appear on her doorstep and offer her $1,000 to buy a song she recorded several decades ago. Gracie Mae gladly accepts their offer. And over the years, she watches Traynor's meteoric rise to rock-and-roll fame as he performs her song to the acclaim of audiences around the world.

It soon becomes evident that Walker's story is a reimagining of Elvis Presley's rise to fame, beginning with his first smash hit, "Hound Dog," originally written for and performed by blues singer Big Mama Thornton, a reported rival of Bessie Smith. (Beginning in 1955, the story's narrative time frame encompasses significant events in Presley's life, ranging from 1956, when he released "Hound Dog," to 1977, the year of his death.)

But events soon take a strange turn as Traynor acknowledges his indebtedness to Gracie Mae and begins to see her as a surrogate mother figure. Consequently, over the next two decades, he showers her with lavish gifts, including a white Cadillac, a mink coat, a new house, and a 500-acre farm. But the gifts have little impact on Gracie Mae, who remains in her modest home and only occasionally drives her Cadillac through the neighborhood. The story ends when Gracie Mae learns of Traynor's death and finds herself wondering about his life.

Reflecting on Walker's story, we might be compelled to ask ourselves several questions: Can White guilt ever compensate for the stolen legacy of Black people, especially Black artists? How does the story fit within the larger context of the Civil Rights movement? What is its relevance for us today? At any rate, we must admit that it raises significant questions about race, racism, and cultural appropriation.

WHO IS "QUALIFIED" TO SPEAK?

In 1967, William Styron, a White southerner, published *The Confessions of Nat Turner*, a novel presented as a first-person narrative by Nat Turner, leader of the infamous 1831 slave rebellion in Southampton, Virginia. The book prompted an immediate outcry from Black scholars and historians, who pointed out that Styron had completely distorted the character of Nat Turner, turning him from a defiant Black prophet and revolutionary into an impotent "Uncle Tom" stereotype who lusted after White women. The result was a book of collected essays titled *William Styron's Nat Turner: Ten Black Writers Respond*, published in 1968. In 1997, the book was rereleased as *The Second Crucifixion of Nat Turner*, with a new introduction by renowned historian John Henrik Clarke. In defending his choice of a title, Clarke (1997) explained:

> Nat Turner's first crucifixion was on the gallows in the county of Southampton, Virginia, on November 11, 1831 . . . Nat Turner's second crucifixion was in the misinterpretation of his life . . . by white writers who chose to play down his rebellion to preclude recognizing him as a genuine radical. (p. vii)

The furor surrounding Styron's novel (which won the 1968 Pulitzer Prize for Fiction) raised significant questions concerning freedom of speech versus cultural appropriation and exploitation.

In 2000, Ian Frazier published *On the Rez*, an account of his experiences on the Pine Ridge Reservation in South Dakota, accompanied by his Native American friend who introduces him to reservation life. According to Amazon.com, "*On the Rez* delivers a history of the Oglala Nation that spotlights our paleface population in some of its most shameful, back-stabbing moments, as well as [providing] a quick tour through Indian America."

But Sherman Alexie's (2009) response to Frazier's book articulated the frustrations of many Native Americans: "Non-Indians should stop writing about us until we've established our own voice. . . . If non-Indians stop writing about us they'll have to publish us instead" (p. 98).

Rejecting the argument that his stance seeks to prevent all outsiders from writing about another culture or group of people, Alexie continues:

> The real issue is that Indians' relationship to this country is still that of the colonized, so that when non-Indians write about us, it's colonial literature. And unless it's seen that way, there's a problem . . . The galley had at least fifty historical

errors. And I really had a problem with the point of view. What happens is that anybody can write these kinds of books about Indians, but the same does not hold true with any other group. Indians have so little political power, so little social and cultural power, that this happens to us all the time. (p. 98)

In 2020, Jeanine Cummins published *American Dirt*, the story of Lydia, a Mexican refugee who escapes her violent life in Acapulco, Mexico, and comes to the United States with her son Luca, only to become entrenched in the hardships of immigrant life. Praised for its insight and authenticity, the book became a *New York Times* Best Seller and was selected for Oprah's Book Club. But when it was discovered that the author was a White woman, critics accused her of appropriating the real-life trauma of Mexican immigrants for entertainment and financial gain.

Ironically, two prominent Latina writers, Sandra Cisneros and Isabel Allende, supported the text, which ranked as number six in Hispanic American Literature on Amazon.com. Cisneros points out that Cummins's text will reach a wider audience than her own works are able to. She contends that as long as *American Dirt* raises readers' awareness of America's immigrant crisis, it has done its job. But those who disagree echo Alexie's argument: that as long as White authors are able to benefit financially from writing the stories of others (Cummins reportedly received a $1 million advance for her novel), immigrant writers will not be adequately compensated for their works.

Clearly, the past several decades have taught us little about where to draw the line between entertainment and exploitation.

Questions for Writers

In his groundbreaking text *A Stranger's Journey: Race, Identity, and Narrative Craft in Writing*, David Mura (2018) poses four significant questions fiction writers must ask themselves concerning their narrators:

- Who is the narrator?
- Whom is the narrator telling her story to?
- When is the narrator telling the story?
- Why is the narrator telling the story? (p. 135)

Although Mura addresses these questions to writers, they are equally relevant for readers. As he points out, for traditional storytellers who told their stories to members of their own tribes gathered around a campfire, the answers to these questions would be readily apparent and revealed in the telling. But for modern readers, the questions have become essential and relevant.

For most readers, questions concerning narrative point of view focus on issues such as evaluating the limitations and benefits inherent in first-person versus third-person narratives or on gauging the effectiveness of single, dual, or multiple narrators. But Mura moves beyond these distinctions, focusing on the narrator's voice as perceived by the reader/listener. To illustrate, he focuses on two texts with radically different narrators: Aravind Adiga's *The White Tiger* and Junot Díaz's *The Brief Wondrous Life of Oscar Wao.* Adiga's narrator, Balram Halwai, a Bangolore entrepreneur and criminal, tells his story of escaping poverty to the emperor of China via a series of letters. Since the emperor allegedly knows little or nothing about modern India's politics and economics, Halwai assumes the role of "native informer," providing numerous detailed explanations about Indian life and culture to his "foreign" reader and, by extension, to his "foreign" Western readers. By contrast, Díaz's narrator Yunior, a young, college-educated Dominican American immigrant, tells his story to other Dominican Americans who can understand his language and relate to his experience. As Mura (2018) points out:

> [W]ith such an audience, the economy of explanation is clear, both for Díaz and for his narrator, Yunior. No Spanish need be translated; a familiarity with Dominican culture is assumed (though Yunior still must footnote an explanation of the reign and history of Trujillo); pop cultural references can be dropped without explanation or context. In contrast to *The White Tiger* and Balram's formal address to the premier of China, Yunior's voice is intimate and alludes to a shared experience. . . . (p. 146)
>
> In his aesthetic choices, Díaz refuses to place either Yunior or Oscar at the margins of his storytelling or of the culture. He also shows other authors from immigrant or marginalized communities how they might tell their tales without resorting to an economy of explanation where everything must be made clear to a White mainstream readership or some vague picture of a majority audience. (pp. 146–147)

Questions for Students

I always encourage my students to begin the process of "interrogating a text" by considering questions suggested by its title. For example, in reading Ralph Ellison's *Invisible Man*, we begin by addressing the question that immediately presents itself: How can a Black man in White America be "invisible"? Once we establish the irony inherent in the narrator's statement, "I am an invisible man," we can proceed to discuss the concept of "social death": a phenomenon experienced by people denied their human dignity by being excluded from society through methods and institutions such as slavery, segregation, persecution, and apartheid.

I then ask students to reflect on a time they felt "invisible," perhaps by being ignored or dismissed by a group or individual from whom they sought approval or validation. Once we have explored this concept, students are better prepared to deal with some of the issues raised by the novel.

To preview Ernest Gaines's novel *A Lesson Before Dying,* which centers on a young Black man who has been wrongly convicted of murder and awaits execution on Death Row, I ask students to consider four questions suggested by the title:

1. What is the lesson?
2. Who learns it?
3. Who is dying?
4. Why should we care?

I also ask them to reflect on the narrator's opening statement: "I was not there, yet I was there," which not only sets the stage for the novel's narrative structure, but also highlights the difference between being a witness and being an observer (Gaines, 1993a, p. 1). Asked to differentiate between the two, James Baldwin (1996) explains, "An observer has no passion. It doesn't mean *I saw it*. It means that *I was there*. I don't have to observe the life and death of Martin Luther King. I am a witness to it" (p. 92).

To highlight and illuminate key themes in the novel such as freedom and literacy, compassion, redemption, and transformation, we read excerpts from texts such as Carter G. Woodson's *The Mis-Education of the Negro;* Franz Kafka's *The Metamorphosis;* Elie Wiesel's *Night;* Richard Wright's *Native Son;* and Dr. Martin Luther King Jr.'s "Letter from Birmingham Jail." We also consider Gaines's (1993b) remarks regarding his novel:

> We all know—at least intellectually—that we're going [to die]. The difference is being told, "Okay, it's tomorrow at 10 a.m." How do you react to that? How do you face it? That, it seems to me, is the ultimate test of life. (para. 36)

Thus armed, students are ready for a close, critical reading of the text that focuses on literary elements such as plot, setting, and character, as well as cultural, historical, and human rights issues such as the legacy of slavery, race relations in the Jim Crow South, the corrupt criminal justice system, and capital punishment. They are also better prepared to receive Gaines's message concerning the inherent worth and dignity of a human life, the importance of "learning to stand" (Hemingway's "grace under pressure"), and the value of friendship and personal relationships, which form the basis of Dr. King's "beloved community."

The Kite Runner, a coming-of-age novel by Afghan American author Khaled Hosseini, tells the story of two childhood friends from different social classes: Amir, the protagonist and narrator, is from a well-to-do Pashtun family, while Hassan is a member of the Hazaras, perceived as an inferior class. Set in Kabul against the backdrop of the war in Afghanistan, the novel opens before the war, when Amir and Hassan enjoy flying kites and participating in kite-fighting tournaments. Following a traumatic event that ends their friendship, the boys are separated and the narrative follows Amir's escape to Pakistan and his subsequent move to the United States. The novel's major conflict involves Amir's guilt over having betrayed his friend and his opportunity "to be good again" by rescuing Hassan's son from an orphanage in Kabul.

To gain a deeper appreciation of the novel, we note that it poses several significant questions:

- Who are the "Hazaras" of this world? The "Pashtuns"?
- What is the price we must pay for the choices we make?
- How do we define love? Loyalty? Friendship?
- Is there a way to atone for our sins and "be good again"?
- How does the past shape our future?

I used a similar approach to introduce my students to Native American literature. In the opening chapter of *Other Destinies: Understanding the American Indian Novel*, Louis Owens (1994) raises several significant questions concerning American Indian novels. As he points out:

> To begin to write about something called "the American Indian novel" is to enter a slippery and uncertain terrain. Take one step into this region and we are confronted with difficult questions of authority and ethnicity: What is an Indian? Must one be one-sixteenth Osage, one-eighth Cherokee, one-quarter Blackfoot, or full-blood Sioux to be Indian? Must one be raised in a traditional "Indian" culture or speak a native language or be on a tribal roll? To identify as Indian—or mixed-blood—and to write about that identity is to confront such questions. (p. 3)

Exploring "Subversive" Texts

In her bestselling memoir, *Reading Lolita in Tehran*, Azar Nafisi (2008) anticipates readers' questions concerning her selection of Vladimir Nabokov's *Lolita* for her women's reading group:

> I have asked you to imagine us, to imagine us in the act of reading *Lolita* in Tehran: a novel about a man who, in order to possess and captivate a twelve-year-old girl, indirectly causes the death of her mother, Charlotte, and keeps her as his little entrapped mistress for two years. Are you bewildered? Why *Lolita*? Why *Lolita* in Tehran? (p. 35)

Nafisi then proceeds to answer her own questions, pointing out that the novel opens with the narrator, Humbert Humbert, in jail, awaiting trial for the murder of the playwright Clare Quilty, with whom Lolita ran away to escape him. As she points out:

Humbert appears to us both as narrator and seducer—not just of Lolita but also of us, his readers . . . As the story unfolds, a deeper crime, more serious than Quilty's murder, is revealed: the entrapment and rape of Lolita . . . Lolita belongs to a category of victims who have no defense and are never given a chance to articulate their own story. As such, she becomes a double victim: not only her life but also her life story is taken from her. We told ourselves we were in that class to prevent ourselves from falling victim to this second crime. (p. 41)

Nafisi also emphasizes that Lolita is Humbert's creation, an identity he imposes on 12-year-old Dolores Haze. Consequently, we see her only through his eyes.

In addition to *Lolita*, Nafisi's students read *1,001 Nights*, F. Scott Fitzgerald's *The Great Gatsby*, and works by Henry James and Jane Austen. I found myself wondering why, given her focus on oppression and liberation, she did not introduce her students to works by writers of color. I was delighted, therefore, when I discovered her latest work, *Read Dangerously: The Subversive Power of Literature in Troubled Times*, in which she discusses the works of 11 "subversive" writers, including Salman Rushdie, Zora Neale Hurston, Toni Morrison, James Baldwin, and Ta-Nehisi Coates.

As illustrated in these examples, not only does encouraging students to ask significant questions about a literary work enable them to forge personal connections with a text and the author's worldview, it also compels them to ask significant questions about their own lives.

PART II

EXPLORING THE LIST PARADIGM: FOUR "KEYS TO CULTURE"

Language is our creation. It reflects our values, ideals, and goals, and the way we see and relate to the world.

—Thich Nhat Hanh

A riot is the language of the unheard.

—Martin Luther King Jr.

War is what happens when language fails.

—Margaret Atwood

CHAPTER 5

Language
"How Does the Author Contextualize Linguistic Signs and Symbols?"

Language: An organized system of linguistic signs and symbols expressed as words that acquire meaning only within specific contexts.

(Note: The definitions provided for Language, Identity, Space, and Time in chapters 5 through 8 are provided as working definitions. They are meant to invite readers to consider their own definitions of these concepts.)

According to Toni Morrison (1990), "The most valuable point of entry into the question of cultural (or racial) distinction . . . is its language—its unpoliced, seditious, confrontational, manipulative, inventive, disruptive, masked and unmasking language" (p. 210).

Morrison's statement illuminates West African author Malidoma Patrice Somé's (1994) comments regarding the difficulties of using the language of one culture to describe events outside that culture:

> The greatest obstacle I encountered [in writing his book, *Of Water and the Spirit*] was finding a suitable way to tell my story . . . the things I talk about here did not happen in English; they happened in a language that has a very different mindset about reality. There is usually a significant violence done to anything being translated from one culture to another. Modern American English, which seems to me better suited for quick fixes and the thrill of a consumer culture, seems to falter when asked to communicate another person's world view. (p. 2)

Both highlight the power and limitations of language.

Language creates our reality and shapes our ability to construct myths and images that reframe the past, transform the present, and help us envision the future. As illustrated in this chapter, language comprises the basis of culture, be it Black culture, feminist culture, military culture, prison culture, LGBTQ+ culture, or the culture of violence. Within these contexts, we can speak of body language, sign language, racist language, sexist language, culturally biased language, or "politically correct" language. Similarly, we can also explore the language of music, the language of protest, the language of humor, and the language of love.

LANGUAGE AS RESISTANCE

In spring 1997, I had an opportunity to attend the International Multi-Ethnic Literature of the U.S. (MELUS) Conference in Honolulu, Hawaii. The first thing you learn upon your arrival in the Aloha State is not to refer to the locals as "natives." The second is that Pidgin (Hawaiian English Creole) is the language of the Indigenous Hawaiian people and not a form of substandard American English. One of my favorite souvenirs from that trip is an illustrated dictionary/comic book titled *Pidgin To Da Max*. Clearly aimed at *haole* (White) tourists intrigued or amused by the local dialect, it was more than that to me. Having just learned about the use of pidgin English as a form of political resistance, I found the book both entertaining and informative. I also appreciated its humorous approach to a serious subject: the centrality of pidgin English to Pacific Islanders, a language often dismissed or deemed inferior to Standard English by outsiders.

During the conference, I was introduced to the works of two authors who inspired my appreciation of Hawaiian literature: Milton Murayama (1923–2016) and Haunani-Kay Trask, a political activist and featured conference speaker. During a visit to the University of Hawai'i at Mānoa campus bookstore, I bought copies of Murayama's novel, *All I Asking for Is My Body*, and Trask's poetry collection, *Light in the Crevice Never Seen*. (Admittedly, I also anticipated sharing my newfound knowledge with my son, who had received his Bachelor of Arts degree in Asian Studies from the university 3 years earlier.)

Originally published in 1959, Murayama's novel, set during the 1930s and 1940s, tells the story of the Oyamas, a family of second-generation Japanese Americans (*Nisei*) struggling to survive on an American-owned sugar plantation that exploits the labor of Japanese and Filipino Americans. Narrated by Kiyo Oyama, the younger of two brothers, the novel focuses on the interplay of culture and language in the plantation community. According to critic Rob Wilson, "Part of the accomplishment of the novel is that the language ranges from the vernacular to the literate and standard, and so reflects the cultural and linguistic diversity of Hawaii" (Odo, as cited in Murayama, 1988, p. 106). As Kiyo points out:

> We spoke four languages: good English in school, pidgin English among ourselves, good or pidgin Japanese to our parents and the other old folks. (Murayama, 1959/1988, p. 5)

Rejected by several publishers because of his use of pidgin English, which he was told would alienate mainstream readers, Murayama originally self-published his novel, which was later published by University of Hawaii Press. Today, it stands as a classic of Hawaiian literature and as "the most compelling work done on the Hawaii *nisei* experience" (Odo, as quoted in Murayama, 1959/1988, p. 108). *All I Asking for Is My Body* is the first in a trilogy that includes *Five Years on a Rock* (1994), narrated by Kiyo's mother, and *Plantation Boy* (1998), narrated by Kiyo's older brother, Tosh.

Following in Murayama's footsteps, Trask (1994) also employs pidgin in her literary works. As she explains about one of her poems, "Comin Home":

> This poem is dedicated to my cousin who died shortly before his twenty-seventh birthday of a massive heart attack. The poem is written in pidgin . . . because Ka'ohu and his friends spoke pidgin . . . The use of pidgin by locals is often a political statement, especially in the presence of *haole*. Like Black English, pidgin has also come under attack as a substandard language that must be eradicated from everyday speech. Given the resistance of local people, however, pidgin is likely to remain the basic medium of local speech. (p. 22)

I was reminded of my Hawaii experience more than a decade later when I attended a Toni Morrison Society Conference in Charleston, South Carolina, and bought a copy of *A Gullah Guide to Charleston*. Subtitled "Walking Through Black History," the guide introduced visitors to Gullah, an English-based creolized language spoken by enslaved Africans in South Carolina and Georgia.

LANGUAGE IN POSTCOLONIAL STUDIES

Language is often a central question in postcolonial studies, since colonizers usually imposed their language on colonized peoples and denied them the right to speak their native languages. In his memoir *Long Walk to Freedom*, Nelson Mandela (1994) points out that the Soweto Riot (June 16, 1976) was launched "when fifteen thousand school children gathered in Soweto [South Africa's South West Township] to protest the government's ruling that half of all classes in secondary schools must be taught in Afrikaans . . . the language of the oppressor" (p. 483).

Contemporary writers generally choose one of two options: writing in their native language, or creating new forms of English that subvert Standard English, a process that Kenyan writer Ngũgĩ wa Thiong'o refers to as "decolonizing the mind."

Thiong'o's philosophy of language echoes that of Morrison. When asked how Black writers "write in a world dominated by and informed by their relationship to white culture," Morrison (1993) responds: "By trying to alter language, simply to free it up, not to repress it or confine it, but to open it up. Tease it. Blast its racist straitjacket" (p. 372).

READING OUSMANE SEMBÈNE'S *NIIWAM*

In the summer of 2009, I had an opportunity to explore some of the complex issues surrounding language, culture, and colonialism when I spent 6 weeks in Senegal as a participant in a Fulbright-Hays Seminars Abroad program titled "Senegal: Gateway to West Africa." At the end of the seminar, which consisted primarily of a cultural immersion program for faculty members from various Western countries, including France, Canada, and the United States, we were asked to submit a final project that demonstrated our understanding of a selected aspect of Senegalese culture. My project, "Stories of Senegal: Teaching the Works of Ousmane Sembène Through the LIST Paradigm," focused on the short works of Ousmane Sembène (1923–2007), a Senegalese writer renowned for his highly controversial and politically charged films and heralded as "the father of African cinema." Sembène is perhaps best known for his historical novel *God's Bits of Wood* (1960), a fictional treatment of the events surrounding the 1947–1948 workers' strike on the Dakar–Niger railway. Given the scope and complexity of this text (which has enjoyed a broad range of critical analysis), I decided to focus instead on *Niiwam*, a shorter, more accessible, but equally complex work.

Originally published in French in 1987, the English translation of this text first appeared in 1992 as *Niiwam and Taaw*. In this context, it comprises one of two novellas that explore the social and political problems of a "New Africa" struggling to come to terms with the challenges of "neo-colonialism," a term coined by Kwame Nkrumah, the first president of independent Ghana, in *Neo-colonialism: The Last Stage of Imperialism* (1965). In this text Nkrumah contends that despite having achieved their independence, countries like Ghana were still subject to the control of "superpowers such as the United States," which continued to influence their educational and cultural institutions. Consequently, Nkrumah argued that "neo-colonialism was more insidious and more difficult to detect than the older overt colonialism" (cited in Ashcroft et al., 2002, p. 162).

In *Niiwam*, Sembène paints a harrowing portrait of modern-day Dakar, Senegal's capital city. The story centers on Thierno, a rural peasant whose young son has died due to poverty and disease. To cope with his loss and to atone for his guilt at having been unable to provide for his family, Thierno resolves to bury his son in the Muslim cemetery at Yoff. With the help of an old ragman, Thierno transports his son's body from Dakar to Yoff on a crowded city bus. During the course of his journey, as his emotions vacillate between grief, guilt, and fear of discovery, Thierno studies his fellow passengers, who represent a microcosm of Senegalese society.

On approaching the text, the issue of language quickly becomes apparent, beginning with the novella's title. As the reader soon discovers, Niiwam is not the name of Thierno's son. Rather, it is Wolof for "his corpse." Further analysis reveals that *Niiwam* includes three separate but interrelated languages:

- *French*: The language of the educated elite, as well as the language of the oppressor
- *Wolof*: The language of the people, the primary African language spoken in Senegal
- *Franwolof*: The language of Senegal's largely uneducated young people; a "bastardized" version of Wolof that combines elements of French and Wolof

In addition to its realistic portrayal of contemporary Senegalese culture, *Niiwam* presents a powerful portrait of the dynamics of language in postcolonial literature.

As illustrated in the following pages, fostering an awareness of language as manifested through three interrelated components—Language Creation, Language Validation, and Language Use—is critical to the teaching of multicultural texts, which often explore language as a form of social and political exploitation. Consequently, readers attuned to the nuances of language employed by various characters will enjoy a significantly enhanced reading experience.

LANGUAGE CREATION: CODE-SWITCHING AND CODE-MESHING

As evidenced by our constantly changing language, we create the language we need to reflect our current reality. (Consider the language created during the COVID-19 pandemic, when terms like "social distancing," "antivaxxers," and "N-95s" entered our daily discourse. Similarly, consider the language of technology and social media, which have given us "doomscrolling," "influencer," and "deepfake.") Of course, some of our most vibrant and colorful language comes from hip-hop artists and rappers, who create new words and phrases as soon as their language loses its shock value.

Code-switching refers to the manipulation of language to express alternative views of reality. Authors who employ code-switching generally focus on three approaches: (a) alternating between two or more languages in the same text (e.g., using Spanish words and phrases in an English text); (b) switching back and forth between Standard English and alternate forms of English (e.g., slang, vernacular, regional dialects, etc.); and (c) reclaiming language by redefining terms (e.g., Black, Nigger, Queer). As indicated by the title of their 1997 text focusing on "Contemporary Native Women's Writings of North America," Native American authors Joy Harjo and Gloria Bird refer to this process as *Reinventing the Enemy's Language*.

In *Other People's English*, the authors define *code-meshing* as a blending of vernacular language and dialects of English in speaking and writing. As Young et al. (2014) point out, "Code-meshing challenges the belief that English is a national, prescriptively narrow language, unable to accommodate linguistic influences from other cultures and nations" (p. 76).

Intrigued by their discussion, I began to seek out examples of code-meshing and found it especially prominent in the works of poet Kevin Young, director of the Schomburg Center for Research in Black Culture at the New York Public Library and poetry editor of *The New Yorker*. In his essay "Blacker Than Thou," which explores the bizarre circumstances surrounding Rachel Dolezal, a White woman determined to pass as Black, Young et al. (2014) proclaim:

> When Rachel Dolezal . . . was simply a joke on Black Twitter, I identified some of my favorite Twitter titles for the inevitable, anticipated memoir: "Their Eyes Were Watching Oprah" . . . ; "Imitation of Imitation of Life" . . ."Blackish Like Me" . . . Now things done got serious. (p. 103)

Clearly, code-switching and code-meshing are powerful antidotes to the "standardization" of English.

LANGUAGE VALIDATION: STANDARD ENGLISH
AND VERNACULAR

The validation of Black English and its African origins has been well documented in the works of Geneva Smitherman (1985, 2000). But its unique use in African American literature has received decidedly less attention.

One of the most fascinating aspects of Ralph Ellison's *Invisible Man* is the author's obvious delight in wordplay to achieve what he describes as "bluestoned laughter" (1995b, xvi). If we explore the various types of wordplay—which include allusions, puns, and rhymes as well as powerful metaphors and similes—we discover an added dimension of literary and cultural richness in the novel that we might otherwise overlook.

Ellison bases much of his wordplay on Black vernacular, the ordinary language of Black Americans enriched by colloquial expressions and proverbs, as well as excerpts from songs and stories rooted in African and African American culture. For example, in Chapter 25, one of the leaders of the Harlem riots provides instructions for burning down a tenement building. He closes with the warning, "After that it's every tub on its own black bottom!" (1995b, p. 546). Without grounding this scene in Black culture, he might have used the more common (and much less colorful) phrase, "After that it's every man for himself!" Another example is the vivid simile two winos use to describe Ras the Exhorter as "looking like death eating a sandwich" (p. 562).

His work reflects the sentiment expressed in James Baldwin's classic essay, "If Black English Isn't a Language, Then Tell Me, What Is?"

In *A Lesson Before Dying*, Ernest Gaines demonstrates a profound respect for language as a form of personal expression when he devotes an entire chapter (Chapter 29) to Jefferson's journal, giving the young Death Row inmate an opportunity to speak in his own voice. Gaines does not "translate" Jefferson's language but provides it to us directly, unfiltered, complete with misspellings and grammatical errors. Consequently, we realize that although Jefferson lacks formal education, since he has been compelled to work in the cane fields since childhood to help support his family, he is not ignorant but merely lacks the ability to express his feelings in writing, since he has never had the opportunity to do so. Once given that opportunity, he is able, for the first time, to use his own voice to express his innermost thoughts. In essence, by giving Jefferson a pencil and a notepad, Grant also gives him the opportunity to control the narrative of his life story by "speaking truth to power," a theme that resonates throughout the text.

In teaching the novel, I have students read extensive excerpts from Jefferson's journal out loud. Once they overcome their initial resistance to Jefferson's language and surrender to its rhythm, they begin to connect with his story. To supplement our reading, we also watch clips from the HBO film starring Mekhi Phifer and Don Cheadle.

Jefferson's journal is his legacy. By recording his thoughts and feelings as he awaits execution, Jefferson, in effect, writes himself into history. Consequently, the journal becomes a historical document that records his life story.

In his journal, Jefferson expresses intimate feelings he has not been able to articulate previously, such as his love for his nannan, his affection for Grant, and his fear of dying. Alone with his private thoughts, he is able, for the first time, to acknowledge his part in the tragic events surrounding Alcee Gropé's murder and to accept responsibility for his actions, admitting that he had a choice that fateful night. He realizes that he was not only guilty of being "in the wrong place at the wrong time," but of making the wrong choice. Once he accepts this fact, he is able to release his hatred toward his captors and accept his fate with grace and dignity.

Since Grant saves the journal and shares its contents with his students, it also emerges as an archived prison document, much like Martin Luther King Jr.'s "Letter from Birmingham Jail," Elie Wiesel's *Night*, and Mumia Abu-Jamal's *Live from Death Row*.

LANGUAGE USE: UNLOCKING THE POWER OF LANGUAGE

Proverbs

Brief, popular expressions or folk sayings that capture a truth or sentiment, *proverbs* often reflect cultural beliefs and values. Consequently, they can serve as important "keys to culture." For example, we often hear the African proverb, "It takes a village to raise a child," which contradicts the Western value of rugged individualism. Another African proverb, "If you want to go fast, go alone. If you want to go far, go together," supports this perspective.

Similarly, although the Japanese proverbs "Even monkeys fall from trees" and "The protruding nail gets hammered" echo the American proverbs "Anyone can make a mistake" and "Don't make waves," they provide us with more concrete and colorful images.

An understanding of figurative language is key to unlocking the power of language. But rather than overwhelm students with lists of literary terms, I find that providing them with definitions, examples, and illustrations of the "top four"—metaphor, irony, imagery, and allusion—gives them a solid foundation for literary analysis and piques their interest in discovering other rhetorical devices. It also enhances their awareness of distinctive rhetorical devices employed by writers from diverse cultures and heightens their awareness and appreciation of the nuances of language in literary works.

Metaphor

Asked to describe his creative process, Pulitzer Prize–winning playwright August Wilson explains that "you use metaphor and condense" (Bryer & Hartig, 2006, p. 23). Since Wilson began his writing career as a poet, his response speaks to the power of metaphor to convey complex ideas and concepts.

"War is hell."

"Love is a battlefield."

"Papa was a rollin' stone."

Most of us recognize metaphors as implied comparisons between two dissimilar things designed to evoke an emotional response in a reader. Employing a more eloquent description, one critic proclaims, "A metaphor is a way of getting at a truth that exists beyond the literal" (Miller & Paola, 2004, p. 53).

Central to the study of multicultural literature are *cultural metaphors*, some unique or distinctive elements expressive of a nation's values, such as the Chinese family altar, the Japanese tea ceremony, or American football.

A central metaphor in African American literature is the quilt, a metaphor created by Alice Walker in her classic short story "Everyday Use."

In her essay "In Search of Our Mothers' Gardens," Walker (1983) describes the inspiration for her story:

> [I]n the Smithsonian Institution in Washington, D.C., there hangs a quilt unlike any other in the world. In fanciful, inspired, and yet simple and identifiable figures, it portrays the story of the Crucifixion. It is considered rare, beyond price. Though it follows no known pattern of quilt-making, and though it is made of bits and pieces of worthless rags, it is obviously the work of a person

of powerful imagination and deep spiritual feeling. Below this quilt I saw a note that says it was made by "an anonymous Black woman in Alabama, a hundred years ago."

If we could locate this "anonymous" Black woman from Alabama, she would turn out to be one of our grandmothers—an artist who left her mark in the only materials she could afford, and in the only medium her position in society allowed her to use. (p. 239)

As critic Barbara T. Christian (1994) points out:

"Everyday Use" has remained a cornerstone of [Alice Walker's] work. Her use of quilting as a metaphor for the creative legacy that African Americans inherited from their maternal ancestors changed the way we defined art, women's culture, and African American lives. By putting African American women's voices at the center of the narrative for the first time, "Everyday Use" anticipated the focus on an entire generation of black women writers. (p. xx)

One of those "women writers" was Toni Morrison, whose use of the quilt features prominently in *Song of Solomon*: When we first meet Pilate in the novel's opening scene, she appears wrapped in a quilt, instead of a winter coat. The metaphor of the quilt features prominently in the works of Lucille Clifton. In her poetry collection *Quilting*, each section title is taken from the name of a traditional quilt design. The history of the quilt can also be traced to slavery times, when quilt patterns were used to transmit secret coded information to "passengers" on the Underground Railroad.

Also prominent in African American literature is the metaphor of flight, which appears in the works of numerous poets and writers, including Ralph Ellison (*Flying Home*), Robert Hayden (*Angle of Ascent*), and Ishmael Reed (*Flight to Canada*).

Other examples of cultural metaphors in African American literature include trains (symbolic of the Great Migration, as well as the migratory nature of Black Americans seeking a better life) and the blues guitar, prominent in the poetry of Langston Hughes and the plays of August Wilson.

Irony

Irony relies on "a subtly humorous inconsistency, in which an apparently straightforward statement or event is undermined by its context so as to give it a very different significance" (Baldick, 2015, p. 187).

One of the most infamous examples of *verbal irony* in contemporary literature is the title of Ralph Ellison's novel *Invisible Man*. Clearly, a Black man in White America is highly visible. Consequently, in order to appreciate Ellison's novel, we must understand its context, in which an intelligent, educated Black man who has lived by society's rules is rendered invisible because he is not recognized as a fully human, contributing member of that society. Closely related to verbal irony, *structural irony* involves the use of an unreliable narrator whose views differ wildly from the actual circumstances recognized by the author and reader. Given this context, we immediately recognize Ellison's narrator as "unreliable," since he continually misreads fairly obvious social cues. (Most critics agree that all first-person narrators are unreliable, since their views are limited by their highly restricted perceptions of reality.) *Dramatic irony*, in which the audience knows more about a character's situation than the character does, is also evident in the novel. For example, the novel includes numerous incidents in which characters refer to the narrator's virtual blindness, since he refuses to see things as they are. And if we view Ellison's singular story as an abstraction of real life, in which people's lives often seem governed by a cruel and mocking fate, we can also read it as *cosmic irony*, which entails "a discrepancy . . . between a character's aspiration and the treatment he or she receives in the world" (Kennedy, 2013, p. 39).

Clearly, irony is a critical concept for students to understand, especially since their consumption of news media and genre fiction may have conditioned them to accept what they read at face value. Like metaphor and allusion, irony underscores the ambiguous nature of literature, one of its defining characteristics.

Imagery

Imagery refers to the "uses of language in a literary work that evoke sense-impressions by literal or figurative reference to . . . objects, scenes, actions, or states, as distinct from the language of abstract argument or exposition" (Baldick, 2015, p. 177).

In *The Bluest Eye*, Toni Morrison (1994a) employs nature imagery to illustrate the unnatural phenomenon of Pecola's pregnancy:

> Quiet as it's kept, there were no marigolds in the fall of 1941. We thought, at the time, that it was because Pecola was having her father's baby that the marigolds did not grow. (p. 7)

The absence of marigolds resonates throughout the novel, whose four sections are named after the four seasons of the year, presented out of sequence (Autumn, Winter, Spring, and Summer). The marigolds come to evoke an image of Pecola, whose life, like that of the marigolds, is not allowed to flourish.

In her novel *Maud Martha*, the poet Gwendolyn Brooks (1993) also employs nature imagery to sketch an image of Maud Martha, a young Black girl growing up in Chicago's impoverished South Side neighborhood:

What she liked was candy buttons, and books, and painted music (deep blue, or delicate silver) . . . and dandelions.

She would have liked a lotus, or China asters or the Japanese Iris, or meadow lilies—yes, she would have liked meadow lilies, because the very word meadow made her breathe more deeply, and either fling her arms or want to fling her arms, depending on who was by, rapturously up to whatever was watching in the sky. But dandelions were what she chiefly saw. Yellow jewels for everyday, studding the patched green dress of her back yard. She liked their demure prettiness second to their everydayness; for in that latter quality she thought she saw a picture of herself, and it was comforting to find that what was common could also be a flower. And could be cherished! (pp. 143–144)

Encouraging students to become aware of imagery can greatly enrich and enhance their reading experience.

Allusion

An *allusion* is a brief reference (usually indirect) to a person, place, thing, event, or idea in history or literature that is not explained by the writer but that relies on the reader's familiarity with what is mentioned. "Allusions imply a common knowledge between reader and writer and operate as literary shorthand to enrich the meaning of a text" (Kennedy, 2013, p. 6). Consequently, allusions rely on a well-read audience that will be able to make the connection between a selected text and its literary antecedents.

Students can certainly read and appreciate Salman Rushdie's *Midnight's Children* without recognizing its literary and historical allusions. But their reading experience will be greatly enhanced if they can.

Set in Bombay (Mumbai), India, *Midnight's Children* is the fictional autobiography of narrator and protagonist Saleem Sinai, one of 1,001 children born on the eve of India's independence from Great Britain (August 15, 1947) "at the stroke of the midnight hour," each endowed with special powers such as invisibility, clairvoyance, and teleportation. Through his eyes, we witness the events leading up to and following "the Partition"—the division of the Indian subcontinent into India (Hindu) and Pakistan (Muslim)—marked by triumphs as well as bitter religious and political violence.

They will also benefit from recognizing the literary allusion to *1,001 Arabian Nights*, a collection of Middle Eastern folk tales heralded as a Persian classic. Moreover, by recognizing the narrative structure of *Arabian Nights*—a frame story in which the narrator, Scheherazade, tells 1,001 stories to King Shahryar in order to save her life—they will be more likely to appreciate the narrative structure of *Midnight's Children*, which centers on Saleem Sinai telling his stories to Padma Mangroli, his lover and, eventually, his fiancée.

The Language of Love

In describing her writing, Toni Morrison proclaims:

> I'm interested in how men are educated, how women relate to each other, how
> we are able to love, . . . who survives in certain situations and who doesn't and,
> specifically, how these and other universal issues relate to African-Americans . . .
> The search for love and identity runs through most everything I write. (Micucci,
> 1994, p. 278)

At first, these proclamations may sound strange, coming from a writer
whose works repeatedly explore issues such as rape, murder, incest, and suicide. But upon closer examination, we discover the truth behind these statements. In fact, Morrison's characters often become whole (albeit not *perfect*)
once they recognize their self-worth and learn how to give and receive love.

The Language of Music (Blues Narratives)

According to essayist and critic Walter Pater, "All art aspires to the condition of music." Consequently, African American writers often turn to the
language of music to tell their stories.

In Ellison's *Invisible Man*, the narrator immerses himself in Louis
Armstrong's "What Did I Do to Be So Black and Blue?" as he contemplates
his fate in his underground coal cellar. In Morrison's *Song of Solomon*, the
protagonist, Milkman Dead, experiences a spiritual rebirth after he learns
his great-great-grandfather Solomon's song. And in his signature play, *Joe
Turner's Come and Gone*, August Wilson's protagonist, Herald Loomis,
who returns home after spending 7 years on Joe Turner's chain gang, regains
his sense of human dignity and self-worth only after Bynum Walker, a root
worker and spiritual healer, reminds him of his song. But the epitome of the
"blues narrative" is James Baldwin's classic short story "Sonny's Blues," in
which music provides the catalyst that prompts the reconciliation of two estranged brothers.

Inspired by Baldwin, I use a unique approach to introduce my students
to the language of music: I bring a recording of Jimi Hendrix playing his version of "The Star-Spangled Banner" to class. With its screeches and discordant notes, the piece aptly conveys the chaos and violence of the 1960s Civil
Rights movement. It provides an ideal segue to a discussion on the power of
music to convey the Black experience.

Establishing a connection between a selected text and a piece of music
representative of the author's culture (Japanese koto, African drumming,
Native American prayer chants) can also help students forge emotional connections with literature.

The Language of Violence and Oppression ("Words as Weapons")

In his landmark text, *The Language of Oppression*, cultural critic Haig A. Bosmajian (1983) examines the violence inherent in the Language of Anti-Semitism, the Language of White Racism, the Language of Indian Derision, the Language of Sexism, and the Language of War. He concludes that "Linguistic assaults often are used by persons who show no visible evil intent. While their motivations may not be to deprecate, the effects of what they are saying are damaging. Efforts must be made to make such people conscious that their speech is degrading to other human beings" (p. 139).

Morrison agrees. In her Nobel Lecture, she points out that "Oppressive language does more than represent violence; it is violence. . . . it must be rejected, altered, and exposed" (1994b, p. 16).

The Language of Protest

The definitive statement on protest literature is Amiri Baraka's (2007; originally published in 1965) proclamation in his poem "Black Art" that poems should be "fists," "daggers," and "guns" to "clean out the world for virtue and love" (pp. 302–303). Setting the tone for the Black Arts Movement (BAM), Baraka's stance opened the floodgates for a deluge of openly confrontational "hand grenade poems" by poet/activists such as Sonia Sanchez, Nikki Giovanni, and Dudley Randall.

Baraka's insistence that Black art must be political echoes Richard Wright's philosophy, expressed in "Blueprint for Negro Writing," in which he rails against Black writers—primarily Harlem Renaissance writers—who created art primarily for White audiences, in an effort to "prove" their humanity. As Wright (1995a) points out:

> Generally speaking, Negro writing in the past has been confined to humble novels, poems, and plays, prim and decorous ambassadors who went a-begging to white America. They entered the Court of American Public Opinion dressed in the knee-pants of servility, curtsying to show that the Negro was not inferior, that he was human and that he had a life comparable to that of other people. For the most part these artistic ambassadors were received as though they were French poodles who do clever tricks. (pp. 194–195)

Wright's criticism of the Harlem Renaissance (1919–1940) echoes that of Langston Hughes, who points out that the renaissance of art and culture and the birth of the "New Negro" heralded by Alain Locke was largely driven by the White obsession with "primitive" Black art, a stance supported by writers such as George S. Schuyler ("The Negro-Art Hokum") and Wallace Thurman

(*Infants of the Spring*) that offer harsh critiques of the movement and its literary luminaries. As Hughes (1995e) points out, "The ordinary Negro hadn't heard of the Negro Renaissance. And if they had, it hadn't raised their wages any" (p. 80).

Clearly Hughes, who, like his contemporary Zora Neale Hurston, had enjoyed the sponsorship of White patrons, eventually realized that continuing to accept such support meant compromising his artistic integrity. As a result, his later poems expressed a call to action against racism and violence. Hughes (1995c) proclaims his new philosophy of Black art in his manifesto "The Negro Artist and the Racial Mountain," in which he asserts:

> We younger Negro artists who create now intend to express our individual dark-skinned selves without fear or shame. If white people are pleased we are glad. If they are not, it doesn't matter. We know we are beautiful. And ugly too . . . If colored people are pleased we are glad. If they are not, their displeasure doesn't matter either. We build our temples for tomorrow, strong as we know how, and we stand on top of the mountain, free within ourselves. (p. 95)

Hughes's stance is further articulated in his support of the radical arts journal *Fire!*, which gave voice to a new generation of Black artists. Although the editors managed to publish only one issue of the journal due to lack of funds, it stands as a testament to the energy, creativity, and passion of a radical group of young writers who refused to let themselves be defined by the status quo.

The link between radical writers of the Harlem Renaissance and the Black Arts Movement is undeniable. Consequently, artists who failed to support BAM's political stance and its counterpart, the Black Power Movement, were denounced as traitors.

A case in point is Ernest Gaines, who was often criticized for not participating in Civil Rights protest marches and rallies. But Gaines stood firm in his belief that by documenting the stories and personal histories of Black people through his writing, he was doing his part to support the movement. As Gaines (1995b) points out, "When Bull Connor turned the hoses on the marchers, I just said to myself, 'Write a better paragraph'" (Gaines, 1995b, p. 276).

One of my most vivid memories of the Civil Rights movement—marked by the murders of Medgar Evers, Malcolm X, and Martin Luther King Jr.—is watching the evening news on television highlighted by Black men wearing sandwich-board placards declaring "I am a man!" Recently, I was reminded of that scene when I read Kazuo Ishiguro's *Never Let Me Go*. Set sometime in the future, the novel imagines a utopian society in which death, disease, and disability have been eradicated, thanks to scientists who have created new life-forms whose sole purpose is to serve as organ donors for humans.

When the new life-forms learn to create art, the community is compelled to confront the question of their humanity and address the moral and ethical issues surrounding their role. Teaching Ishiguro's novel alongside the works of writers from the Harlem Renaissance or the Black Arts Movement could help students forge connections between these works, all of which ultimately address issues of human rights and social justice.

A classic example of protest poetry is Margaret Walker's "For My People." Emulating the structure of Walt Whitman's "Song of Myself," it proclaims the courage and resistance of African Americans faced with seemingly insurmountable challenges.

Signifyin(g)

Signifyin(g), or "playing the dozens," is a unique form of subversive wordplay (verbal combat) rooted in African culture and Black vernacular in which the oppressed (Blacks) appropriate and transform the language of the oppressor (Whites) and use it against them without directly confronting or openly challenging the oppressor. Signifyin(g) is a coded language that uses puns, hyperbole, humor, irony, repetition, reversal, sexual innuendo, and understatement to "score points."

The classic work on the history and culture of signifyin(g) is Henry Louis Gates Jr.'s *The Signifying Monkey*. Subtitled *A Theory of African-American Literary Criticism*, it explores the relationship between African and African American vernacular traditions and Black literature. Gates (1988) describes it as:

> A scholarly return to the relationship between black vernacular and formal traditions, a return to the forms of black criticism undertaken in the thirties by Sterling A. Brown and Zora Neale Hurston . . . [whose] reverence for the black vernacular and their use of it as the touchstone for rhetorical excellence provide critical models that I have tried to imitate. (p. xii)

Gates then proceeds to illustrate how African vernacular traditions, beginning with the "origin myth" of Esu-Elegbara and the Signifying Monkey, influence contemporary African American literature.

In *Beloved*, Toni Morrison employs the rhetoric of signifying to affirm the dignity of enslaved Africans by resurrecting one of its anonymous victims (symbolized by the character Beloved). She also frames the story of Margaret Garner, an enslaved woman who killed her children to save them from slavery, and uses code-switching to reverse the stereotypes of "civilized" Whites and "savage" Blacks.

The classic example of a "signifyin(g)" text is Ishmael Reed's *Flight to Canada*, a parody of the slave narrative. In the introduction, a short poem (also titled "Flight to Canada") provides a parody of Frederick Douglass's letter to his former "master," Thomas Auld. Later, in the body of the text, Reed signifies on the notion of the kind slavemaster with his depiction of Mr. Davis. As his trickster protagonist, Raven Quickskill, observes:

> Davis' slaves are the only ones I know of who take mineral baths. And when hooped skirts became popular he gave some to the slave women, and when this made it awkward for them to move through the rows of cotton, he widened the rows. (Reed, 1989, p. 24)

One of the most striking (albeit lesser-known) examples of signifyin(g) is Langston Hughes's 1961 poetry cycle "Ask Your Mama: 12 Moods for Jazz." According to the creators of the Langston Hughes Project (n.d.), "Ask Your Mama: 12 Moods for Jazz" is "a kaleidoscopic jazz poem suite" that represents "Hughes' homage to the struggle for artistic and social freedom at home and abroad at the beginning of the 1960s."

Dedicated to Louis Armstrong, "Ask Your Mama"—meant to be performed on stage, accompanied by live music—employs jazz as a central metaphor for Black life and signifyin(g) ("playing the dozens") as a form of social protest. The work consists of 12 interconnected poems, or "moods," that portray 12 vignettes highlighting significant people, places, and events in the struggle for human rights, each accompanied by a select piece of music. For example, Mood #1, "Cultural Exchange" (accompanied by "When the Saints Go Marching In"), imagines a time when "Wealthy Negroes have white servants, white sharecroppers work the Black plantations, and colored children have white mammies" (Hughes, 1995a, p. 480). Mood #4, "Ode to Dinah" (accompanied by "Hesitation Blues"), directs our attention to Black families trapped in Harlem's housing projects, and Mood #8, "Gospel Cha-Cha" (accompanied by "Gospel music with a very heavy beat as if marching forward against great odds, climbing a high hill"; p. 504), offers a searing satire of the Black church. Since this is a complex and challenging work, teachers may want to preface it with some of Hughes's other "protest poetry," such as "Good Morning Revolution" and "Kids Who Die." To set the tone, they may have students listen to the music of Louis Armstrong, such as "When the Saints Go Marching In" or "What Did I Do to Be So Black and Blue?," which provides the soundtrack for Ralph Ellison's *Invisible Man*. To emphasize the work as "performance poetry," they may also want to introduce students to Ntozake Shange's choreopoem, "For Colored Girls Who Have Considered Suicide / When the Rainbow Is Enuf."

A more recent example is Ta-Nehisi Coates's *Between the World and Me*, in which Coates signifies on two classic African American texts to tell his story of violence and institutional racism in America: Richard Wright's lynching poem, "Between the World and Me," and James Baldwin's "Letter to My Nephew" from *The Fire Next Time*.

Racist Language (Calibanic Discourse)

Racist language degrades the human dignity of individuals who identify with a designated racial or ethnic group and often depicts them as subhuman or inferior.

In *Black Male Fiction and the Legacy of Caliban*, James W. Coleman defines racist language as "Calibanic discourse," an allusion to Caliban in Shakespeare's *The Tempest*, a deformed misanthrope who represents "the untamed force of natural man." As Coleman (2001) explains:

> Calibanic discourse is the perceived history and story of the black male in Western culture that has its genesis and tradition in language and nonlinguistic signs. It denotes slavery, proscribed freedom, proscribed sexuality, inferior character, and inferior voice. In summary, the black male is the slave or servant who is the antithesis of reason, civilized development, entitlement, freedom, and power of white men, and he never learns the civilized use of language. His voice is unreliable; his words fail to signify his humanity. He also preys on civilization and represents bestial, contaminating sexuality. (p. 3)

In Toni Morrison's *Beloved*, this "bestial, contaminating sexuality" is attributed to schoolteacher's nephews, White men who sexually abuse Sethe, thereby reversing the racist stereotype of "savage" Blacks and "civilized" Whites. But schoolteacher's contempt for the Sweet Home men (enslaved Africans bound to the Garner's plantation) best exemplifies the dehumanizing violence of racist language. As Paul D recalls:

> It was schoolteacher who taught them . . . [that] they were only Sweet Home men at Sweet Home. One step off that ground and they were trespassers among the human race. Watchdogs without teeth; steer bulls without horns; gelded workhorses whose neigh and whinny could not be translated into a language responsible humans spoke. (Morrison, 2004, pp. 147–148)

Sermonic Language

Sermonic language emulates the language of the traditional Black Southern preacher with its emphasis on Biblical allusions, repetition, and call-and-response.

In *The Sermon and the African American Literary Imagination*, Dolan Hubbard (1994) defines sermonic language as "spiritually and emotionally charged symbolic language . . . molded by the Black experience—one whose central impulse is survival and resistance" (p. 6).

The definitive text on sermonic language is James Weldon Johnson's *God's Trombones: Seven Negro Sermons in Verse,* which includes the powerful sermons "The Creation" and "Go Down, Death." In his preface, Johnson (1927) describes the unique role of "the old-time Negro preacher":

> [He] . . . was above all an orator and . . . an actor. . . . He preached a personal and anthropomorphic God, a sure-enough heaven and a red-hot hell . . . He had the power to sweep his hearers before him; and so himself was often swept away. At such times his language was not prose but poetry. It was from memories of such preachers there grew the idea of this book of poems. (p. 5)

To understand and appreciate the power of sermonic language, we need only recall the rhetorical prowess of two of our most powerful civil rights leaders—Malcolm X and Martin Luther King Jr.—and some of their most memorable speeches, such as Malcolm's "The Ballot or the Bullet" and King's "I Have a Dream."

Ellison's *Invisible Man* includes some of the most powerful examples of sermonic language in Black fiction: Rev. Homer A. Barbee's sermon on "The Founder"; Dr. Bledsoe's sermon on "The Politics of Power"; Ras the Exhorter's satiric sermon on "The Blackness of Blackness," and (my personal favorite) the Invisible Man's eulogy for Tod Clifton.

In *Beloved*, Toni Morrison illustrates the power of sermonic language through Baby Suggs's Sermon in the Clearing, during which she rejects Christianity's justification for slavery and its promise of a better life in the "hereafter." Instead, Morrison (2004) urges her congregation to "Love your heart. For this is the prize" (p. 104). Baby Suggs's sermon signifies on Jesus's Sermon on the Mount ("The Beatitudes," Matthew 5: 1–12) by reversing the message of this biblical sermon.

Sermonic language also plays a central role in N. Scott Momaday's *House Made of Dawn*, which tells the story of Abel, a man sickened by alcoholism and wartime trauma, struggling to reintegrate himself into his Native community. Like Morrison, Momaday draws on the Bible for inspiration and then moves beyond the text to illustrate his point: that language is sacred. The novel consists of four parts. Part 2, "The Priest of the Sun," consists of two sermons delivered by "The Right Reverend John Big Bluff Tosamah," Pastor and Priest of the Sun. The first sermon, "The Gospel According to John," draws on the opening lines of Genesis 1:1: "In the beginning was the Word." It then illustrates how the sacred language of the Bible has been corrupted by Whites, who ignore its sanctity and use it to lie, steal, and make false promises. The second sermon, "The Way to Rainy Mountain," centers on Tosamah's memories of his Kiowa grandmother.

As illustrated in this chapter, language is a powerful tool that forms the foundation of culture. As Toni Morrison (1994b) proclaims in her Nobel Lecture, "We die. That may be the *meaning* of life. But we do language. That may be the *measure* of our lives" (p. 22).

SIGNIFICANT QUESTIONS—GENERAL

- What is the author's native language?
- Is the author bilingual/multilingual? If so, does the author use code-switching/code-meshing? To what effect?
- What is the protagonist's native language? If the characters speak English (either as their native language or in translation), do they use Standard English? Nonstandard (undervalued) English? Slang? Regional dialects (e.g., Pidgin, Gullah, Yiddish)? Do they use vernacular? Idioms? Proverbs? Folk sayings? If so, to what effect?
- Is this a work in translation? If so, what may have been "lost in translation"?
- What myths and stories define the narrative's culture ("classic" texts; sacred or secular texts; oral narratives [folk tales, songs, chants, etc.])?
- How would you describe the author's writing style? (Consider diction [word choice], syntax [sentence structure], dialogue, description, imagery, characterization, etc.)
- Is the language symbolic? Consider the author's use of figurative language (metaphors, similes, etc.). Does the author employ literary, historical, or religious allusions (e.g., to the Bible, the Qur'an, the Torah, the Heart Sutra)? Color or number symbolism? Archetypes? Humor? Satire? Irony? If so, how do these impact the texture of the work?
- Do characters speak for themselves, or does the narrator (or another character) frequently speak for them?
- Are the characters' conversations or dialogues often interrupted? If so, who or what causes the interruptions? To what effect?
- Do characters seem comfortable with their use of language? Are they articulate or unable to express themselves clearly? To what effect?
- Are there references to letters, notes, songs, etc., that provide clues to the character's identity or illuminate the plot?
- What does the characters' use of language reveal about their background, education, history, or culture?
- Do characters speak freely, or is their language limited or restricted in any way? Are characters assertive or afraid of expressing themselves? To what effect?

SIGNIFICANT QUESTIONS—MUSIC

As students explore the language of music, they may find it helpful to visualize a selected text as a film and consider questions such as the following:

- Given the tone of the narrative (somber, humorous, violent), what type of music would provide an effective "soundtrack": Blues? Gospel? Country? Classical? Rock? Rap? (A soundtrack for Ernest Gaines's *A Lesson Before Dying* might be Aaron Neville's "I Shall Be Released"; a soundtrack for Ellison's *Invisible Man* might be Curtis Mayfield's "Invisible.")
- Are there references or allusions to singers, songs, musical instruments, or musical compositions? To dancers or dances? If so, how do these impact the narrative?
- If the main characters were actors in a movie, what would be their theme song?
- Does the narrative include terms that allude to music (notes, records, chords, etc.)?
- How would you describe the narrative's pace and rhythm: Fast? Slow? Measured? Smooth? Discordant?

My color is not my country. I am a human being before being an American. I am a human being before being a Negro; and if I deal with racial problems, it is because those problems were created without my consent and permission.

—Richard Wright

We cannot escape our origins however hard we try, those origins which contain the key—could we but find it—to all that we later become.

—James Baldwin

We are what we imagine.

—N. Scott Momaday

CHAPTER 6

Identity

"Who Are These People and What Do They Want?"

Identity: A fluid, elusive concept shaped by society that attributes positive or negative qualities to individuals based on perceived differences that determine their place in that society's power structure.

"Who am I?"

"Where do I belong?"

Coming to terms with our identity involves creating a positive self-image and treating others with respect and dignity. An important step in this process is learning to identify, dismantle, and reject cultural stereotypes, while reminding ourselves that our identities are fluid and dynamic and, therefore, constantly subject to change.

With the current emphasis on a multicultural (or "post-racial") society, American identity has undergone countless permutations, especially for "hyphenated" Americans (Mexican-American, Asian-American, African-American, etc.), who often struggle to validate their status as "American" while maintaining their cultural and historical roots. In many respects, the focus on fluid, shifting, or multiple identities has complicated the issues of identity construction, deconstruction, and reintegration. An exploration of identity enables students to examine how issues such as race, gender, and ethnicity impact identity and self-image and contribute to our perceptions of "self" and "other."

To introduce the concept of identity, I begin by asking students to contemplate their own identity. To generate discussion, I often bring in a form adapted from a questionnaire distributed by the Census Bureau that asks, "What is your racial or ethnic identity?" and expects readers to check the "correct" box: Black, White, Hispanic/Spanish, Asian or Pacific Islander, Native American, Other. After discussing the absurdity of having to limit our identities to a single group or category, students are better prepared to engage in broader explorations of identity.

To continue our discussion, we read "identity poems" such as Maya Angelou's "Phenomenal Woman" and Nikki Giovanni's "Ego Tripping." I also encourage students to write an "I am" poem, a formula poem that begins with phrases such as, "I am," "I wonder," "I hope," or "I dream" and prompts students to complete the statements by filling in their own thoughts, ideas, and feelings. If I were to teach the class today, I would also introduce students to *The Universal Declaration of Human Rights*, which presents fundamental rights guaranteed to all human beings and offers an excellent opportunity to engage students in a discussion of contemporary human rights issues (United Nations, 1948).

After encouraging students to reflect on their own identities, I point out that an important aspect of critical reading is contemplating the author's identity and worldview. In this way, we will be better prepared to connect with a work's narrator(s) and characters. Moreover, we will be able to consider how our own stance and worldview align or conflict with the author's.

As illustrated in the following pages, coming to terms with our identity is a complex process that demands an awareness of numerous issues, including identity politics and cultural markers as well as an understanding of literary archetypes and cultural stereotypes.

IDENTITY POLITICS (RACE, RACISM, AND COLORISM)

Identity politics is generally defined as

> political activity . . . grounded in the shared experiences of injustice [among] certain social groups. . . . [that] aim to secure the political freedom of a specific constituency marginalized within its larger context. Members of that constituency assert or reclaim ways of understanding their distinctiveness that challenge dominant oppressive characterizations, with the goal of greater self-determination. (*The Stanford Encyclopedia of Philosophy*, 2007)

Those who embrace identity politics often reject the labels imposed on them by the dominant culture ("colored," "Negro," "Native American," "Asian American," "Hispanic") and redefine themselves by assuming new names. In recent years, the acronym BIPOC (Black, Indigenous, and People of Color) has been adopted by communities of color that believe in presenting a united front that identifies them as people who have been historically oppressed and victimized by racism and prejudice. However, it has been rejected by people of color who do not identify with marginalized groups.

As illustrated in the following paragraphs, identities are fluid and shift as we move in and out of designated groups. In her classic essay "How It Feels to be Colored Me," Zora Neale Hurston illustrates this process of "identity performance" as she describes how her identity changes based on whether she finds herself in the company of Whites or other Blacks (Hurston, 1979).

Masking and Passing

Paul Laurence Dunbar's "We Wear the Mask" (1896) paints a painful portrait of a people compelled to disguise their true identities in order to be accepted by the dominant society. An extreme form of masking is "passing," a term originally used to describe the ability of light-skinned Blacks to "pass" as White. It has since been adapted by the LGBTQ+ community to refer to the ability of gays to "pass" as straight. And in 2008, in the bizarre case of Rachel Dolezal, it was used to describe the attempts of a White woman to "pass" as Black.

In the early 20th century, with its strict taboos against "race mixing" and "miscegenation," passing narratives—first-person stories of individuals who describe their experiences of passing as White—enjoyed notoriety. Titles include works such as Langston Hughes's short story "Passing"; Charles W. Chesnutt's *The House Behind the Cedars*; James Weldon Johnson's *The Autobiography of an Ex-Colored Man*; and Nella Larsen's *Passing* (the basis of the 2021 Netflix film).

Central to the passing narrative is the cultural stereotype of the "tragic mulatto," a person of mixed racial heritage perceived as "almost white, but not quite," whose "tragic" existence stems from their alienation from both identity groups. The stereotype is portrayed in films such as *Pinky* and *Imitation of Life*, and in novels such as William Faulkner's *Light in August* and Toni Morrison's *Jazz*, which feature the "passing" characters Joe Christmas and Golden Gray, respectively.

In her essay "The Politics of Passing," Elaine K. Ginsberg (1996) contends that

> . . . passing is about identities: their creation or imposition, their adoption or rejection, their accompanying rewards or penalties. Passing is also about the boundaries between identity categories and about the individual and cultural anxieties induced by boundary crossing. Finally, passing is about specularity: the visible and the invisible, the seen and the unseen. (p. 2)

Clearly, for individuals identified as Black, the "rewards" of passing entail the social and economic benefits of White Privilege. In her classic essay "White Privilege: Unpacking the Invisible Knapsack," Peggy McIntosh (1985) contends that Whites in Western society enjoy advantages that non-Whites do not experience as "an invisible package of unearned assets" (para. 3).

In his 1950 essay "Portrait of the Inauthentic Negro: How Prejudice Distorts the Victim's Personality," renowned *New York Times* critic Anatole Broyard (1920–1990), a Black man who spent his entire life "passing" as White, explores the painful situation of a man forced to mask his true identity. According to Broyard (1950), "distorting [social] pressures" prevent "the Negro" from maintaining his "authenticity" and expressing his "essential self," which he defines as "his innate qualities and developed characteristics as an individual, as distinguished from his preponderantly defensive reactions as a member of an embattled minority" (p. 5). (Broyard's life inspired Philip Roth's (2001) novel *The Human Stain*, in which the protagonist, Coleman Silk, makes the fatal error of trying to pass as Jewish.)

In his essay "The Passing of Anatole Broyard" (originally titled "White Like Me"), renowned scholar and historian Henry Louis Gates Jr. (1998) speculates on Broyard's motives:

> So here is a man who passed for white because he wanted to be a writer and he did not want to be a Negro writer . . . In his terms, he did not want to write about black love, black passion, black suffering, black joy; he wanted to write about love and passion and suffering and joy. We give lip service to the idea of the writer who happens to be black, but had anyone, in the postwar era, ever seen such a thing? (p. 208)

Broyard's story echoes that of Harlem Renaissance writer Jean Toomer (1894–1967), best known for *Cane*, a collection of poems, stories, and vignettes about rural Black life in the South, whose innovative narrative structure anticipates Ernest Hemingway's *In Our Time*. Published in 1923 and reissued in 1967 at the height of the Black Arts/Black Power Movement, *Cane* has been—and continues to be—one of the most widely critiqued works of contemporary American literature.

Apparently, for both writers, the pressures of maintaining their "inauthentic" lives took an enormous toll on their creativity, as neither managed to achieve their ultimate goals. Toomer, who had been accepted into White literary circles, stopped writing for more than a decade after an editor he trusted labeled him as a "Negro" writer. (In 1936, he published his long narrative poem, "Blue Meridian." Written in a free-verse style reminiscent of Walt Whitman's "Song of Myself," the poem argues for "a new America" in which all barriers separating human beings from each other and from God, including race and gender, have been overcome.) Broyard, who revealed his identity to his children only on his deathbed, never managed to write his long-anticipated novel, which, some speculate, stemmed from his inability to express his "essential self."

Names as Cultural Markers

In *The Language of Oppression* (cited earlier), Haig A. Bosmajian explores the power of names and naming. As he points out:

> Our identities, who we are, how others see us, are greatly affected by the names we are called and the words with which we are labeled. The names, labels, and phrases employed to "identify" a people may in the end determine their

survival. . . . One of the first acts of an oppressor is to redefine the "enemy" so they will be looked upon as creatures warranting separation, suppression, and even eradication. (pp. 5–6)

If we reflect on the aftermath of 9/11, which spawned virulent hatred and violence toward Muslims, with many Westerners suspecting anyone with a Muslim name of being a potential terrorist, we find it difficult to deny Bosmajian's argument.

In 2010, the Hindi-language film *My Name Is Khan*, starring Bollywood icon Shah Rukh Khan, explored this phenomenon. Set in the United States, the film tells the story of Rizvan "Rizzu" Khan, an autistic Muslim man married to a Hindu woman, whose stepson is killed during a racially motivated fight at his school. Devastated by his loss, Khan embarks on a journey to meet the American president to share his story. While detained at the San Francisco International Airport for reciting verses from the Qu'ran, he tells the Transportation Security Administration, "My name is Khan and I am not a terrorist."

Asked about the film, Shah Rukh Khan described it as being about "the journey of one family and how it changes because of 9/11." Khan (2009) also stated:

It's not about a disabled man's fight against disability. It's a disabled man's fight against the disability that exists in the world—terrorism, hatred, fighting . . . *My Name Is Khan* is also about Islam and the way the world looks at Islam but we are not taking any sides. We are only trying to say that there are only good people and bad people. . . . Religion is not the criterion, humanity is. (para. 10)

In a similar attempt to dismantle the stereotype of the Muslim terrorist, Mohsin Hamid exploits the concept of "Islamic fundamentalism" in *The Reluctant Fundamentalist*, the story of Changez, a Pakistani man from Lahore who immigrated to the United States to pursue the American Dream as a student. After graduating from Princeton, he embarks on a professional career and proceeds to live "the good life" until 9/11 drastically disrupts his life. The novel is the basis of a film released in 2012.

Reflecting on the power of names for African Americans, Toni Morrison points out:

If you come from Africa, your name is gone. It is particularly problematic because it is not just *your* name but your family, your tribe. When you die, how can you connect with your ancestors if you have lost your name? That's a huge psychological scar. (LeClair, 1981, p. 126)

And in *The House on Mango Street*, Sandra Cisneros (1991) approaches the issue from a Latinx perspective through her narrator, Esperanza:

In English, my name means hope. In Spanish, it means too many letters. It means sadness. It means waiting. It is like the number nine. A muddy color. It is the Mexican records my father plays on Sunday mornings when he is shaving, songs like sobbing. . . . At school they say my name funny as if the syllables were made out of tin and hurt the roof of your mouth. But in Spanish, my name is made out of a softer something, like silver. (pp. 10–11)

In *The Namesake*, Jhumpa Lahiri explores the power of names through the story of Gogol Ganguli, a first-generation Indian American named after his father's favorite author, Nikolai Gogol. However, the narrator informs us that Gogol's name is the result of a series of unfortunate incidents, beginning with a missing letter from his Indian grandmother that would have established his true namesake.

Since Gogol hates his name, he decides to change it before leaving for college, but soon discovers that adopting a new name—Nikhil—doesn't change his identity. As he reflects:

[E]ven though his new driver's license says "Nikhil," . . . everyone he knows in the world still calls him Gogol. He is aware that his parents and their friends, and the children of their friends, and all his own friends from high school, will never call him anything but Gogol. He will remain Gogol during holidays and in summer; Gogol will revisit him on each of his birthdays. Everyone who comes to his going-away-to-college party writes "Good Luck, Gogol" on the cards. (Lahiri, 2003, p. 103)

The Politics of Hair

Hair has long been recognized as a cultural marker for people of color. As Angela Ards (2005) points out in her profile of Malcolm Gladwell:

Race in America often comes down to the politics of hair: the tighter the curl, the blacker the experience. A few years back, literary phenomenon Malcolm Gladwell discovered this absurd truism when he let his close-cut, blondish locks bolt into an Afro. The son of an English father and a Jamaican mother, Gladwell doesn't "look particularly black, especially to white people," he says, for in terms of skin color, he inherited his father's. Once he grew out that hair, his Jamaican heritage stood out, quite literally, and police officers began giving him undue special attention: more speeding tickets, more street stops, even once accosting him as a suspected rapist on the loose. (p. 21)

For Gladwell, who had earlier stated that he chose not to define himself by race, it was a rude awakening that informed his bestseller *Blink: The Power of Thinking Without Thinking*. Reflecting on the incident, Gladwell states:

The one takeaway I have from *Blink* . . . in its explorations of race, is an appreciation for how racial prejudice doesn't respect those kinds of fine distinctions . . . That to the cop looking at you in that split second . . . black is black is black. (Ards, 2005, p. 23)

Hair has long been a topic of discourse among Black writers. Examples include Bebe Moore Campbell's 1982 essay, "What to Wear to the Revolution," in which she reflects on the 1960s, when "the Afro was a black woman's revolutionary I.D." (n.p.). In "Hairpeace," a 1993 essay in *African American Review*, journalist Pearl Cleage takes a humorous approach to the subject. As Cleage (1993) points out, "You can't be a black woman writer in America and not talk about hair. They won't renew your license and, well, a black woman writing without a license in America? I guess you know the penalty for *that*" (p. 37). And in his memoir *Colored People*, in a chapter titled "In the Kitchen," Henry Louis Gates Jr. describes hair straightening as a rite of passage for Black girls (Gates, 1994).

More recently, the subject has been addressed by writers like Zadie Smith, who offers a hilarious portrait of the black hair salon in her novel *White Teeth*, and by comedian Chris Rock in his 2009 documentary, *Good Hair*.

LITERARY ARCHETYPES

Archetypes are universal symbols (motifs and images) "that recur in the myths of peoples widely separated in time and place [that] tend to have a common meaning . . . and . . . serve similar cultural functions" (Guerin et al., 2005, p. 184). Examples include images such as water (purification and redemption), the rising and setting sun (birth and death), trees (life, growth, regeneration), and the circle (wholeness, unity) and recur in literature across cultures. Perhaps the greatest differences across cultures occur in color imagery, especially in regard to black, white, red, and green.

Other examples of literary archetypes include the following:

The Hero

The classic hero who slays the proverbial dragon and saves humanity is a familiar figure in classic literature. Consequently, the classic hero's journey in Homer's *Odyssey*, which depicts the 10-year journey of Odysseus (Ulysses), a Greek hero of the Trojan War, from Troy to his home on the island of Ithaca, resurfaces in James Joyce's *Ulysses*, in which Odysseus's 10-year journey is collapsed into the 1-day journey of Joyce's antihero, Leopold Bloom, across his native Dublin.

But the hero's journey also appears in Toni Morrison's *Beloved*, depicted by Paul D's journey from Sweet Home to Sethe's home at 124 Bluestone

Road; in Sherman Alexie's short story "This Is What It Means to Say Phoenix, Arizona," depicted by Victor and Thomas's journey from the Spokane Indian Reservation ("the rez") to Phoenix, Arizona; and in George Lucas's *Star Wars* trilogy, depicted by Luke Skywalker's journey across the galaxy to destroy the Evil Empire.

The Antihero

The antihero lacks the conventional qualities attributed to a hero. "Instead of being dignified, brave, idealistic, or purposeful, the antihero may be cowardly, self-interested, alienated or weak" (Kennedy, 2013, p. 9). However, even in this capacity, he functions as protagonist. The quintessential antihero is Cervantes's Don Quixote. Other examples include Willy Loman (*Death of a Salesman*), Alexander Portnoy (*Portnoy's Complaint*), and the aforementioned Leopold Bloom (*Ulysses*).

The Code Hero

A phrase coined by Ernest Hemingway, the code hero describes a nontraditional hero who undergoes an almost ritualistic initiation to achieve "grace under pressure," which enables him to meet life's challenges. In his text *Ernest Hemingway: A Reconsideration*, critic Philip Young (2000) defines the code hero as follows:

> [He is] sensitive, masculine, impressionable, honest . . . a boy, then a man who had come up against violence and evil and had been wounded by them. The manhood he had attained was thus complicated and insecure, but he was learning a code with which he might maneuver, though crippled, and he was practicing the rites which might exorcise the terrors born of the events that crippled him. (p. 63)

The philosophy of the code hero is perhaps best articulated by Frederic Henry, the protagonist of *A Farewell to Arms*, as he struggles to regain his sense of self in the midst of death and destruction in wartime Italy: "The world breaks everyone and afterwards many are strong at the broken places" (Hemingway, 2003, p. 249).

Interestingly, the heroes in works by writers of color often possess attributes of the code hero, such as Jefferson in Ernest Gaines's *A Lesson Before Dying*, Celie in Alice Walker's *The Color Purple*, and Victor Thomas in Sherman Alexie's *The Lone Ranger and Tonto Fistfight in Heaven*.

The Ancestor

The ancestor is often depicted as a wise old man or woman who represents ancient wisdom and offers guidance to characters whose suffering can often be traced to a severance with the past and a lack of knowledge about the culture that shaped them. Consequently, the ancestor serves as a bridge that connects past and present.

In her seminal essay "Rootedness: The Ancestor as Foundation," Toni Morrison cites the presence of an ancestor as one of the defining characteristics of Black literature. As Morrison (1984) points out:

> There is always an elder there. And these ancestors are not just parents, they are sort of timeless people whose relationships to the characters are benevolent, instructive, and protective. (p. 343)

It is no wonder, then, that "the ancestor" looms large in Morrison's fiction, as portrayed by characters such as Pilate in *Song of Solomon* and Baby Suggs in *Beloved*.

In August Wilson's "century cycle" plays, the ancestor appears as Aunt Ester, a seemingly ageless woman who provides wisdom and spiritual healing for the community. Wilson (2005) describes her as follows:

> Aunt Ester has emerged for me as the most significant persona of the cycle. The characters, after all, are her children. The wisdom and tradition she embodies are valuable tools for the reconstruction of their personality and for dealing with a society in which the contradictions, over the decades, have grown more fierce, and for exposing all the places it is lacking in virtue. (p. x)

Aunt Ester is introduced in *Two Trains Running*. She appears as a central character in *Gem of the Ocean*. And she dies in *King Hedley II*.

Other examples of the ancestor in contemporary fiction include The Grandfather (Ralph Ellison's *Invisible Man*), Ultima (Rudolfo Anaya's *Bless Me, Ultima*), Miss Emma and Tante Lou (Ernest Gaines's *A Lesson Before Dying*), Mrs. Johnson (Alice Walker's "Everyday Use"), and La Inca (Junot Díaz's *The Brief Wondrous Life of Oscar Wao*).

The Trickster

The trickster, a variation of Shakespeare's "wise fool," often emerges as the most insightful and intelligent person in a narrative. Modeled on the role of the medieval court jester, employed to entertain royalty, the trickster often enjoys a privileged place in the hierarchy of the dominant power structure because, through his deft use of language—which relies heavily on irony, sarcasm, puns, and double entendres—he is the only one able to point out the flaws and shortcomings of his superiors without suffering the consequences of direct confrontation.

Each culture has its trickster tales (such as "The Tortoise and the Hare"). But African American trickster tales often involve animals, such as Brer

Rabbit, who consistently outwits Brer Fox. According to folklorist Julius Lester (1987), the trickster's function "is to add disorder to order and so make a whole, to render possible, within the fixed bounds of what is permitted, an experience of what is not permitted" (para. 3).

Examples of the trickster figure in West African folklore include the Signifying Monkey and Anansi the spider. The epitome of the trickster in contemporary African American fiction is Raven Quickskill in Ishmael Reed's *Flight to Canada*.

The Underground Man

The Underground Man is a figure who—literally or metaphorically—lives hidden away from society. Symbolically, "going underground" suggests moving from external to internal reality. Examples of the Underground Man in contemporary literature include Fred Daniels in Richard Wright's *The Man Who Lived Underground*; the unnamed narrator in Ralph Ellison's *Invisible Man*; and "the man of two minds" in Viet Thanh Nguyen's *The Sympathizer*.

CULTURAL STEREOTYPES

Stereotypes are oversimplified images of particular types of people (the prostitute with the heart of gold, the sanctified "church lady," the John Henry "superman") that are rooted in reality but grossly exaggerated. Cultural stereotypes grounded in racist images of Black people abound in literature, as illustrated in the following paragraphs.

The Black Man

Cultural stereotypes of Black men include Caliban (the Savage/Primitive); Uncle Tom (often depicted as "the good Nigger"); "Sambo"/The Clown (plays the fool to entertain Whites; often cited as the origin of Jim Crow and the Minstrel Tradition); "The Buck" (perceived as sexually insatiable and extremely well endowed, who consequently presents a danger to White women); and the Preacher (often portrayed as both a charismatic, articulate leader as well as a con man who uses his position to line his own pockets and seduce women). But the most pervasive stereotype, depicted in movies such as *Boyz n the Hood* and *Menace II Society*, and perpetuated by "gangsta rap," which glorifies sex, violence, and the drug culture, is "The Bad Nigger," a violent, dangerous "monster" who poses a threat to "civilized" society.

In his poetry collection *Brutal Imagination*, Cornelius Eady explores the stereotype of the violent Black male held by some Whites. In two of the most powerful poems, "Susan Smith's Police Report" and "Charles Stuart in the Hospital," Eady draws on two notorious criminal cases that exposed a chilling truth about American society: Most White Americans are willing to accept the stereotype of the violent Black male as a defining characteristic of Black male identity.

- On October 25, 1994, Susan Smith drowned her two sons, ages 3 and 14 months, in an act of vengeance against her former husband. She claimed that a Black man had kidnapped her children.
- On October 23, 1989, Charles Stuart shot himself and killed his pregnant wife in an effort to collect insurance money. He blamed his crime on a Black man.

Both poems are narrated by a Black man in prison, contemplating his fate. In his 1999 young adult novel *Monster*, Walter Dean Myers also explores the stereotype of the violent Black male in his story of a young Black man falsely accused of murder, portrayed as a "monster" by the judicial system.

The Black Woman

In her exploration of race and gender, *No Crystal Stair*, Gloria Wade-Gayles (1997) contends that "an intricate web of misconceptions and stereotypes defines Black women in many roles and, simultaneously, creates the monolithic 'Black woman'" (p. 3). Citing Michelle Wallace's classic essay, "Black Macho and the Myth of the Super Woman," Wade-Gayles lists the following characteristics associated with the stereotype:

> Sapphire. Mammy. Tragic mulatto wench . . . A wonderful housekeeper. Excellent with children. Very clean. Very religious. A terrific mother. A great little singer and dancer and a devoted teacher and social worker. She's always had more opportunities than the black man because she was no threat to the white man so he made it easy for her. Curiously enough, she frequently ends up on welfare. Not beautiful, rather hard-looking unless she has white blood, but then very beautiful. The black ones are very exotic though, great in bed, tigers. And very fertile. . . . Very strong. Sorrow rolls right off her brow like so much rain. Tough, unfeminine. Opposed to women's rights movements, considers herself already liberated. (p. 3)

Unfortunately, racist stereotypes persist across cultural groups. For Native Americans, they include images of the stoic Indian and the tomahawk-wielding savage. Stereotypes persist in the names of athletic teams, such as the Atlanta Braves and the Washington Redskins, which have recently come under fire. (To their credit, on February 2, 2022, the Washington Redskins unveiled their new name: the Washington Commanders. Hopefully, the Atlanta Braves will follow suit.) They also persist in phrases such as "sitting Indian style," being an "Indian giver," and in children's rhymes such as "Ten Little Indians."

Asian American stereotypes also persist in American culture. As Jessica Hagedorn (1993), a Filipino American author best known for her first novel, *Dogeaters*, points out:

> Charlie Chan is our most famous fake "Asian" pop icon—known for his obsequious manner, fractured English, and dainty walk. Absurdly cryptic sayings rolled off his tongue . . . Ingrained in American popular culture, Charlie Chan is as much a part of the demeaning legacy of stereotypes that includes Fu Manchu, Stepin' Fetchit, Sambo, Aunt Jemima, Amos N' Andy, Speedy Gonzalez, Tonto, and Little Brown Brother. (p. xxi)

Hagedorn contends that although some of the most obvious Asian stereotypes are starting to fade, they have evolved into subtler stereotypes, such as "the clever *Japanese Businessman*," "the *Ultimate Nerd*" ("model minority Asian American student excelling in math and computer science, obsessed with work, work, work"), and "*Miss Saigon*, the contemporary version of Madame Butterfly—tragic victim/whore of wartorn Vietnam, eternally longing for the white boy soldier who has abandoned her and her son" (p. xxii).

The Other/Outsider

Both these figures exist on the margins of society, having been denied the opportunity to participate in the mainstream. However, while the Outsider may be simply a rogue or maverick who refuses to conform to society's norms, the Other is generally a member of a marginalized racial or ethnic group, such as Meursault in Albert Camus's *The Stranger* and Cross Damon in Richard Wright's *The Outsider*.

The term "othering," used to identify an individual perceived as an outsider or "alien" who is systematically excluded from the dominant group, was coined by Palestinian American scholar Edward W. Said (1935–2003). In his landmark text *Orientalism* (1978), Said contends that individuals not viewed as part of Western Eurocentric culture are excluded from global society and perceived as "the Other" (a concept sometimes paraphrased as "The West and the rest"). "Othering" has been explored in the works of writers such as Toni Morrison, Ernest Gaines, Sherman Alexie, Frank Chin, Sandra Cisneros, Salman Rushdie, Edwidge Danticat, Junot Díaz, and Viet Thanh Nguyen.

In his award-winning novel *Interior Chinatown*, a satire on the treatment of Asian Americans in Hollywood (see Chapter 1), Charles Yu presents a portrait of the outsider from an Asian perspective.

Yu's message: Despite the phenomenal success of films such as *The Joy Luck Club* and *Crazy Rich Asians*, the majority of Asian American actors are still trapped in roles that portray them as stereotypes.

As explored in this chapter, identity is a key component of culture. Encouraging students to explore identity through multicultural literature can give them the tools to fight prejudice and racism and become more compassionate world citizens.

SIGNIFICANT QUESTIONS

- Is the work autobiographical? If so, how do characters reflect the author's experience?
- What rhetorical devices does the author employ to reveal a character's race or ethnicity?
- Does the text exploit *cultural stereotypes* and/or *literary archetypes*? If so, to what end?
- How would you describe the relationships among author, narrator(s), and readers?
- Does the author embrace or reject the role of *native informer*? How do you know?
- What do the names of characters reveal about their identity? Are they called by different names? Why?
- How are characters treated in the story? What is their role in society?
- How are characters defined by society? Their family? The community? Themselves?
- How do characters see themselves? What is the relationship between their self-image and their public image? Do these visions conflict? In what way?
- What defines the relationships between and among characters? Are the relationships empty or fulfilling? Close or distant? Are family members loving? Supportive? Distant? Estranged?
- What external characteristics or attributes define the characters' personalities?
- What beliefs and values appear to guide and motivate the characters' actions?
- Would you describe the major characters as whole or fragmented? Why?
- Do characters appear to suffer an identity crisis? If so, do they have the tools necessary to resolve the crisis?
- What roles do various characters play? Are they heroes? Victims? Villains? Martyrs? Outsiders? How do you know?
- Are characters changed or transformed through the course of the narrative? If so, what prompts the transformation? If not, does the narrator provide readers with information that enables them to change their attitudes toward the characters?

The serious fiction writer always writes about the whole world no matter how limited his particular scene.

—Flannery O'Connor

I have to provide the places and spaces so that the reader can participate.

—Toni Morrison

CHAPTER 7

Space

"How Do Characters Negotiate the Text's Physical, Psychological, and Cultural Landscapes?"

Space: The unlimited realm of physical and psychological components that extends beyond artificially constructed borders and boundaries and offers humans a vision of endless vistas to explore.

James Joyce's Dublin. Fyodor Dostoevsky's St. Petersburg. William Faulkner's Yoknapatawpha County. Ernest Gaines's Louisiana. Rudolfo Anaya's New Mexico. August Wilson's Pittsburgh. Gabriel Garcia Márquez's Macondo. Ryan Coogler's Wakanda.

The physical spaces—real or imagined—writers select for their stories set the stage for their characters, often presenting them with challenges they must meet in order to survive and thrive. But within these physical settings, characters also encounter psychological spaces that test their endurance, especially those perceived as outsiders by the dominant culture. Moreover, many must cope with *cultural landscapes*, or "sites of memory" embedded in their subconscious, such as the trauma of war or the legacy of slavery.

*   *   *

Culture impacts perceptions of space. Consequently, how characters engage with physical and psychological space can help reveal or conceal their identities. Do they have "room to bloom," or are they locked out or hemmed in? Do they assertively claim their space, or are they somehow constrained or limited by it?

Exploring the concept of Space focuses on issues such as the process of creating and transforming physical and psychological space to create *counterspaces* or *racialized space* (the ghetto, the barrio, Chinatown, the reservation). It also involves the concept of *narrative space*, created by the author to allow the reader to enter the text.

As noted in Chapter 1, the emphasis on ecocriticism in Native American literature challenges the Myth of the Frontier. By focusing on the relationship between literature and the physical environment, ecocriticism acknowledges that people are part of the natural landscape. Consequently, land cannot be owned and people cannot be forced from the land on which they live.

Acknowledging Indigenous people and their native lands has captured the attention of critics and scholars during the past decade, prompted by organizations such as the LANDBACK Movement, which calls for the return of Native lands to Native peoples, and the NDN Collective, an Indigenous-led organization "dedicated to building Indigenous power through organizing, activism, philanthropy, grantmaking, capacity-building and narrative change" in the tristate area of North Dakota, South Dakota, and Minnesota (NDN Collective, 2022, para. 1). But Native American literature has traditionally focused on a respect for ancestral land, a reverence for its people, and the importance of living in harmony with nature, as illustrated by works such as N. Scott Momaday's *House Made of Dawn*, Leslie Marmon Silko's *Ceremony*, and Sherman Alexie's *Smoke Signals*.

PHYSICAL SPACE

To introduce the concept of physical space, and the ability of individuals to alter space, I have my students read the essay "Black Men and Public Space" by African American journalist Brent Staples (2000), in which he describes a unique method he has devised to make himself appear less threatening to Whites while walking the streets of New York City:

> I move about with care, particularly late in the evening. I give wide berth to nervous people on subway platforms during the wee hours, particularly when I have exchanged business clothes for jeans. . . . And on late-evening constitutionals, I employ what has proved to be an excellent tension-reducing measure: I whistle melodies from Beethoven and Vivaldi and the more popular classical composers . . . my equivalent of the cowbell that hikers wear when they know they are in bear country. (p. 170)

As illustrated in this example, exploring physical space involves examining the concept of "center versus margin," in which "the center" represents the space allocated to—and claimed by—the dominant society, whereas "the margin" is relegated to "minorities" or "outsiders."

Exploring physical space also involves examining the impact of geographical locations on fictional characters portrayed in contemporary literature.

The South: Rural Roots

An ideal place to begin the exploration of Black Southern literature is Jean Toomer's *Cane*. Consisting of a collection of songs, stories, and vignettes about the South, *Cane* captures both the beauty and the horror of Black Southern life in the 1920s. Published in 1923, *Cane* is often cited as one of the major literary works of the Harlem Renaissance. It was reissued in 1967 at the height of the Black Arts/Black Power Movement and continues to rank as one of the most widely critiqued works of contemporary American literature.

With its circular narrative structure, which begins and ends in the South, *Cane* serves as a metaphor for Blacks who left the South during the Great Migration, the movement of 6 million African Americans out of the rural South to the urban North, a historical period portrayed in Richard Wright's *12 Million Black Voices*, and more recently captured in Isabel Wilkerson's national bestseller *The Warmth of Other Suns*.

Other works that highlight the challenges of living in the South include the following:

- Zora Neale Hurston's *Their Eyes Were Watching God*
- Richard Wright's *Black Boy (American Hunger)*
- Alice Walker's *The Color Purple*
- Maya Angelou's *I Know Why the Caged Bird Sings*
- Ernest Gaines's *A Lesson Before Dying*

The North: Urban Landscapes

Some of the most popular literature about the Black experience in the North is set in Harlem, New York, an area also known as "Black Manhattan." These works include Ralph Ellison's *Invisible Man*, Ann Petry's *The Street*, and James Baldwin's "Sonny's Blues."

In fact, it is the quintessential ghetto depicted in James Baldwin's essay "The Harlem Ghetto: Winter 1948" and Ralph Ellison's "Harlem Is Nowhere."

Another popular location for works set in the urban North is Chicago's South Side neighborhood, alternatively referred to as Woodlawn or Bronzeville, the historic center of African American culture in the city since the early 20th century.

Other works that highlight the challenges of living in the North include Richard Wright's *Native Son*, Gwendolyn Brooks's *Maud Martha* and *A Street in Bronzeville*, Lorraine Hansberry's *A Raisin in the Sun*, and the plays of August Wilson.

DOMESTIC SPACE ("HOME")

Contemporary literature often depicts the house or home as a safe space, especially for female characters. But immigrants, refugees, or outsiders, forced to move repeatedly and create a home "elsewhere," may have quite a different experience. In her essay "Becoming a Latina Writer," Sandra Cisneros (2002) recalls an experience while attending the University of Iowa's Writers' Workshop during the 1970s when the discussion focused on the archetypal "house of the imagination":

> Everyone seemed to have some communal knowledge which I did not have—and then I realized that the metaphor of house was totally wrong for me. Suddenly I was homeless . . . I had no such house in my memories. As a child I had read of such things in books, and my family had promised such a house, but the best they could do was offer the miserable bungalow I was embarrassed with all my life. (p. 247)

Realizing she could never fit in with her affluent White classmates, Cisneros experienced an epiphany:

> It was not until this moment when I separated myself, when I considered myself truly distinct, that my writing acquired a voice. I knew I was a Mexican woman, but I didn't think it had anything to do with why I felt so much imbalance in my life, whereas it had everything to do with it! My race, my gender, my class! That's when I decided I would write about something my classmates couldn't write about. (p. 247)

The result was her bestselling novel, *The House on Mango Street.*

Commenting on her women's reading group, Azar Nafasi, who has lived in both Iran and the United States, offers her definition of home:

> The books became our world, and they became our home, and they opened us up to ourselves. . . . The real home we have transcends ethnicity and nationality, gender, sex, and religion. It is a universal space where we can all live. (Nafisi, 2008, pp. 353–354)

Domestic spaces as sanctuaries are often highlighted in African American fiction. For example, Toni Morrison readers will readily recognize 124 Bluestone Road as the home of Baby Suggs (Sethe's mother-in-law in *Beloved*), which serves as a sanctuary and gathering place for the Black community. When Sethe escapes from Sweet Home, she finds refuge for herself and her four children at 124 Bluestone Road. But as the narrative unfolds, the house becomes the site of a murder and, eventually, a space haunted by the ghost of Beloved. Until the arrival of Paul D, it is occupied only by Sethe and her daughter Denver. As we trace the history of the house, we watch it evolve through a series of stages, much like the characters who occupy its physical space.

Similarly, August Wilson afficionados will recognize 1839 Wylie Road as the home of Aunt Ester, an ancient healer and pillar of the Black community. She first appears in *Gem of the Ocean*, where she welcomes two "outsiders" into her home: Solly Two Kings, an old man born into slavery who scouted for the Union Army, and Citizen Barlow, a young man from Alabama searching for a new life.

RACIALIZED SPACE

In his classic text *The Souls of Black Folk*, W. E. B. Du Bois (1903/1995) presents a graphic description of racialized space, the Jim Crow car:

> If you wish to ride with me you must come into the "Jim Crow Car." There will be no objection—already four White men, and a little White girl with her nurse, are in there. Usually the races are mixed in there; but the White coach is all White. Of course this car is not so good as the other, but it is fairly clean and comfortable. The discomfort lies chiefly in the hearts of those four black men yonder—and in mine. (p. 142)

In *The Lone Ranger and Tonto Fistfight in Heaven*, Sherman Alexie portrays life on "the Rez," a racialized space occupied by numerous Native Americans. As Alexie points out: "I am a Spokane/Couer d'Alene Indian from Wellpinit, Washington, where I live on the Spokane Indian Reservation. Everything I do now, writing and otherwise, has its origin in that" (Charters, 2003, p. 14).

One of the key stories in *The Lone Ranger* is "This Is What It Means to Say Phoenix, Arizona" (the basis of the award-winning film *Smoke Signals*). The story centers on two friends—Victor Joseph and Thomas-Builds-the-Fire—who travel from their reservation in Wellpinit, Washington, to Phoenix, Arizona, to retrieve the ashes of Victor's estranged father.

In preparing students to read "Phoenix, Arizona," I provide them with some background on Alexie, whose writings juxtapose images of American popular culture (John Wayne movies, country-western music, and Denny's Grand Slam Breakfast) with significant events in U.S. history (the Trail of Tears, the Sand Creek Massacre, and Custer's Last Stand), presenting both against a backdrop of Native American culture and heritage.

We also consider that Sherman Alexie's works explore American Indian boys trying to find their place in both their reservation community as well as their neighboring White community. Given this background, students are better prepared to approach "Phoenix, Arizona" through the lens of Native American culture and to understand the journey of Victor and Thomas as a postmodern quest narrative.

Edwidge Danticat, a Haitian American writer, often explores the racialized spaces occupied by Haitian immigrants. But unlike some immigrant writers (with whom she identifies), Danticat's works focus on Haiti but do not idealize it. As Danticat (2011) points out:

> We Haitians like to remind the world that Haiti was the first black republic in the Western Hemisphere, home to the only slave revolt that succeeded in producing a nation. What we would rather not say . . . is that this same country has continued to fail to reach its full potential, in part because of foreign interference, but also because of internal strife and cruelty. (p. xx)

In her short story "Hot Air Balloons," two Haitian American girls (Neah and Lucy) who have never been to Haiti live in a Haitian community in Miami, Florida. Neah joins a women's program whose members volunteer to go to Haiti to provide humanitarian services, but Lucy refuses to join her, opting instead to preserve the idealistic vision of Haiti she inherited from her parents. After seeing posters and fliers that depict Haiti as a Third World country plagued by AIDS, poverty, and corruption, Lucy wonders:

> Where were the idyllic beaches with fine white sand that my parents were always dreaming and talking about, and that I had also seen online? Where were the dewy mountaintops, Haiti being the land of mountains and all? Where was the Citadelle Laferriere, one of the world's greatest forts? Where were the caves and grottoes, the waterfalls, the cathedrals, churches, Vodou temples, museums, and art galleries college students should be visiting? (Danticat, 2020, p. 114)

Like Alexie, Danticat strives to present a realistic portrait of her home without succumbing to the racist stereotypes created by White society.

Other examples of racialized spaces portrayed in contemporary literature include "the quarters" in Ernest Gaines's *A Lesson Before Dying* (shacks that once housed slaves but still serve as "home" to their descendants) and the perilous spaces reserved for Koreans living in Japan after World War II, portrayed in Min Jin Lee's *Pachinko*.

COUNTERSPACES (THIRD SPACE THEORY)

In *The Location of Culture*, Homi Bhabha (1994) describes his concept of "third space theory" as:

The creation by formerly colonized people of an identity space that resists limitations imposed by racist, classist, and other oppressive forces in their lives." (pp. 1–2)

As Bhabha says, "instead of limiting thinking to boundaries set by outside institutions, oppressed people create a new space within official space that functions under rules more beneficial to them" (pp. 1–2).

In his award-winning novel *On Earth We're Briefly Gorgeous*, Ocean Vuong (2019) presents a graphic portrait of a racialized "third space"—the Vietnamese nail salon—which he describes as:

[A] cramped space with aromas of cloves, cinnamon, ginger, mint, and cardamon mixing with formaldehyde, toluene, acetone, Pine-Sol, and bleach. A place where folklore, rumors, tall tales, and jokes from the old country are told, . . . It's a makeshift classroom where we arrive, fresh off the boat, the plane, the depths, hoping the salon would be a temporary stop—until we get on our feet, or rather, until our jaws soften around English syllables—bend over workbooks at manicure desks, finishing homework for nighttime ESL classes that cost a quarter of our wages. (pp. 79–80)

As illustrated in this passage, the image of the Vietnamese nail salon as perceived by the dominant society is a far cry from the racialized "third space" it represents for the Vietnamese community.

PSYCHOLOGICAL SPACE

In her introduction to *No Crystal Stair: Visions of Race and Gender in Black Women's Fiction*, Gloria Wade-Gayles (1997) describes the psychological space occupied by Black women in White America:

There are three major circles of reality in our nation, which reflect degrees of power and influence. There is a large circle in which white people, most of them men, experience influence and power. Far away from it is a smaller circle, a narrow space, in which black people, regardless of sex, experience uncertainty, exploitation, and powerlessness. Hidden in this second circle is a third, a small, dark enclosure in which black women experience pain, isolation, and vulnerability. These are the distinguishing marks of black womanhood in white America. (p. xx)

Wade-Gayles's depiction of the "narrow space" and "dark enclosure" occupied by Black women clearly alludes to Harriet Jacobs's description of "The Loophole of Retreat" (in *Incidents in the Life of a Slave Girl*), a cramped crawlspace in her grandmother's attic in which she spent 7 years hiding from her "master." It also addresses the concept of "contact zones," spaces where cultures meet and contend with each other, in situations where one group has more power than the other.

THE SUBALTERN

A term coined by Italian Marxist intellectual Antonio Gramsci (1891–1937), the *subaltern* refers to the psychological space occupied by individuals excluded from mainstream society, often depicted as "underground."

In his essay "The Psychological Reactions of Oppressed People," Richard Wright contemplates the psychological distance between oppressed Blacks and their White oppressors. Drawing on Nietzsche's concept of "Frog Perspectives" (used "to describe someone looking from below upward, a sense of someone who feels himself lower than others"), Wright (1995) claims that "this psychological reality can be readily found in the expression of oppressed people" (p. 6). To illustrate, he contends that "If you ask an American Negro to describe his situation, he will almost always tell you, 'We are rising.' Against what or whom is he measuring his 'rising'? It is beyond doubt his hostile white neighbor" (p. 6).

In his novella *The Man Who Lived Underground*, Wright explores the experience of the subaltern through his protagonist, Fred Daniels, who, in order to escape the police who had tortured him into confessing to a murder he did not commit, seeks refuge in the sewer system of a fictional, unnamed city. (Fred Daniels alludes to both Frederick Douglass, a primary "conductor" on the Underground Railroad, and Fyodor Dostoevsky, whose *Notes from Underground* inspired Wright's work.)

As the story opens, Daniels is the quintessential outsider who has suffered a "social death" that further separates him from dominant (White) society. But as the story progresses, we realize that Daniels's escape to "the underground" symbolizes his inward journey to discover his true essence as a human being. His experience illustrates that of enslaved Blacks who escaped to free states and, alternatively, of Black expatriates (such as Wright) living in Europe. In his autobiography *Along This Way*, James Weldon Johnson (2000) describes his experience living abroad:

> From the day I set foot in France, I became aware of the working of a miracle within me. I became aware of a quick readjustment to life and to environment. I recaptured for the first time since childhood the sense of just being a human being. . . . I was suddenly free, free from the conflict within the Negro-man dualism and the innumerable maneuvers in thought and behavior that it compels; free from the special scorn, special tolerance, special condescension, special commiseration; free to be merely a man. (p. 209)

In essence, Daniels's experience mirrors that of Ralph Ellison's (1994) Invisible Man, whose retreat into a coal cellar symbolizes his "rising to an understanding of the human condition" (p. 110).

The concept of invisibility looms large in African American literature. The poet Adrienne Rich (1986) describes it as follows:

> Invisibility is a dangerous and painful condition. . . . When those who have the power to name and to socially construct reality choose not to see you or hear you, whether you are dark-skinned, old, disabled, female, or speak with a different accent or dialect than theirs, when someone with the authority of a teacher, say, describes the world and you are not in it, there is a moment of psychic disequilibrium, as if you looked into a mirror and saw nothing. (p. 199)

CULTURAL LANDSCAPES: THE SLAVE SHIP

The slave ship as cultural landscape appears throughout African American and Afro-Caribbean literature, including Derek Walcott's "The Schooner Flight," Toni Morrison's *Beloved*, Henry Dumas's "Ark of Bones," and August Wilson's *Gem of the Ocean*. In each work, it appears as a ship of death, in marked contrast to the biblical Noah's Ark, the mythical ship of life.

NARRATIVE SPACE

In *The Cambridge Introduction to Narrative*, H. Porter Abbott (2015) defines narrative space as "The inevitable voids, large or small, in any narrative that the reader is called upon to fill from his or her experience or imagination" (p. 234).

In February 2022, I was one of an estimated 30,000 people across the globe who attended a virtual public reading of Morrison's first novel, *The Bluest Eye*. Sponsored by the Literacy Network in conjunction with the Toni Morrison Society, the event featured a new generation of Black women writers, including Edwidge Danticat, Tayari Jones, and Jesmyn Ward, reading Morrison's work and paying tribute to the Nobel Laureate as mentor and role model. It also included civil rights icon Angela Davis, who recounted working with Morrison as her editor to publish her autobiography.

As I followed along in my battered copy of the novel, I was struck anew by the beauty of Morrison's language, and I recalled my first encounter with the text decades earlier when I was transfixed by its power to portray the brutalities of racism through the eyes of a child.

Upon reflecting on the reading, I felt that I had missed the scene in which Pauline Breedlove sits in a darkened movie theater watching *Imitation of Life*. As I searched for the scene without success, I realized that it was not part of the narrative. Instead, it existed only in my imagination, where I had constructed it by filling in the spaces provided by Morrison in two previous scenes: (1) a conversation between Claudia MacTeer, the primary narrator, and Maureen Peal, "the high-yellow dream child," concerning *Imitation of Life*; and (2) a monologue in which Pauline reminisces about sitting in a darkened movie theater watching films featuring White actresses who represented a beautiful, privileged life she could only dream of. The latter scene had transported me back to my childhood when my parents took me to see *Imitation of Life*. Having long struggled with a perpetual identity crisis concerning my biracial identity, I was traumatized by the scene in which Peola (renamed Sarah Jane in a later version of the film) is barred from attending her Black mother's funeral because she had lived her life "passing" for White.

I also recalled that *Pecola* was a term often used to describe light-skinned Black girls. Consequently, by naming her dark-skinned daughter Peola, Pauline had erred on two levels: she had burdened her with a false identity she could never fulfill, and by misspelling her name, she had compounded her futile attempt to impose an identity on her daughter that was itself an imitation.

Learning to negotiate a text's physical, psychological, and cultural landscapes enables us to explore uncharted territory and to remind ourselves that the borders and boundaries between texts—and between cultures—are arbitrary, often created by those who seek to control and dominate. Moreover, reflecting on the intertextuality of literature can help us cross those boundaries and continue our journey of discovery in the infinite universe.

SIGNIFICANT QUESTIONS

- What is the physical setting for the narrative? The psychological setting?
- How does setting impact the development of plot and characters?
- Does the setting shift? If so, how does this affect the characters' development?
- How do characters interact with their space? Do they feel comfortable, or are they desperately trying to escape or "fit in"?
- How do characters define, create, claim, and/or occupy their space? (For example, a character may be physically confined to a prison cell, yet remain psychologically free.)
- Are characters free to explore their own space, or are they confined or trapped in some way? If so, what defines their entrapment? How do they cope with it?
- How is the primary physical space defined? Is it friendly? Threatening? Ominous? Open? Expansive? Restricted? Claustrophobic?

- Do characters occupy *racialized space* (ghettos, plantations, barrios, prisons, reservations, etc.)? If so, how do they cope with their confinement?
- What devices does the author use to define *physical spaces* or establish their boundaries? Are there references to bodies of water (rivers, lakes, oceans, etc.)? Bridges? Borders? Crossings? Fences? Mountains? Walls? Cages?
- What devices does the author use to define *psychological spaces* or establish their boundaries? Do characters appear isolated? Alienated? Suffocated? Free? Happy? Depressed?
- Are characters marginalized, or are they part of the mainstream of the fictional community?
- What are the physical attributes of the novel? Is it divided into parts or sections? If so, why? Is there an introduction? A prologue and epilogue? How many chapters are there? Are the chapters titled or numbered? How much space (in terms of pages) is allocated to each chapter? To each major character? To each significant event?
- Do characters experience dreams or visions? If so, what do they reveal about their psychological state?

We cannot possibly leave it to history as a discipline nor to sociology nor science nor economics to tell the story of our people.

—Nikki Giovanni

If a race has no history, if it has no worthwhile tradition, it becomes a negligible factor in the thought of the world and it stands in danger of being exterminated.

—Carter G. Woodson

Sometimes the past deserves a second chance.

—Malcolm Gladwell

CHAPTER 8

Time

"How Does the Author Manipulate Time?"

Time: An infinite continuum, often expressed in terms of eons, epochs, or ages, that provides a sense of continuity for human experience, but exists outside "history."

As documented in films such as *Black History: Lost, Stolen, or Strayed*, and in texts such as Ivan Van Sertima's *They Came Before Columbus: The African Presence in Ancient America*; Ronald Takaki's *A Different Mirror: A History of Multicultural America*; and, most recently, Nikole Hannah-Jones's *The 1619 Project*, much of the history concerning people of color has been erased, distorted, or simply omitted from history books, which focus on the histories of dominant cultures (e.g., White, Eurocentric people).

CULTURAL PERCEPTIONS OF TIME

A critical concept integral to the study of history—but often ignored—is the conflict between Eastern (Afrocentric) and Western (Eurocentric) perceptions of time, which can be described as follows.

Western (Eurocentric) Perspective: Social Progress

Time is a commodity (e.g., "Time is money"). It can be spent, saved, lost, managed, and so forth. *Time is linear*, consisting of the past, present, and future, each separated by distinct barriers. Death is the end of life. Consequently, "history" is a series of "significant events" that document the accomplishments of "heroes."

Eastern (Afrocentric) Perspective: Cultural Memory

Time is a continuum (e.g., an endless river). It cannot be controlled, contained, or manipulated. *Time is cyclic*, consisting of the past and present. Events that have not yet occurred exist in a separate realm of "no time." All elements of time are interconnected. Death is a part of life. Consequently, "history" is a series of interrelated stories that celebrate the lives of ordinary people.

The late South African singer Miriam Makeba (1991) summarizes these perspectives as follows:

> When a Westerner is born, he or she enters a stream of time that is always flowing. When a point in life is passed, it is finished. When a Westerner dies, he leaves the stream, which flows on without him. But for us, birth plunges us into a pool in which the waters of past, present, and future swirl around together. Things happen and are done with, but they are not dead. After we splash about a bit in life, our mortal beings leave the pool, but our spirits remain. (p. 380)

HISTORIOGRAPHY

As discussed in Loewen's example of "heroification," the process of documenting history—who records it, how it is recorded, and who decides what is worth recording—must be considered in the study of history. In the age of smartphones, the Internet, and social media, virtually anyone can record an event and share it almost instantaneously with millions across the globe. But in the age of print media, events that were deemed "worthy" of recording in history books were often drawn from the pages of newspapers, magazines, and individual reports. Consequently, since the power of the press was largely controlled by the White dominant culture, stories concerning communities of color were simply omitted or distorted to fit the dominant narrative.

HISTORICITY

In his seminal text *Literature and Existentialism*, Jean Paul Sartre (1994) explains the concept of historicity as follows:

> If I were to tell an audience of Americans about the German occupation, there would have to be a great deal of analysis and precaution. I would waste twenty pages in dispelling preconceptions, prejudices, and legends. Afterward, I would have to be sure of my position at every step; I would have to look for images and symbols in American history which would enable them to understand ours; . . . If I were to write about the same subject for Frenchmen, we are "entre nous" [between us]. For example, it would be enough to say: "A concert of German military music in the band-stand of a public garden;" everything is there: a raw spring day, a park in the provinces, men with shaven skulls blowing away at their brasses, blind and deaf passers-by who quicken their steps, two or three sullen-looking listeners under the trees, this useless serenade to France which

drifts off into the sky, our shame and our anguish, our anger and our pride too. . . . (p. 69)

Interestingly, David Mura's "economy of explanation" (see Chapter 4) bears a striking resemblance to Sartre's "historicity." In exploring these concepts with students, teachers will want to emphasize these similarities and point out that although the terminology has changed, the concepts described within the context of these two vastly different cultures remain relatively unchanged.

As discussed in the following paragraphs, Time has a profound impact on a novel's narrative structure.

EXPLORING TIME IN CONTEMPORARY FICTION

A Tale for the Time Being

In her *New York Times* bestselling novel, *A Tale for the Time Being,* Ruth Ozeki, a Zen Buddhist priest, tells the story of Ruth, a writer living on a remote island in the Pacific Northwest who finds a mysterious diary washed ashore in a Hello Kitty lunchbox. Believing it to be debris from the Tōhoku earthquake and tsunami (March 11, 2011), the most powerful earthquake ever recorded in Japan, she takes it home and discovers that the diary was written by Naoko "Nao" Yasutani, a troubled teenager living in Tokyo who, depressed over having to relocate from her home in the United States and tormented by her Japanese classmates, who view her as an outsider, has resolved to commit suicide. Obsessed with the diary and determined to alter Nao's fate, Ruth sets out to connect with her across space and time. A fictional exploration of time and impermanence as discussed in ancient Buddhist texts, the novel is also a meditation on the "magical" connections between readers and writers.

To "unlock" Ozeki's novel, we must begin with its title: This is not A Tale for the Time *Being* (something temporary and transitory), but A Tale for the *Time Being,* which Ozeki (n.d.) defines as follows:

> A time being is you and me and every one of us who is, and was, and ever will be. But it's not just people who are time beings. Everything that exists in the universe is a time being, because everything, from subatomic particles to galaxies, comes and goes. We are all fluid and constantly changing. This is our identity, not to have a fixed identity. We are temporal beings, and we flow from one form to another. ("A Conversation with Ruth Ozeki," para. 27)

Through her dual narrators, Ruth and Nao, supported by a cast of colorful characters, Ozeki takes us through several decades of history spanning three generations, presented from both Western and Eastern perspectives. Key characters include Nao's father, a former Silicon Valley engineer, whose failed suicide attempt creates unbearable hardships for his family; her grandfather, who is forced to abandon his passion for French literature and philosophy to become a Kamikaze pilot during World War II; and her 104-year-old great-grandmother, a Zen Buddhist nun, who teaches Nao the "superpower" of meditation. In addition to contemporary Japanese history and pop culture (such as manga, anime, and cosplay), historical events highlighted include the Japanese bombing of Pearl Harbor; the U.S. bombings of Tokyo, Nagasaki, and Hiroshima; 9/11; and the 1990's "dot.com" crash. But Ozeki not only alludes to these events; she cites them as evidence of *cultural memory*, the belief that memories of traumatic events are embedded in our DNA. Consequently, we come to realize that a major source of Nao's suicidal tendencies is her cultural memory of World War II and its aftermath, exacerbated by Japan's culture of suicide, presumably influenced by the culture of the samurai warrior for whom the ultimate act of courage and sacrifice was *seppuku*, a form of ceremonial suicide. (The culture of suicide is highlighted in the 2015 film *The Sea of Trees*.)

One of the most intriguing aspects of the novel is Ozeki's commentary on how she came to write it. In an interview with *Chatelaine*, she reveals that after having spent 5 years working on the manuscript, she was on the verge of submitting it to her publisher. But after learning about the Tōhoku earthquake and tsunami, she felt compelled to discard more than half of her manuscript and rewrite it, placing the earthquake at the heart of her narrative and making Nao a primary narrator.

Although her novel is more fantasy than historical fiction, Ozeki joins the ranks of writers whose works document the history of Japan after World War II such as Masuji Ibuse's *Black Rain*, Hisaye Yamamoto's *Seventeen Syllables*, Joy Kogawa's *Obasan*, Jeanne Wakatsuki Houston's *Farewell to Manzanar*, and John Okada's *No-No Boy*.

By playing on the narrator's name (Nao/Now), Ozeki also exploits the concept of "time zones," described by literary critic Marjorie Garber (2012) as follows:

> The word *now* is what linguists call a shifter: *now* in 1920 meant 1920; *now* in 2019 will, presumably, mean 2019. To put the case in literary-historical terms, Shakespeare's *Henry V* exists in at least three time zones—the time in which it was written (the end of the sixteenth century), the time in which it is set (the medieval kingship of Henry V, 1413–22), and the time in which it is being read, interpreted, or performed. (p. 173)

In short, in Ozeki's world, time is infinite; depending on a character's perspective, it can be compressed, expanded, or collapsed, with little or no distinctions between past, present, and future.

Song of Solomon

In *Song of Solomon*, Toni Morrison performs a similar feat by documenting African American history. Set in an unnamed town in Michigan and inspired by an African American folk tale about enslaved Africans who escape slavery by flying back to Africa, *Song of Solomon* explores the quest for cultural identity. The novel tells the story of Macon "Milkman" Dead, a young Black man alienated from himself and estranged from his family, his community, and his historical and cultural roots. But with the help of his eccentric Aunt Pilate and his best friend, Guitar Bains, Milkman embarks on a physical and spiritual journey in search of his "inheritance" that enables him to reconnect with his past and realize his self-worth.

Although the action of the novel spans approximately 32 years (from Milkman's birth to his "flight" from Solomon's Leap), the narration spans over 100 years, documenting the Dead family's history over three generations. Thus, it encompasses two major historical eras: Emancipation and Reconstruction (1865 to 1877) and the 1960s Civil Rights movement (1955 to 1970). Moreover, the novel begins in 1931 and ends around 1963. Thus, it also encompasses two major literary movements: the Harlem Renaissance (1919 to 1940) and the Black Arts/Black Power movement (1960 to 1970).

In addition to flashbacks and foreshadowing, Morrison employs numerous historical allusions to mark the passage of time, which fall into four general categories:

- *Allusions to historical documents*: The Emancipation Proclamation, the Constitution, the Declaration of Independence, newspaper articles
- *Allusions to historical characters*: Black pilots in the military, Father Divine, Malcolm X, Martin Luther King Jr., Charles Drew ("the Blood Bank"), Robert Smalls ("a riverboat pilot")
- *Allusions to historical sites*: Pennsylvania, the Freedmen's Bureau, Michigan, Accra
- *Allusions to historical events*: the Birmingham church bombing ("scraps of Sunday dresses"), the murder of Emmett Till, the Depression, the Great Migration

She challenges the Eurocentric perspective of history as a progressive series of "significant events" that document the accomplishments of "heroes," and she compels us to consider the Afrocentric perspective of history as a series of individual and collective stories that document the accomplishments of ordinary people.

In fact, both Ozeki and Morrison eschew the Western "heroes and holidays" approach to history. In "Handicapped by History: The Process of

Hero-making," included in his classic text *Lies My Teacher Told Me*, James W. Loewen (1995) describes this approach as "heroification," which he defines as "a degenerative process (much like calcification) that makes people over into heroes" (p. 19). To illustrate, he cites numerous examples, including that of former President Woodrow Wilson, often cited as a hero who reluctantly led the United States into World War I and who, after the war, championed the struggle to establish the League of Nations. But in fact, Loewen points out, Wilson's heroic persona contradicted his true character, noting that he was "an outspoken white supremacist . . . who ordered that white and black workers in federal government jobs be segregated from one another" (p. 27).

Loewen's concept of "heroification" echoes the philosophy of Leo Tolstoy, who insisted on a clear distinction between historians and artists as recorders of history. As Tolstoy (2008) points out in the preface to *War and Peace*:

> A historian and an artist, describing an historical epoch, have two completely different objects. As a historian would be wrong if he should try to present a historical figure in all his entirety, . . . so an artist would not fulfill his task by always presenting a figure in his historical significance. . . . For a historian, considering the contribution rendered by some person towards a certain goal, there are heroes; for the artist, considering the correspondence of this person to all sides of life, there cannot and should not be any heroes, but there should be people. . . . And so the tasks of the artist and the historian are completely different. . . . (pp. 1217–1224)

Tolstoy's observations, in turn, reflect Morrison's: "[T]he crucial distinction for me is not the difference between fact and fiction, but the distinction between fact and truth. Because facts can exist without human intelligence, but truth cannot" (Morrison, 1998, pp. 112–113).

As illustrated in these examples, the exploration of a people's history must include an acknowledgment of and respect for their culture, as well as an awareness of *historiography* (the process of documenting historical events) and *historicity* (a sense of shared knowledge among people who share a common history).

A Lesson Before Dying

Set in the fictional community of Bayonne, Louisiana, *A Lesson Before Dying* tells the story of Jefferson, a 21-year-old uneducated Black field worker sentenced to death by electrocution after being wrongfully accused and convicted of the robbery and murder of a White man. At his trial, Jefferson's court-appointed attorney argues that Jefferson lacks the intelligence to plan a robbery and that sentencing him to death would be like putting a hog in the electric chair. Despite this "defense," the all-White jury finds Jefferson guilty.

To compound the horror of his situation, Jefferson internalizes the attorney's racist depiction of him as a dumb animal.

Determined that Jefferson will die with dignity, his godmother, Miss Emma, coerces Grant Wiggins—Jefferson's former teacher and the novel's primary narrator—to teach Jefferson to "stand up" and be a man. Although convinced that there is nothing he can do, Grant reluctantly agrees to visit Jefferson in jail. Over the next several months, while Jefferson awaits his impending execution, he and Grant forge a bond that enables both men to regain their dignity, reconnect with their community, and learn "the importance of standing."

Although the action of the novel spans approximately 5½ months (from Jefferson's trial to his execution), the narration spans over 100 years, documenting "significant events" in U.S. history that chronicle the journey of enslaved Africans from slavery to freedom. To help students view the novel's narrative time frame from a historical perspective, we construct a timeline that highlights key dates in the Civil Rights struggle.

We also note that the slow passage of time at the beginning of the novel reflects the relaxed, leisurely pace of life in the rural South. But as Jefferson's impending execution draws nearer, the passage of time not only accelerates; it acquires a profound sense of urgency.

I encourage students to visualize the novel's narrative structure as a series of 10 concentric circles depicting progressively smaller units of time in which the largest (outer) circle represents the post–Civil War/pre–Civil Rights era. This circle encompasses a series of smaller circles that depict progressively smaller units of time, which we label as follows:

1. The post–Civil War/pre–Civil Rights era (1865–1965)
2. The late 1940s
3. "The Grinding Season" (December 1948–April 1949)
4. Annual Events: Christmas, Easter, Mardi Gras, Dr. Joseph's visits to Grant's school, etc.
5. Monthly Events: Termination Sunday
6. Weekly Events: Church services, visits with Jefferson
7. Daily Events ("The Daily Grind"): Work, school, etc. The text's division into 31 chapters emphasizes the focus on daily events.
8. Specific days: Sunday, Monday, Friday
9. The day of Jefferson's execution: Friday, April 8
10. The final hours, minutes, and seconds of Jefferson's life: noon to 3:00 p.m.

We also note that the novel's narrative time frame (December 1948 to April 1949) not only moves from Christmas (the birth of Jesus) to Easter (Jesus's resurrection); it also emulates two seasonal cycles that depict the

rituals of life, death, and rebirth: the agricultural cycle of the Louisiana sugar cane plantation, from planting to harvesting to "the grinding season."
The time frame also reflects the cycle of the truncated school year for Black
children who—like Jefferson—work in the cane fields to help support their
families, thus sacrificing their only opportunity to escape the crushing cycle
of poverty and illiteracy.

To underscore the significance of time, we also consider the observations
of Sister Helen Prejean (1994) in her chilling account of life on Death Row,
Dead Man Walking:

> Time rushes by and yet time is frozen. Funny how we get so exact about time at
> the end of life and at its beginning. She died at 6:08 or 3:46, we say, or the baby
> was born at 4:02. But in between we slosh through huge swatches of time—
> weeks, months, years, decades, even. (p. 85)

Clearly, Gaines embraces the Eastern/Afrocentric perspective of history,
since Jefferson's story is passed on to succeeding generations through Grant
and his students. Moreover, by recording his prison experience in his journal, Jefferson follows in the footsteps of other inmates whose prison writings
have become historical documents, such as Martin Luther King Jr.'s "Letter
from Birmingham Jail," George Jackson's *Soledad Brother*, and Mumia
Abu-Jamal's *Live from Death Row*. Jefferson also joins the ranks of political prisoners such as Elie Wiesel, Viktor Frankl, and Malcolm X, whose in-
carcerations resulted in profound spiritual transformations. Viewing the text
from an even broader perspective, we might also consider Jefferson's story
alongside that of Anthony Ray Hinton (*The Sun Does Shine: How I Found
Freedom on Death Row*) and in light of Michelle Alexander's *The New Jim
Crow: Mass Incarceration in the Age of Colorblindness*.

Each text centers on one or more "significant events," as defined by the
author, that anchor their stories in time: the Tōhoku earthquake and tsunami; Milkman's birth and "flight" from Solomon's Leap; Jefferson's trial
and execution. Moreover, each author demonstrates that the past continues
to influence the present and future. Consequently, they support William
Faulkner's oft-quoted statement, "The past isn't dead. It's not even past." Or,
as the irreverent Raven Quickskill observes in Ishmael Reed's (1989) *Flight
to Canada*, "Strange, history. Complicated, too. It will always be a mystery,
history. New disclosures are as bizarre as the most bizarre fantasy" (p. 8).

SIGNIFICANT QUESTIONS

- What is the setting for this narrative: The past? The present?
  The future? No time?

- How much time elapses during the course of the narrative? (Minutes? Hours? Days? Weeks? Months? Years? Decades? Centuries?) How do you know?
- What *historical characters or events* does the author reference to establish a sense of *real time*? (Frederick Douglass, Malcolm X, Michelle Obama; World War II, the Harlem Renaissance, the Civil Rights movement, etc.)
- What *rhetorical devices* does the author employ to convey a sense of *narrative time*? (Flashbacks? Foreshadowing? References or allusions to historical issues, events, or characters? References to songs, movies, or books that reflect a designated era? Letters? Photographs? Diaries?)
- Does the author focus primarily on a Western (Eurocentric) or an Eastern (Afrocentric) perspective of history? How do you know?
- Does the author expand or compress time? If so, what methods or techniques does she use? How do these techniques affect the development of the narrative?
- Does the narrative incorporate elements of fantasy, magic, or surrealism? (Mystical symbols or images? Dreams or visions? Ghosts or spirits?)
- How does the text's *narrative structure* impact the plot?
- How does the author's manipulation of narrative time impact the portrayal of "significant events"?

EXPLORING THE LIST PARADIGM: UNLOCKING THE TEXT

CHAPTER 9

Cultural Contexts for *The Brief Wondrous Life of Oscar Wao*

I don't speak Spanish.

I abhor violence.

I know nothing about comic books, video games, or the Fantastic Four.

And as a Black/biracial female who has only recently (and reluctantly) embraced my role as "village elder," I am clearly not Junot Díaz's "ideal reader."

So why *Oscar Wao*?

My initial encounter with the novel mirrored that of Natalie Goldberg's initial encounter with Silko's *Ceremony*: "This was stretching my brain—I was afraid it would snap" (2000, p. 112). But I was intrigued by this strange and wonderful novel that challenged me to enter its magical universe while making it clear that the journey would not be easy. And as a lifelong reader and decades-long Morrison scholar, I know that the most challenging and "difficult" novels ultimately offer the most rewarding reading experience.

Like Goldberg, I decided to take it slow. And once I focused on finding ways to connect with the author, I began to realize that despite our differences in race, age, and gender, we actually did have some things in common: Díaz came to the United States from the Dominican Republic at age 6 and struggled to learn English. I came to the United States from Germany at age 7 and struggled to learn English. Díaz sought solace in books, which opened up whole new worlds to him. I sought solace in books, which opened up whole new worlds to me. And—taking a giant leap forward—Díaz taught literature and creative writing at MIT, an elite, predominantly White institution dedicated to the study of science and technology. I taught literature and composition at the Air Force Academy, an elite, predominantly White institution dedicated to the study of science and technology. I began to feel that if I could connect with Díaz on such seemingly superficial levels, I could connect with his novel.

I initially encountered the genius of Junot Díaz through two of his short stories: "Fiesta, 1980," about a young boy who struggles to cope with his father's infidelity, and "Edison, New Jersey," about a young man who narrates his experience of delivering custom-made pool tables to wealthy clients.

I remember being immediately captivated by the young narrators' seemingly effortless, conversational language and struck by their insight and ability to cope with life.

After purchasing my copy of *Drown,* Díaz's first short story collection, and reading the first story, "Ysrael," about a bully who harasses and humiliates a boy with a serious facial deformity, I was once again compelled to ask myself what attracted me to these dark stories told from the perspective of a brash young narrator who, through a rare combination of intuition, intelligence, and street smarts, encounters the most soul-crushing experiences and emerges battered, but unbroken.

As I read the rest of the stories, I realized that I had met Yunior de la Casas, the primary narrator of *Oscar Wao.*

READING *OSCAR WAO*

Published in 2007 and winner of the 2008 Pulitzer Prize for Fiction, *The Brief Wondrous Life of Oscar Wao,* with its blend of history, mythology, and "comic book realism," defies our attempts to classify and categorize (Bautista, 2010, p. 42). In fact, Díaz openly rejects traditional notions of genre (fiction, poetry, and drama), opting instead for his own version of "the genres": comics, science fiction, and fantasy (Díaz, 2008, p. 15). Consequently, once we abandon our efforts to fit the novel into a preconceived category of what a novel "should be," we can begin to appreciate it for what it is: an innovative reframing of the immigrant narrative that casts its characters as comic book heroes and villains. Instead of Rafael Trujillo, the Dominican Republic's ruthless dictator, we have Rafael Trujillo as Galactus, the comic book villain. And instead of four Dominican American immigrants, we have new incarnations of the Marvel comic series *Fantastic Four*: Oscar (Mister Fantastic); Oscar's mother, Belicia (The Human Torch); Oscar's sister, Lola (The Thing); and Oscar's adopted grandmother, La Inca (The Invisible Woman).

In a *New York Times* interview, Díaz (2012a) explains that patterning his four main characters on the Fantastic Four was a stylistic choice that forms "the deep structure of the book" (p. 28). Once we recognize this structure, we gain a fresh perspective on the novel as a character-driven narrative that unfolds as a series of episodes featuring four ordinary individuals forced to use their "superpowers" to survive. (We may also find ourselves pondering the potential of our own superpowers, should we be called upon to unleash them.) In creating this unique structure, Díaz elevates the world of comics to the level of literary fiction. In essence, he reverses the popular trend of converting complex literary works to graphic novels.

In reflecting on his inspiration for writing the novel, Díaz (2012a) recalls finding a small black-and-white photo of his father dressed in a fascist uniform:

This sent me into Oscar Wao—discovering this photo. That's my dad . . . a total pro-Trujillo lunatic. And how happy and normalized this was, you know, to go get your picture taken. And yet that was the uniform of terror. He was so proud of it. He's a baby here, about 19. At this age, I was delivering pool tables and reading *Granta*. And he could have been torturing people. I handled this again and again and again in *Oscar Wao*. (p. 29)

In 1999 Díaz received a Guggenheim Fellowship. But despite the award and his accolades for *Drown*, he found himself unable to write in Syracuse. Consequently, he decided to spend some of his grant money on a trip to Mexico City with his friend, novelist Francisco Goldman. At the time, Díaz was working on his "Akira" novel, *Monstro*, inspired by the Japanese comics series and 1987 film about the destruction of New York City and its aftermath. But although he wrote thousands of words, he had trouble completing it. Then, when he least expected it, a character appeared to him who would become the narrator of his long-anticipated novel, *The Brief Wondrous Life of Oscar Wao*, which took him 11 years to write (Bures, 2007, p. 54).

According to *New York Times* literary critic Michiko Kakutani (2012), *Oscar Wao* enjoys a broad readership among young people, especially Black and Latino males who respond to the "limber, streetwise, caffeinated and wonderfully eclectic" voice that drives the novel (para. 1). But it is precisely this "wonderfully eclectic" voice that presents a challenge for readers used to a more conventional style.

LANGUAGE IN *OSCAR WAO*

In *Oscar Wao*, Díaz combines code-switching the language of music with the languages of love, racism, and violence. In describing his innovative use of language, Díaz (2008) explains:

> I was trying to see how far I could push English to the edge of disintegration, but still be, for the large part, entirely coherent. In other words, could I make the unintelligibility gap for any one reader as wide as I could, but still have it hold together, still be able to communicate the experience? (p. 14)

(I must confess that for help in translating some of the Spanish words and phrases and identifying some of the more obscure references and allusions in *Oscar Wao*, I frequently consulted Kim Flournoy's 2008 "The Annotated *Oscar Wao*: Notes and Translations for *The Brief Wondrous Life of Oscar Wao*.")

Clearly, Díaz rejects the role of "native informer." As he points out:

> I'm not . . . a native informer. I don't explain cultural things with italics or with exclamation points or sidebars or asides. I was aggressive about that [in *Oscar Wao*] because I had so many negative models, so many Latinos and black writers who are writing to White audiences, who are not writing for their own people. If you are not writing to your own people, I'm disturbed because of what that says about your relationship to the community you are in one way or another indebted to. (Céspedes &Torres-Saillant, 2000, p. 900)

HISTORY: THE PARSLEY MASSACRE

Much of Díaz's novel is informed by historical events impacting the Dominican Republic, such as the U.S. occupation of the Dominican Republic (1916–1924), which played a major role in creating the Trujillo regime (1930–1961), and the Dominican Diaspora, which saw thousands of Dominicans fleeing the Dominican Republic in the wake of Trujillo's assassination.

Díaz seems especially obsessed with the Parsley Massacre/Haitian Genocide (October 2–8, 1937), during which an estimated 20,000 Haitians were killed by Trujillo's henchmen because they could not pronounce the letter "r" in *perejil*, the Spanish word for parsley. In *Oscar Wao*, Díaz establishes the Parsley Massacre as a significant historical event. Consequently, he aligns himself with other African American and Afro-Caribbean writers who have documented the massacre in their works, including Rita Dove ("Parsley"); René Philoctète (*Massacre River*), and Julia Alvarez (*In the Time of the Butterflies*). The massacre is also documented in the works of Haitian American writer Edwidge Danticat, who tells the story from the Haitian perspective in her novel *The Farming of Bones*, and in her short story "Nineteen Thirty-Seven," included in her first short story collection, *Krik? Krak!*

But Díaz goes even further: He combines history and mythology with fantasy. Instead of merely recounting the myths of the dictator some saw as superhuman, he creates a new myth that casts Trujillo as a comic book villain obsessed with controlling the universe.

MAJOR INFLUENCES

During an interview with Toni Morrison at the New York Public Library, Díaz (2013b) confessed that when he read *Song of Solomon* during his first semester at Rutgers, "the axis of my world shifted and it has never returned." In fact, *Oscar Wao* shares several similarities with *Song of Solomon*: Both explore the devastating impact of racism and colorism on communities of color; both feature a formidable cast of strong female characters, including an ancestor who serves as healer and guardian; and both trace the histories of families through several generations.

Díaz also cites Sandra Cisneros's *The House on Mango Street* as a key influence. Like Cisneros, Díaz finds his voice in the real voices of his people, his family, and the extended family of the Latinx community. In fact, his philosophy echoes that of Cisneros (2002), who proclaims, "I'm trying to write the stories that haven't been written. I feel like a cartographer; I'm determined to fill a literary void" (p. 246).

Other works that influence his writing include Patrick Chamoiseau's *Texaco*, Derek Walcott's "The Schooner *Flight*," Herman Melville's *Moby-Dick*, Alan Moore's *Watchmen*, and J. R. R. Tolkien's *Lord of the Rings*.

AUTHOR BACKGROUND

Born December 31, 1968, in Santo Domingo, the Dominican Republic, Junot Díaz moved with his family to Parlin, New Jersey, at age 6. Díaz (2008) recalls the experience as a kind of surreal time travel:

> How in the world [do you] describe the extreme experience of being an immigrant in the United States, the extreme experience of coming from the Third World and suddenly appearing in New Jersey . . . [E]very time I tried to use a narrative to take me from here to there, it disintegrated . . . But science fiction, fantasy, and comic books are meant to do this kind of stupid stuff, they're meant to talk about these extreme, ludicrous transformations, and so I really wanted to use them. (p. 15)

As a child, Díaz read voraciously and spent much of his time at the public library. He recalls struggling with the English language, a subject he addresses in several interviews. As a young man, he worked various menial jobs, including delivering pool tables, an experience that inspired "Edison, New Jersey."

In 1996, at age 28, Junot Díaz burst onto the literary landscape with his debut short story collection, *Drown*, a slim volume of 10 stories that explore the Dominican immigrant experience through the eyes of several young narrators struggling to come to terms with their "cultural schizophrenia." He then spent several years teaching creative writing at Syracuse University alongside his colleague George Saunders.

In 2012, Díaz published his second short story collection, *This Is How You Lose Her*, which includes "Alma" and "The Pura Principle," as well as "Miss Lora," about a high school student coming of age in 1980s New Jersey who struggles to overcome his guilt and shame after being sexually molested by an older woman (Díaz, 2012d). He also received a $500,000

MacArthur "genius grant." In 2013, Díaz won the "world's richest short sto-ry prize" for "Miss Lora," for which he was awarded 30,000 British pounds, or $36,055.95 (Flood, 2013).

"Miss Lora," which originally appeared in the April 23, 2012, issue of *The New Yorker*, is included in *This Is How You Lose Her*. In reflecting on "Miss Lora," Díaz described it as a "challenging" story to write. As he points out:

> We tend, as a culture, to think of boys having underage sex quite differently to how we think of girls. I find that quite disturbing, and wanted to question the log-ic of that. . . . If a boy has sex with his teacher, people under their breath are kind of high-fiving the kid. If a 16- or 15-year-old girl has sex with an older teacher—forget about it. No one's celebrating. That seemed really strange. (Flood, 2013)

That same year, his dystopian short story "Monstro," about the destruc-tion of New York City by a mysterious force, appeared in the June issue of *The New Yorker*.

In a 2013 interview, Díaz explains the allusion to Oscar Wilde in the novel's title:

> [O]ne time after a night of partying I picked up a copy of *The Importance of Being Earnest*, and I said Oscar Wilde's name in Dominican and it came out "Oscar Wao." A quick joke, but the name stayed with me, and next thing you know, I had this vision of a poor, doomed ghetto nerd, the kind of ghetto nerd I would have been had I not been discovered by girls the first year out of high school. (Díaz, 2013a)

An excellent resource on the life and works of Junot Díaz is *Junot Díaz and the Decolonial Imagination* (Hanna, Vargas, & Saldívar, 2016).

Sexual Abuse Allegations

On May 4, 2018, Díaz was accused "of forcibly kissing the writer Zinzi Clemmons, as well as behaving inappropriately towards two other female writers" (Flood, 2018). As a result, he voluntarily resigned from his post as chairman of the Pulitzer board while the organization launched a review of the allegations. He also encountered problems with his colleagues at VONA (Voices of Our Nations Arts Foundation), an organization he co-founded, who failed to support him. Consequently, his reputation suffered and several of his lectures and appearances were canceled. Ironically, the charges were filed less than 1 month after Díaz published his controversial essay, "The Silence: The Legacy of Childhood Trauma," in the April 16, 2018, issue of *The New Yorker*, in which he describes his experience of being raped at the age of 8 and reflects on the aftermath of the traumatic event on his later life and relationships (Díaz, 2018c).

In November 2018, following an "exhaustive" 5-month investigation, Díaz was cleared of all charges and invited to resume his post as chairman of the Pulitzer committee. He was also exonerated by his colleagues at MIT, where he continued to teach, and by the *Boston Review*, which retained him as fiction editor.

Career Highlights

Díaz is a prolific writer whose work has been applauded by both readers and critics. Over the years, four of his short stories have been included in *The Best American Short Stories* annual anthology: "Ysrael" (1996) and "Fiesta, 1980" (1997), from *Drown*; and "The Sun, the Moon, the Stars" (1999) and "Nilda" (2000), from *This Is How You Lose Her*.

He is also a frequent contributor to *The New Yorker*, which published his short stories "Alma" (December 24 and 31, 2007) and "The Pura Principle" (March 2010), as well as "Wildwood" (June 11 and 18, 2007), which appears as Chapter 2 of *Oscar Wao*. As noted, Díaz has won numerous prestigious awards including a Guggenheim Fellowship (1999), the National Book Critics Circle Award (2007), and the Pulitzer Prize for Fiction (2008).

In 2016, Díaz served as guest editor for *The Best American Short Stories*. At this writing, he still serves as fiction editor for the *Boston Review*. He also served on the board of advisers for Freedom University, a volunteer organization in Georgia that offers educational assistance to undocumented immigrants. In 2017, he was inducted into the American Academy of Arts and Letters. And in 2018, Díaz published the children's book *Islandborn*, which tells the story of Lola, a young girl born on "the Island" and raised in the United States who can't remember her homeland. Through the stories of her relatives, she begins to imagine her past. Threaded throughout the book are themes of home and belonging. For as Lola's *abuela* points out, "Just because you don't remember a place doesn't mean it's not in you." But even in this book, Trujillo looms large as "the most dreadful monster anyone had ever seen" (Díaz, 2018a).

Given this formidable track record, I find it odd that it is George Saunders—not Junot Díaz—who is heralded as "the master of the American short story."

At this writing, Díaz is still at work on *Monstro*, his highly anticipated next novel. Reflecting on his work-in-progress, Díaz (2013a) confesses, "I'm trying to write my 'Psychic Terrorist kills New York City' novel. Guess I'm stubborn as hell. Or just stupid" (para. 34).

CHAPTER 10

Exploring the LIST Paradigm

Reading *The Brief Wondrous Life of Oscar Wao*

In the fall 2014 semester, I taught *Oscar Wao* as part of an introductory literature course titled "Literature and Intermediate Composition" at the U.S.
Air Force Academy (USAFA). A required English course designed primarily
for three-degree cadets (sophomores), the course focused on enhancing cadets' writing skills and introducing them to the three literary genres: fiction,
poetry, and drama.

One of the drawbacks of teaching at the Academy is that, in the interest of
maintaining uniformity across the curriculum, instructors have little control
over their syllabi. Consequently, creating a course that met USAFA require-
ments but included some of my favorite texts often presented a challenge.

My syllabus, created by my course director, required me to teach the
following texts:

- Several poems, including Walt Whitman's *Song of Myself*
- Two short stories (I chose Flannery O'Connor's "Everything That
  Rises Must Converge" and Alice Walker's "Everyday Use")
- Toni Morrison's *Beloved*
- Sophocles's *Antigone*
- Shakespeare's *Othello*

To supplement these readings, I was allowed to add one novel as my "flex
text." Without hesitation, I chose Junot Díaz's *The Brief Wondrous Life of
Oscar Wao*.

A semester at the Academy consists of forty 50-minute sessions. Allowing
for course introductions, student conferences, writing workshops, class presentations, and course evaluations, I was left with 29 sessions to teach five
major texts and several shorter works. Of those 29 sessions, I dedicated six
to teaching *Oscar Wao*, which meant students had roughly 6 hours of class
time to focus on this complex text. Given these restrictions, I was pleasantly
surprised by the overwhelmingly positive student responses to the novel. (See
"Coda.")

The Academy offers no Bachelor of Arts degree. (Cadets graduate with
a Bachelor of Science degree.) Consequently, teaching literature to cadets

focused primarily on STEM courses presents a challenge. That challenge is compounded for instructors like me—Black, female, civilian—who teach at this predominantly White, male, military institution.

My class consisted of 20 cadets: 14 male, six female. Sixteen identified as White, three as Black (including one international cadet from Rwanda), and one as Hispanic.

Following our first session on *Oscar Wao*, at which point students were to have completed a first reading of the novel, I presented them with a hand-out of the LIST Paradigm I had created specifically for our critical reading of the novel. I also distributed a list of discussion questions designed to encourage class participation and generate ideas for research papers. Armed with these two handouts, we embarked on our exploration of the novel.

INTRODUCING THE NOVEL

Who is Oscar Wao? What made his life both "brief" and "wondrous"? And what inspired Díaz to write this novel? To begin our exploration of *Oscar Wao*, we considered the title, first focusing on the name "Oscar Wao," which, I point out, alludes to the flamboyant writer and critic Oscar Wilde.

We then focus on the first epigraph from the Marvel comic series *Fantastic Four*: "Of what import are brief, nameless lives . . . to Galactus?" (Díaz, 2007a). We note that Galactus is a cosmic villain who threatens the Marvel Comics universe defended by the Fantastic Four and that Oscar Wao may have been one of his nameless victims. We also note that by naming Oscar in the title of his novel, Díaz gives his life "import" and restores his humanity.

We note that the second epigraph is an excerpt from "The Schooner *Flight*," a narrative poem by West Indian Nobel laureate Derek Walcott (1930–2017). The poem tells the story of Shabine, a disillusioned sailor from St. Lucia who embarks on a perilous voyage to ports unknown in a desperate search for freedom and identity. Cut off from family and community, he soon realizes, "I had no nation now but the imagination" (Walcott, 2014, p. 251). After witnessing a series of horrific visions—including a vision of his enslaved ancestors drowning during the Middle Passage—Shabine meets a similar fate, achieving freedom only in death.

Reflecting on both epigraphs, we realize that in order to connect with the novel, we must explore the links between the culture of comics, represented by Galactus and the Fantastic Four, and the culture of the Caribbean, represented by Oscar Wao, whose family hails from the Dominican Republic.

But what is this novel about? To address this question, we turn to the author:

> It's about the Dominican version of the cursed House of Atreus [and] . . . this young nerd, Oscar, who risks his whole life on the chance of finding love. It's

also about New Jersey and about Rutgers and about a crazy dictator and about cheating-dog men. . . . And it's about the foundational women in Oscar's life: his mother and his sister. (Díaz, 2013a, para. 13)

This leads us to the central question that drives the narrative: Is Oscar's life—and, by extension, the lives of his family members—controlled by an ancient Dominican curse (Fukú) or guided by a divine blessing (Zafa)? Or is it, as Díaz seems to suggest, merely a matter of personal choice and circumstance?

To illuminate key themes and motifs, we read several short works by Latinx authors: Rhina Espaillat's "Bilingual/Bilingue" (to illustrate the challenges faced by bilingual writers and to introduce the concept of code-switching); Sandra Cisneros's "My Name" (to introduce the power of names and naming of both groups and individuals); and Jimmy Santiago Baca's "Immigrants in Our Own Land" (to demonstrate what Díaz describes as "the American Doom" that haunts countless "Third World" immigrants pursuing the American Dream). Finally, to underscore the impact of two works Díaz describes as his "cultural touchstones"—J. R. R. Tolkien's *Lord of the Rings* trilogy and Alan Moore's graphic novel *Watchmen*—I bring in both for "show and tell."

NARRATIVE STRUCTURE

My course introduction always includes an overview of the elements of fiction and a discussion on narrative structure. I also point out that most modern and postmodern texts defy our attempts to classify and categorize. To establish a broader context for the novel, I note that *Oscar Wao* is a postcolonial text that explores the impact of colonialism on subjugated peoples and offers an alternative perspective to the White, Western value system. To highlight the far-reaching impact of colonialism, I share the opening line from the seminal text on postcolonial literatures, *The Empire Writes Back*: "More than three-quarters of the people living in the world today have had their lives shaped by the experience of colonialism" (Ashcroft et al., 2002, p. 1).

Given this background, students are prepared to "unlock" the text and explore some of its complex themes and motifs by focusing on each component of the LIST Paradigm: Language, Identity, Space, and Time.

LANGUAGE: *"HOW DOES THE AUTHOR CONTEXTUALIZE LINGUISTIC SIGNS AND SYMBOLS?"*

To explore the concept of Language in *Oscar Wao*, we discuss Díaz's use of rhetorical devices such as the following:

Code-Switching

Díaz's use of code-switching (from Standard English, to Black vernacular, to Spanish, to Elfin, to Dominican vernacular) is one of the most distinctive aspects of his writing style. Through his liberal use of Spanish words and phrases, as well as frequent references to his implied reader as "Nigger," he reverses the trend of mainstream writers who assume a White reading audience. He also rejects conventional White standards of female beauty by challenging the concept of colorism in the Black community. In describing Belicia's birth, the narrator observes that she "was born black. And not just any kind of black. But *black* black . . . and no amount of fancy Dominican racial legerdemain was going to obscure the fact" (Díaz, 2007a, p. 248). Having established this irrefutable fact, he not only portrays Belicia as a stunningly beautiful woman; he also presents us with a diverse cast of Black female characters ranging from "golden mulatas" to "morenos."

The Language of Violence

Díaz's graphic depictions of violence can sometimes seem excessive. But as he points out:

> Allowing the Spanish to exist in my text without the benefit of italics or quo-
> tation marks was a very important political move. Spanish is not a minority
> language . . . So why treat it like one? . . . About the violence. When I learned
> English in the States, this was a violent enterprise. And by forcing Spanish back
> onto English, forcing it to deal with the language it tried to exterminate in me,
> I've tried to represent a mirror-image of that violence on the page. Call it my
> revenge on English. (Céspedes & Torres-Saillant, 2000, p. 892)

Proverbs and Folk Sayings

As noted in Chapter 5, proverbs and folk sayings often serve as important keys to culture. Díaz shares some unique proverbs (in Spanish) that highlight the beliefs and values of Dominican culture, leaving it up to his readers to translate and interpret them. Examples include "One nail drives out another" (Díaz, 2007a, p. 124); "No matter how far a mule travels it can never come back as a horse" (p. 163); and "Ripe bananas are not green" (p. 208).

Extensive Footnotes

Díaz's extensive footnotes comment on the text and comprise an integral component of the narrative. The footnotes also enable the narrator to inter-rupt the narrative and address readers directly. For example, when Yunior first introduces us to "Our then dictator for life Rafael Leónidas Trujillo Molina," a footnote explains:

> For those of you who missed your mandatory two seconds of Dominican history: Trujillo, one of the twentieth century's most infamous dictators, ruled the Dominican Republic between 1930 and 1961 with an implacable ruthless brutality. (Díaz, 2007a, p. 2)

We soon realize that the footnotes not only enable Yunior to comment on the narrative, thereby contributing to the "conversation" between reader and narrator; they also allow Díaz to provide historical context for his novel by highlighting the fact that dominant cultures often attempt to erase the histories of oppressed peoples by reducing them to footnotes in global history.

The Language of Humor

Díaz often uses humor to deflect the horror of the novel's most violent scenes. For example, when Yunior describes the two thugs who savagely beat Belicia, he depicts them as "two Elvises with matching pompadours" (Díaz, 2007a, p. 140). Later, when two of the "the captain's" henchmen abduct Oscar and drive him to the cane fields where he endures a brutal beating, Yunior wryly observes, "In situations like these he had always assumed his secret hero would emerge and snap necks, à la Jim Kelly, but clearly his secret hero was out having some pie" (p. 297).

Literary Allusions

Díaz uses literary allusions in fresh and surprising ways. For example, to illustrate Belicia's stubborn insistence on pursuing men who ultimately abuse her, Yunior compares her relentless pursuit of "the albino boy" Jack Pujols to Ahab's pursuit of the great white whale in Melville's *Moby-Dick*: "Wonder ye then at the fiery hunt?" (Díaz, 2007a, p. 95). Similarly, the narrator's frequent references to Belicia (Beli) as "the third and final daughter" resonate on a deeper level when we recognize the allusions to the four Mirabal sisters—Patria, Minerva, Dede, and María Teresa—whose legendary defiance of Trujillo led to the deaths of three of the sisters and their husbands, and whose lives are reimagined in Julia Alvarez's 2010 novel *In the Time of the Butterflies*. Dede—the third and final daughter of the Mirabal family—lives to tell the story of her sisters' murders. Similarly, Beli—the "third and final daughter" of Abelard and Socorro Cabral—lives to tell the story of the Cabral-de Leon family.

Another example centers on Oscar's last letter to Lola, which ends with "The beauty! The beauty!" (p. 335), clearly a reversal of Kurtz's final words ("The horror! The horror!") in Joseph Conrad's *Heart of Darkness*. By alluding to Conrad's novel, Díaz not only challenges Kurtz's (and Conrad's) racist depiction of Black "savages"; he shifts the perspective from colonizer to colonized, thereby granting agency and restoring humanity to Conrad's "savages." He also reminds us that, ultimately, despite the horror, beauty prevails.

Once students recognize some of Díaz's unique rhetorical devices, they are better prepared to appreciate the power and beauty of his novel.

IDENTITY: "WHO ARE THESE PEOPLE AND WHAT DO THEY WANT?"

To introduce the concept of Identity in *Oscar Wao*, I begin with a brief introduction to Junot Díaz as a Dominican American writer who is renowned as one of the best fiction writers in the world. As part of the introduction, we watch several video clips (readily available on YouTube) of Díaz discussing *Oscar Wao*. I also introduce students to some of the historical characters Díaz refers to in his novel, including Oscar Wilde, Rafael Trujillo, John F. Kennedy, and the Mirabal sisters.

To introduce key characters, we create a character map that identifies characters and explores the relationships among them. We also focus on the characters' names, which offer profound insights into their identities. And we examine the roles various characters play in advancing the narrative.

Yunior ("The Watcher")

Yunior plays multiple roles in the novel: as primary narrator, as Oscar's fickle friend and college roommate, and as Lola's cheating boyfriend. Although not omniscient, he moves through time and witnesses events from the past, such as Belicia's birth, her disastrous love affair with "the Gangster," and the torture of Dr. Abelard Cabral (Oscar's grandfather). He can also see future events such as Oscar's death and Lola's inconsolable grief, which finally compels her to end her relationship with Yunior. Consequently, although Yunior is powerless to effect history, he provides us with a running commentary on events as they unfold and fills in the *paginas blanca* (blank pages) of the characters' histories.

Oscar (Mister Fantastic)

In Chapter 1, "Ghetto Nerd at the End of the World, 1974–1987" (subtitled "The Golden Age"), Yunior introduces us to Oscar at age 7, a charming, precocious boy who loves to dance. When we meet him again a decade later as a student at Rutgers University, he is an overweight, depressed, suicidal nerd who "talked like a *Star Trek* computer" (Díaz, 2007a, p. 173) and "knew more about the Marvel Universe than Stan Lee" (p. 21). But Oscar's superpower enables him to transform into a slimmed-down, courageous man who—having learned that "Fear is the mind killer" (p. 297)—pursues his dreams of becoming "the Dominican Tolkien" and sacrifices his life for love.

In her essay on the poetry of Derek Walcott, Pulitzer prize–winning poet Rita Dove (2003) observes that "Colonialism imposes on its subjects many indignities, but the most insidious one is a spiritual and cultural schizophrenia" (p. 58). Díaz explores the impact of this "cultural schizophrenia" on Dominican Americans:

> You come to the United States and the United States begins immediately, systematically, to erase you in every way, to suppress those things which it considers not digestible. You spend a lot of time being colonized. Then, if you've got the opportunity and the breathing space and the guidance, you immediately—when you realize it—begin to decolonize yourself. And in that process, you relearn names for yourself that you had forgotten. (Céspedes & Torres-Saillant, 2000, p. 902)

For Oscar, this process of decolonizing the mind occurs during his summer vacation in Santo Domingo when he learns his Dominican name: Huáscar (p. 276). Armed with this knowledge, he begins to take control of his life, regains his human dignity, and assumes responsibility for his actions.

Belicia (The Human Torch)

For Belicia (Beli), the process of "decolonizing" is inextricably linked to her "inextinguishable longing for elsewheres" (Díaz, 2007a, p. 77), which keeps her continually searching for something just out of reach. By returning to Santo Domingo and reclaiming her heritage, she, too, comes to terms with her "cultural schizophrenia."

A hot-tempered "child of the Apocalypse" whose black skin and scarred back mark her as an outsider in her conservative, color-conscious Dominican community, Belicia emerges as the Human Torch, "one of the most popular Marvel superheroes of the 1940s." In short, Belicia—who (to her family's amusement) is often mistaken for Haitian—uses her beauty and sexuality to survive in a violent, hostile world while fighting the evils that threaten to annihilate her. Ultimately, through her renewed respect for and reconciliation with La Inca, Hypatia Belicia Cabral de Leon becomes the matriarch who continues the legacy of the Cabral-de Leon family in the United States.

Lola (Thing)

Determined to conceal her compassion and vulnerability behind a tough-as-nails persona, Lola—much like Thing—uses her superpower to continually reinvent herself. At one point, Yunior notes that "She'd shaved her head down to the bone, Sinéad-style, and now everybody, including their mother, was convinced she'd turned into a lesbiana" (Díaz, 2007a, p. 37). Later, he observes that, in college, "she was a Big Woman on Campus and knew just about everybody with any pigment, had her hand on every protest and every march" (p. 50). And as an adult, he depicts her as "one of those tough Jersey dominicanas, a long-distance runner who drove her own car, had her own checkbook, called men bitches, and would eat a fat cat in front of you without a speck of verguenza" (p. 25). Lola's final transformation occurs when she returns to the United States, takes charge of her life, and reclaims her full name—Dolores de Leon—which enables her to finally break free from Yunior, move to Miami, and embrace a traditional role as wife and mother.

La Inca (The Invisible Woman)

La Inca's superpower enables her to watch over her family from afar. As her name implies, La Inca is a descendant of the Incas, an American Indian people of Peru whose domain once included parts of Ecuador, Peru, Bolivia, Chile, and Argentina. La Inca—who has "a mind like a mongoose" (Díaz, 2007a, p. 157)—is also a "shape shifter." As "the mongoose with the golden eyes," she saves Belicia—and initially Oscar—from death in the cane fields. She also rescues Belicia after "the burning," heals her through the power of prayer, and sends her to the United States on the eve of Trujillo's assassination to escape the wrath of his henchmen. Ultimately, La Inca gives Belicia "the greatest gift": a fierce and unwavering pride in her family heritage. In short, La Inca is the ancestor who nurtures future generations and provides a link between the past and present.

Dr. Abelard Cabral

Dr. Abelard Cabral, Oscar's grandfather, is one of the victims of Trujillo's brutality. Determined to protect his young daughters from the lecherous dictator, Dr. Cabral finds himself falsely accused of treason, imprisoned, and tortured. His fate is especially tragic because he is depicted as a "good citizen" who, although not openly supportive of Trujillo's regime, does his best to adhere to "El Jefe's" demands, all the while refusing to face the horror of his situation. Dr. Cabral has a profound impact on Oscar's life. Like his grandfather, Oscar loves books and aspires to be a writer. He also fails to heed the dangers surrounding him, which leads to his untimely death.

Trujillo (Galactus)

Díaz depicts Trujillo primarily as a menacing force that hovers in the background of the narrative, thus denying him agency as a central character. In fact, Trujillo appears in only two key scenes that demonstrate his monstrous brutality: the imprisonment and torture of Dr. Abelard Cabral, and Belicia's savage beating in the cane fields. To underscore Trujillo's unlimited capacity for evil, Díaz also compares him to Darkseid, the archenemy of the Justice League, and to Sauron, the "Dark Lord" from *Lord of the Rings*, who, thanks to his "Omega Effect," has the power to make people disappear.

SPACE: "HOW DO CHARACTERS NEGOTIATE THE TEXT'S PHYSICAL, PSYCHOLOGICAL, AND CULTURAL LANDSCAPES?"

To explore the concept of Space in *Oscar Wao*, we begin by studying maps of Haiti and the Dominican Republic. Students should know that the Dominican Republic shares its border with Haiti; that both countries together comprise the Caribbean island of Hispaniola; and that the unfortunately named Massacre River forms the border between them. In order to appreciate the extent of Belicia's travels throughout the Dominican Republic, they should also know the locations of some of the places referenced in the novel (Azua, Bani, Santo Domingo, Higuey, and Samaná), as well as some of the specific spaces the narrator describes (Casa Hatuey, La Cuerenta, La Casa Amarillo, El Redentor, and La Inca's bakery).

We note that the island of Hispaniola was a single country until 1697, when the French colonized the western portion of the island (now Haiti), while the Spanish claimed the eastern portion (the Dominican Republic). We also note that during the Dominican Diaspora (1960s–2000), many Dominicans en route to the United States settled in Puerto Rico. And we note the social, economic, and political conflicts that continue to plague both countries as they struggle with the dual legacies of slavery and colonialism.

Physical Space

In his portrayal of "the D.R.," Díaz contrasts the tourists' romanticized vision of the country as an exotic vacation paradise to the Watcher's menacing depiction of the D.R. during the Trujillo regime as "The Land of the Lost" and "The Alcatraz of the Antilles."

Juxtaposed against these two extremes is Oscar's description of modern-day Santo Domingo and "the surreal whirligig that was life in La Capital" (Díaz, 2007a, p. 277):

> The guaguas, the cops, the mind-boggling poverty, the Dunkin' Donuts, the beggars, the Haitians selling roasted peanuts at the intersections, the mind-boggling poverty, the asshole tourists hogging up all the beaches . . . the mind-boggling poverty . . . the skinny watchmen standing in front of stores with their brokedown shotguns, the music, . . . the mind-boggling poverty, . . . the music . . . the

unforgettable beauty of the Cibao, . . . [the] political propaganda plastered up on every spare wall. (277)

In the wake of this sensory assault, which he experiences during a family visit with La Inca, Oscar decides to stay on the island for the rest of the summer. Consequently, he recovers his identity by reconnecting with his culture.

Similarly, to get a better sense of the United States from a Dominican perspective, we note La Inca's vision of the U.S. (symbolized by "Nueva York") as "[A] país overrun by gangsters, putas, and no-accounts. Its cities [swarming] with machines and industry, . . . the glittering promise of coin deep in the cold lightless shaft of its eyes" (p. 158).

We then compare La Inca's vision of New York with Oscar's experiences in Paterson, New Jersey. We also compare Paterson to surrounding cities and neighborhoods referenced in the text such as Camden, Washington Heights, and Wildwood. And since much of Oscar's story centers on his reeducation, Don Bosco, his old New Jersey high school (aka "the Moronic Inferno") (p. 264), and Rutgers University, his alma mater, also emerge as significant spaces.

Psychological Space

To begin our exploration of psychological space, we discuss the characters' dreams and visions, especially those involving the mongoose with the golden eyes and the man without a face. By delving deeper into these two surreal images, we note that they evoke aspects of magical realism, a literary style that, although generally attributed to Latin American writers such as Mario Vargas Llosa and Gabriel García Márquez, is also evident in the works of writers such as Octavia Butler, Franz Kafka, and Toni Morrison.

Cultural Landscapes

To explore the concept of cultural landscapes, we discuss the differences between traditional and contemporary perspectives of Latin American writers, which Díaz describes as Macondo versus McCondo. In the untitled prologue, the narrator contends that "Zafa [the "counterspell" to Fukú] . . . used to be more popular in the old days, bigger, so to speak, in Macondo than in McCondo" (Díaz, 2007a, p. 7). To help students grasp these concepts, we note that Macondo refers to the fictional town in Márquez's novel *One Hundred Years of Solitude*, whereas McCondo refers to the works of more modern, contemporary Latinx authors. We also note Díaz's description of *Oscar Wao* as "an attempt to put Macondo and McOndo on the same page, . . . to prove that you can't write the American experience, our American experience, by banning one set of passports in the process of privileging another" (Díaz, 2013a, para. 11).

TIME: "HOW DOES THE AUTHOR MANIPULATE TIME?"

To begin our exploration of Time, we ponder Oscar Wilde's wry observation that "The one duty we owe to history is to rewrite it." We then read a brief biography of "the crazy dictator," Rafael Trujillo (1891–1961), and discuss the Dominican Diaspora that followed in the wake of his assassination. We also note that *Oscar Wao* responds to and expands on the cultural, political, and psychological landscapes of two earlier works about the Trujillo regime and its aftermath: Julia Alvarez's *In the Time of the Butterflies* (1994) and Edwidge Danticat's *The Farming of Bones* (1998). Having established these connections, we move on to a discussion of Real Time versus Narrative Time.

Real Time

We note that Díaz privileges the Eastern (Afrocentric) perspective of time, since he creates his family history by merging the past, present, and future. We also note that although Yunior narrates much of Oscar's story, Lola and Belicia tell their own stories, while much of Dr. Abelard Cabral's story is told by La Inca, with "The Watcher" filling in "la pagina blanca" (Díaz, 2007a, p. 90).

Oscar's story begins in 1974 in Paterson, New Jersey (with Oscar at age 7) and ends in 1995 with his death in the cane fields of the Dominican Republic. Between these two significant events, which frame the narrative, we learn the stories of Dr. Cabral, La Inca, Belicia, and Lola. Thus, although Oscar's story encompasses roughly 28 years (1967–1995), the novel spans centuries and encompasses four generations, including the lives of La Inca and Oscar's grandparents, Abelard and Socorro Cabral; Oscar's parents and aunts, Jackie and Astrid; and Oscar's future niece, Isis. But since Díaz does not provide us with either the birth or death dates of his characters, we are compelled to view their individual lives as a series of interconnected stories that comprise episodes in the continuing saga of the Cabral-de Leon family.

Within this broad swath of time, Díaz highlights key events in Dominican history, such as the arrival of "the Admiral" (Christopher Columbus) in 1492; the country's colonization by Spain; its occupation by Haiti; its reign of terror under the Trujillo regime (1930–1961); and its current status as an impoverished "Third World" country largely ignored by Western society. He also documents (via footnotes) the lives of several individuals who died for daring to oppose the Trujillo regime. To emphasize that Trujillo's death did not, in fact, mark the end of suffering for Dominicans, Díaz includes a footnote referencing "that other Caribbean nightmare, the Haitian dictator Francois 'Papa Doc' Duvalier" (p. 111).

As noted in Chapter 9, Díaz seems especially haunted by the Haitian genocide (October 2–8, 1937), often referred to as "the Parsley Massacre," when an estimated 20,000 Haitians were killed by Trujillo's soldiers because they could not pronounce *perejil*, the Spanish word for parsley, a shibboleth that identified them as Haitian immigrants rather than native Dominicans. To provide students with a literary and historical context for the Parsley Massacre, we discuss the Old Testament story of the Gileadites and Ephraimites (Judges 12: 4–6), whose lives depended on their ability to pronounce the word "shibboleth." We also read Rita Dove's poem "Parsley," which centers on the devastating power of "a single, beautiful word" (Dove, 1993, p. 135).

To illustrate the power of "a single, beautiful word" and help students internalize the concept of language as an identity marker, I conducted a brief role-play exercise. I asked my native Spanish speaker to give us the correct pronunciation of *perejil*. At our next class meeting, I brought in a sprig of parsley and handed it to my native speaker. I then had him ask each student, "What is this?" and, based on their responses, identify them as either Haitians or Dominicans. (Given my cadets' powerful emotional responses to this exercise, I consider it one of my most successful teaching moments.)

To highlight the power of documents to preserve history, we note that the destruction (and preservation) of historical documents (books, manuscripts, letters, photographs, etc.) plays an important role in *Oscar Wao*, underscoring some of the novel's key themes. For example, while Trujillo's henchmen try to "erase" all traces of Dr. Abelard Cabral by destroying his books and documents, Yunior honors Oscar's memory by preserving his comic books and manuscripts in four refrigerators in his basement. We also note the novel's final irony: In the end, both Oscar's book on fúku and his grandfather's book on Trujillo are lost. Consequently, the task of filling in "la pagina blanca" rests on future generations.

Narrative Time

To explore the power of narrative time in *Oscar Wao*, we begin with Díaz's memory of immigrating to the United States at age 6, an experience he recalls as a kind of surreal time travel.

To prepare students for the story of the cursed Casa Hatuey and the fall of Dr. Abelard Cabral, we consider these events in light of "the cursed House of Atreus" and the fall of Agamemnon and Menelaus.

To provide a broader literary and historical context for *Oscar Wao* and its treatment of cyclical history, we note that Díaz's novel echoes the sentiments of activist and author Gerald Vizenor, who coined the term "survivance"—a compilation of survival and resistance—to describe their power to endure and prevail despite the violence of the White dominant culture. I also point out two contemporary works that illustrate the concept of survivance: Toni Morrison's *Song of Solomon,* a narrative of ascent that begins and ends in flight, and Alan Moore's graphic novel *Watchmen*, which ends with a call for "a stronger loving world" (Moore, 1987).

In summarizing *Oscar Wao*, we discuss how Díaz intertwines the various strands of the narrative to trace the legacy of the Cabral-de Leon family through four generations. We also note that, through his characters, he provides a voice for the thousands of Dominican Americans who could not speak for themselves. As Díaz (2012b) explains:

> The biggest megaphones want to talk about the person on top. They want to talk about the hero, the winner. But . . . there are all these other little megaphones that are telling you and whispering that "This is beauty, this is humanity, this is America." (p. 1)

CODA

One of the most gratifying aspects of teaching this novel was the overwhelmingly positive feedback I received from my students on their reading experience. In fact, even students who generally don't read or who merely skim texts to glean enough information to discuss the plot and characters became actively engaged in reading *Oscar Wao*.

One student raves, "*The Brief Wondrous Life of Oscar Wao* was by far the best book we read [in this class]." Another notes, "Junot Díaz has a completely unique style. At times I was shocked [by] his use of language . . . , but this is what made the book memorable and fun to read." And my favorite (from one of my least engaged students):

> I enjoyed this book and I wish we could have read it earlier in the semester. I like the way the narrator tells the story. It's the way you would tell your buddy a story when you go home for Christmas and you are both just catching up. . . . I don't know much about comics and superheroes, so a lot of the allusions were lost on me, but I still enjoyed reading this book. (Washington, class notes, n/d)

I believe that for many of my students, one of the novel's major attractions was Díaz's exploration of comics, graphic novels, and video games, topics they were surprised to encounter in a literature course. The issue of identity politics as perceived through racism and colorism, the use of language as an identity marker, and cultural perceptions of history also generated animated discussions, provocative questions, and insightful essays.

For me, one of the most memorable moments of the semester was a conversation with my cadet from Rwanda regarding his response to the Parsley Massacre. Being two generations removed from the Rwandan genocide (April 7 to July 15, 1994), during which an estimated 800,000 Tutsis were slaughtered by Hutu extremists, he resolved to research this aspect of his history and to interview his relatives about the genocide upon his return to Rwanda.

In short, adding *Oscar Wao* to my syllabus at the Air Force Academy proved to be one of my most rewarding teaching experiences, since it enabled me to offer my students a fresh perspective on multicultural literature. It also reminded me of an old adage about effective teaching—that before you can hope to teach students anything, you have to get their attention.

Oscar Wao definitely got my students' attention, primarily because they were surprised to discover that "literature" could explore issues such as war, torture, and immigration alongside topics such as comics, fantasy, and video games within a single text. In other words, reading *Oscar Wao* compelled them to reconsider their preconceived notions of literature.

The novel also resonated with cadets attuned to reading war literature. Several commented on the narrator's observation that "Santo Domingo was Iraq before Iraq was Iraq" (Díaz, 2007a, p. 4).

In summary, I would highly recommend *Oscar Wao* to any instructor seeking to expand their curriculum and willing to accept the challenges the text presents.

Exploring the LIST Paradigm
A Reader's Guide

> The purpose of all art is to lay bare the questions which have been hidden by the answers.
>
> —James Baldwin

The LIST Paradigm provides a culturally responsive approach to reading (or teaching) literature that prompts readers to *access* and *analyze* a text by *asking significant questions* designed to foster close reading and critical thinking. By combining aspects of *literary analysis* (exploring the elements of fiction, such as plot, setting, and character) and *literary criticism* (exploring works from multiple perspectives, such as historical, psychological, and archetypal), the LIST Paradigm helps readers unlock the power of literature with four *keys to culture*: Language, Identity, Space, and Time.

LANGUAGE: "HOW DOES THE AUTHOR CONTEXTUALIZE LINGUISTIC SIGNS AND SYMBOLS?"

- What is the author's native language? If this text is a work in translation, what cultural elements or rhetorical devices might have been lost or misconstrued?
- How does the author's use of language (the language of music, violence, protest, etc.) establish the narrative's *Weltanschauung* (worldview)? What beliefs and values define it?
- What does language (slang, dialect, vernacular, etc.) reveal about a character's race, culture, and ethnicity?
- Does the author employ literary or historical allusions? Cultural metaphors? Code-switching? Color or number symbolism? Parody? Irony? To what end?

IDENTITY: "WHO ARE THESE PEOPLE AND WHAT DO THEY WANT?"

- Is the work autobiographical? If so, how do characters reflect the author's experience?
- What rhetorical devices does the author use to reveal a character's race or ethnicity?
- How would you describe the relationships among author, narrator(s), and readers?
- Does the author appear to embrace or reject the role of "native informer"?
- What do the names of characters reveal about their identity? Are they called by different names?
- How do characters see themselves (as heroes, victims, villains, outsiders)?
- How does the narrator reveal potential conflicts between a character's self-image and public image?

SPACE: "HOW DO CHARACTERS NEGOTIATE THE TEXT'S PHYSICAL, PSYCHOLOGICAL, AND CULTURAL LANDSCAPES?"

- What is the physical setting for the text? The psychological setting?
- Do characters enjoy the freedom to explore their space, or are they confined or trapped in some way? If so, what defines their entrapment? How do they cope with it?
- Are characters marginalized, or are they part of the mainstream of the fictional community?
- How does the work's narrative structure impact plot development?

TIME: "HOW DOES THE AUTHOR MANIPULATE TIME?"

- What rhetorical devices does the author employ to establish a sense of time: Flashback? Foreshadowing? References or allusions to historical issues, events, or characters? References to songs, movies, or books that reflect a designated era?
- What is the author's perspective of history? Does he focus primarily on a *linear* (Western/Eurocentric) or a *cyclical* (Eastern/Afrocentric) approach to history?
- Does the author expand or compress time? If so, what methods or techniques does the author use? How do these techniques shape the text's narrative structure?
- How does the author's manipulation of *real time* and *narrative time* impact the portrayal of significant events?

LIST Paradigm Worksheet

Directions: Please use this Worksheet in conjunction with Handout 1 *("Exploring the LIST Paradigm: A Reader's Guide")* to conduct a close, critical reading of your text. Citing key words and passages from the text (including page numbers) for each LIST component will help you focus on distinctive elements of style and narrative structure.

Title: _____

Author/Date Published: _____

Synopsis: _____

_____

_____

Questions/Comments/Observations: _____

_____

_____

_____

Language: "How does the author contextualize linguistics signs and symbols?

_____

_____

_____

_____

Identity: "Who are these people and what do they want?"

_____

_____

_____

_____

Space: "How do characters negotiate the text's physical, psychological, and cultural landscapes?"

_____

_____

_____

_____

Time: "How does the author manipulate time?"

_____

_____

_____

_____

Defining Elements of Morrison's Fiction

In reflecting on her works, Toni Morrison asserts,

> I think long and carefully about what my novels ought to do. They should clarify the roles that have become obscured; they ought to identify those things in the past that are useful and those things that are not; and they ought to give nourishment. (LeClair, 1994, p. 121)

To that end, we can cite elements such as the following to help us define Morrison's fiction:

A FOCUS ON FOLKLORE AND ORAL TRADITION

As evidenced by her 1993 Nobel lecture, Morrison draws heavily on story-telling as the basis of narrative, which she perceives as "one of the principal ways in which we absorb knowledge."

A FOCUS ON BLACK CULTURE AND THE AFRICAN AMERICAN COMMUNITY

Morrison has stated that her work is for and about African Americans:

> I'm interested in how men are educated, how women relate to each other, how we are able to love, how we balance political and personal forces, who survives in certain situations and who doesn't and, specifically, how these and other universal issues relate to African Americans. . . . The search for love and identity runs through most everything I write. (Micucci, 1994, p. 278)

She believes that the universal resides in the personal. Therefore, she defines her literature as "universal" only in the sense that it appeals to universal truths such as love, life, and death.

A REJECTION OF BINARY THINKING

Morrison believes that the human tendency to view the world in terms of opposites (good/evil, black/white, right/wrong) limits our ability to see things clearly and understand shades of meaning. She emphasizes *complex thinking*, which emphasizes wholeness and unity, over binary thinking, which focuses on fragmentation and duality.

A BELIEF IN THE POLITICAL NATURE OF ART

Morrison contends that "the best art is political and you ought to make it unquestionably political and irrevocably beautiful at the same time." Although her novels incorporate both fantasy and reality, she rejects the concept of "magical realism," which she believes "dilutes the politics" (Morrison, 1984, pp. 339–345).

A REVERENCE FOR BLACK HISTORY, TRADITION, AND CULTURE (E.G., A RESPECT FOR "THE ANCESTORS")

Morrison draws on numerous elements of Black culture: African griots and oral tradition; voodoo and magic; the bad man hero/trickster; Negro sermons and spirituals; slave narratives; blues and jazz rhythms; Black vernacular; and the uniquely Black form of wordplay known as "signifying." These elements play a vital role in the development of the narrative.

A BELIEF IN PERSONAL CHOICE AND MORAL RESPONSIBILITY

Morrison believes that, regardless of external circumstances, people have the power to create their own reality. And although she implies that most of the problems faced by her characters can be traced to systemic racism and the legacy of slavery, she also emphasizes that each has a personal responsibility to make valid choices. Like Zora Neale Hurston and Ernest Gaines, Morrison rejects the victim mentality, which holds that African Americans are "tragically Black." Thus, she defines freedom not as the absence of responsibility, but as an opportunity to choose one's responsibilities.

A BELIEF IN "PARTICIPATORY READING"

In her Nobel lecture, Morrisons states that "Narrative is radical, creating us at the very moment it is being created." Consequently, she wants her readers to take an active role in the reading process by "fill[ing] in the spaces" in the narrative, based on their own knowledge and experience. In keeping with this belief, the endings to her novels are often ambiguous and open for interpretation (Morrison, 1994b, p. 27).

A TRAGICOMIC VISION OF LIFE

In Morrison's novels, characters often cope with painful experiences through humor. This tragicomic approach to life reflects the attitude of "the blues," which Ralph Ellison (1994) defined as "an impulse to keep the painful details and episodes of a brutal experience alive in one's aching consciousness, to finger its jagged grain, and to transcend it, not by the consolation of philosophy, but by squeezing from it a near-tragic, near-comic lyricism" (pp. 78–79).

A BELIEF IN UNLOCKING THE POWER OF LANGUAGE

Morrison believes that language shapes and transforms reality. Therefore, she often uses Black vernacular to describe "the Black experience" and relies heavily on the use of metaphor. In her Nobel lecture, she spoke of the lasting power of language: "We die. That may be the *meaning* of life. But we do language. That may be the *measure* of our lives" (Morrison, 1994b, p. 22).

Notes on Narrative Structure

Much frustration and confusion regarding the reading of non-Western and postmodern literature arises from the reader's lack of knowledge concerning *narrative structure*: the shape of a narrative created by the order and development of key scenes. (Narrative structure also relates to the physical components of a text, such as sections and chapters.)

Introducing students to narrative structure near the beginning of a literature course enables them to approach texts from a broader perspective and to identify some of the similarities and differences between Western and non-Western texts. For example, students familiar with the structure of the slave narrative, which begins with flight (escape) and traces the narrator's quest for freedom and literacy from "down South" to "up North," will be better prepared to approach African American literature.

As discussed in Chapter 4, identifying a work's narrative structure begins with identifying the narrator (or narrators) and their role(s).

According to the traditional view, a successful story meets three criteria:

- It centers on conflict (external or internal).
- It progresses from rising action to climax to resolution.
- A main character undergoes a change or transformation.

This *linear, chronological structure* ("the narrative arc") is illustrated by the *Freytag Pyramid*, which holds that narrative events unfold sequentially and the story has a clear beginning, middle, and end. (The narrative moves through five stages: inciting action, rising action, climax, resolution, and denouement.) Novels that follow this narrative structure include Western classics and Victorian novels such as the following:

- *David Copperfield* (Charles Dickens)
- *The Adventures of Huckleberry Finn* (Mark Twain)
- *The Great Gatsby* (F. Scott Fitzgerald)

Modern and postmodern literature employs a variety of narrative structures such as the following.

THE QUEST NARRATIVE

A narrative structure inspired by the psychology of Carl Jung and the mythological studies of Joseph Campbell in his landmark text *The Hero with a Thousand Faces*. The narrative traces the hero's journey, which consists of 12 stages. It begins with the hero's Call to Adventure (which he initially refuses) and traces his journey through a series of challenges (such as battles with monsters and a trip to the Underworld.). It ends with the hero's redemption/transformation and his return to the Ordinary World with the Elixir (a boon or treasure to benefit others). Examples of the Quest Narrative include:

- *The Odyssey* (Homer)
- *Ulysses* (James Joyce)
- *Star Wars* (George Lucas)

THE COMING-OF-AGE NARRATIVE (*"BILDUNGSROMAN"*)

The narrative moves from innocence to experience, such as Charles Dickens's *David Copperfield* and James Joyce's *Portrait of the Artist as a Young Man*. For writers of color, the coming-of-age narrative often takes the form of memoir or autobiography. Examples include:

- *Black Boy/American Hunger* (Richard Wright)
- *The Autobiography of Malcolm X* (Malcolm X, with Alex Haley)
- *Hunger of Memory* (Richard Rodriguez)
- *The Woman Warrior* (Maxine Hong Kingston)
- *Paper Bullets* (Kip Fulbeck)

THE FRAMED NARRATIVE

A story (or series of stories) are told within the "frame" of a larger story. The quintessential framed narrative is *The Arabian Nights* (best known as *1,001 Arabian Nights*), based on the text of a 14th-century Syrian manuscript that includes stories drawn from various ethnic origins including Indian, Persian, and Arabic. A contemporary response to *1,001 Arabian Nights* is Salman Rushdie's *Midnight's Children*, in which 1,001 children, each endowed with special powers, are born on the eve of India's liberation ("The Partition"). Here are some other examples:

- *Heart of Darkness* (Joseph Conrad)
- *Invisible Man* (Ralph Ellison)
- *Their Eyes Were Watching God* (Zora Neale Hurston)
- *The Sympathizer* (Viet Thanh Nguyen)

IN MEDIAS RES

The narrative begins "in the middle of things," with no explanation of events leading up to the present moment.

- *The Metamorphosis* (Franz Kafka)
- *Song of Solomon* (Toni Morrison)
- *A Lesson Before Dying* (Ernest Gaines)

THE CIRCLE/SPIRAL

After recounting numerous events, the narrative ends where it began.

- *Ceremony* (Leslie Marmon Silko)
- *House Made of Dawn* (N. Scott Momaday)
- *Indian Killer* (Sherman Alexie)

THE COLLAGE/MOSAIC

The narrative consists of seemingly unrelated/disconnected fragments (bits and pieces of stories, anecdotes, events, etc.). To obtain a coherent picture of the whole, readers must assemble the fragments and "fill in" spaces in the narrative.

- *Beloved* (Toni Morrison)
- *The Brief Wondrous Life of Oscar Wao* (Junot Díaz)
- *The Things They Carried* (Tim O'Brien)

MULTIVOCALITY

The narrative employs multiple narrators, each of whom describes a key incident from their particular perspective.

- *As I Lay Dying* (William Faulkner)
- *The Brief Wondrous Life of Oscar Wao* (Junot Díaz)
- *Paradise* (Toni Morrison)

STREAM-OF-CONSCIOUSNESS

The narrative consists of a continuous flow of sense perceptions, thoughts, feelings, and memories, presented in a disjointed form of *interior monologue*.

- *Ulysses* (James Joyce)
- *Mrs. Dalloway* (Virginia Woolf)
- *Remembrance of Things Past* (Marcel Proust)

MAGICAL REALISM

The narrative blends realism with surreal events and miraculous scenes.

- *One Hundred Years of Solitude* (Gabriel Garcia Márquez)
- *Jazz* (Toni Morrison)
- *The Satanic Verses* (Salman Rushdie)

EPISTOLARY NARRATIVE

The narrative consists of a series of letters from the narrator to various characters. Popular during the Victorian period, this structure is rarely used in modern literature. Three notable exceptions are Alice Walker's *The Color Purple*, Aravind Adiga's *The White Tiger*, and Ocean Vuong's *On Earth We're Briefly Gorgeous*, written in the form of a letter from the narrator to his illiterate mother, who will never be able to read it.

SHORT-STORY CYCLE

A series of connected stories, often featuring the same characters.

- *Cane* (Jean Toomer)
- *Bloodline* (Ernest Gaines)
- *The House on Mango Street* (Sandra Cisneros)
- *The Lone Ranger and Tonto Fistfight in Heaven* (Sherman Alexie)

Some authors may combine two or more narrative structures to create a unique approach (a framed narrative may employ multiple narrators, or a collage/mosaic may lapse into stream-of-consciousness). "Experimental" novels may dispense with structure altogether, opting instead to explore alternate ways of storytelling that create innovative forms.

AFRICAN AMERICAN NARRATIVES

Rooted in the slave narratives, African American literature includes a broad range of forms and genres, such as the sonnets of Claude McKay and Countee Cullen, the Afrofuturistic fiction of Samuel Delany and Octavia Butler, and the experimental works of Jean Toomer and Henry Dumas. The following narratives are unique to African American culture.

The Slave Narrative: An autobiographical text that documents the narrator's quest for *freedom* and *literacy.* These texts generally involve a physical movement from "down South" to "up North." Examples include Frederick Douglass's *Narrative,* Harriet Jacobs's *Incidents in the Life of a Slave Girl,* and Booker T. Washington's *Up from Slavery.*

The Black Folktale: Although made popular by White folklorist Joel Chandler Harris and his Uncle Remus stories, Black folktales originated in rural communities of the Black South. Contemporary folktale collections include Virginia Hamilton's *The People Could Fly* and Julius Lester's *Black Folktales.*

The Trickster Tale: Trickster tales often involve animals such as B'rer Rabbit, who consistently outwits B'rer Fox. According to folklorist Julius Lester (1987), through the trickster, we "add disorder to order and so make a whole to render possible, within the fixed bounds of what is permitted, an experience of what is not permitted" (para. 3). Some African American trickster tales are noted for their obscenity and include some incarnation of the "Signifying Monkey," who appears as Shine, Stagolee, or High John the Conqueror. (A classic example is "Shine and the Titanic.")

The Fictional Slave Narrative ("Narrative of Ascent"): Incorporates elements of the slave narrative into fiction. Examples include Frederick Douglass's "The Heroic Slave," Toni Morrison's *Song of Solomon,* Ernest Gaines's *The Autobiography of Miss Jane Pittman,* and Colson Whitehead's *The Underground Railroad.* A notable text in this tradition is Ishmael Reed's *Flight to Canada,* which parodies the traditional slave narrative.

The Neoslave Narrative: Memoirs and autobiographies that exploit the "up from slavery" motif of the slave narrative. Examples include Richard Wright's *Black Boy/American Hunger,* Maya Angelou's *I Know Why the Caged Bird Sings,* and *The Autobiography of Malcolm X.*

The Jim Crow Narrative: This narrative emerged in response to the Jim Crow "separate but equal" laws that enforced segregation and discrimination throughout the United States in the wake of the Supreme Court's ruling in

Plessy v. Ferguson (1896) and remained in effect until 1965. Examples include Langston Hughes's "My Most Humiliating Jim Crow Experience," Richard Wright's "The Ethics of Living Jim Crow," and Sarah Delany's *Having Our Say: The Delany Sisters' First 100 Years*.

The Passing Narrative: A text (fiction or nonfiction) that documents the Black protagonist's struggle to "pass" as White and explores the concept of "masking" as a means of survival. It centers on the stereotype of the "tragic mulatto," featured in films such as *Pinky* and *Imitation of Life*. Examples include Charles W. Chesnutt's "The Wife of His Youth," Langston Hughes's "Passing," and Nella Larsen's *Passing*. It includes James Weldon Johnson's *The Autobiography of an Ex-Colored Man*, which served as the inspiration for Philip Roth's *The Human Stain*.

The Protest Novel: Generally categorized as "social criticism," this narrative protests the racism and violence experienced by Blacks in White America. Examples include Richard Wright's *Native Son* and Ann Petry's *The Street*.

The Blues Narrative: These works seek to emulate the art of music ("the blues") through the art of language. Blues narratives generally incorporate rhetorical devices such as repetition, call-and-response, and improvisation. Examples include Langston Hughes's "The Weary Blues," James Baldwin's "Sonny's Blues," Ralph Ellison's *Invisible Man*, and August Wilson's play *Seven Guitars*.

The Womanist Narrative: These narratives address sexism as well as racism and colorism (color prejudice among Blacks that privileges light-skinned individuals). Examples include Zora Neale Hurston's *Their Eyes Were Watching God* and Alice Walker's *The Color Purple*.

Suggestions for Pairing Texts

Pairing texts—engaging in a comparative reading of two texts that address similar themes or present conflicting worldviews—can be a valuable strategy for exploring the intertextuality of literature. The following list provides suggestions for pairing texts that explore a diverse range of themes and genres.

Theme/Genre	Texts
Historical Fiction/Mythology	*Song of Solomon* (Toni Morrison) *The Brief Wondrous Life of Oscar Wao* (Junot Díaz)
Magical Realism	*One Hundred Years of Solitude* (Gabriel Garcia Marquez) *Midnight's Children* (Salman Rushdie)
Social Realism	*Native Son* (Richard Wright) *The Street* (Ann Petry)
Autobiography	*Black Boy/American Hunger* (Richard Wright) *The Autobiography of Malcolm X* (Malcolm X)
Transformation	*The Metamorphosis* (Franz Kafka) *A Lesson Before Dying* (Ernest Gaines)
Blues Narrative	"Sonny's Blues" (James Baldwin) *Ma Rainey's Black Bottom* (August Wilson)

Theme/Genre	Texts
Identity/Democracy	"Song of Myself" (Walt Whitman) "Yo Soy Joaquin/"I Am Joaquin" (Rodolfo Gonzales)
Passing	*The Autobiography of an Ex-Colored Man* (James Weldon Johnson) *The Human Stain* (Philip Roth)
Community	*Elbow Room* (James Alan McPherson) *Bloodline* (Ernest Gaines)
Racism/Crime/Criminal Justice	*Native Son* (Richard Wright) *A Lesson Before Dying* (Ernest Gaines)
Independence/Identity	*Maud Martha* (Gwendolyn Brooks) *The House on Mango Street* (Sandra Cisneros)
The American Dream	*A Raisin in the Sun* (Lorraine Hansberry) *The Piano Lesson* (August Wilson)
Caribbean Literature	*The Brief Wondrous Life of Oscar Wao* (Junot Díaz) *The Farming of Bones* (Edwidge Danticat)
Slave Narratives	*Narrative* (Frederick Douglass) *Incidents in the Life of a Slave Girl* (Harriet Jacobs)
Legacy of Slavery	*Beloved* (Toni Morrison) *Kindred* (Octavia Butler)

Theme/Genre	Texts
Mob Violence/Lynching	"Between the World and Me" (Richard Wright) "Going to Meet the Man" (James Baldwin)
Vietnam War	*The Things They Carried* (Tim O'Brien) *The Sympathizer* (Viet Thanh Nguyen)
Fathers & Sons	"Those Winter Sundays" (Robert Hayden) "My Father Is a Simple Man" (Luis Omar Salinas)
Mothers & Daughters	"Everyday Use" (Alice Walker) "Seventeen Syllables" (Hisaye Yamamoto)
Immigrant Narratives	*The Namesake* (Jhumpa Lahiri) *Americanah* (Chimamanda Ngozi Adichie)
Colonialism	*Heart of Darkness* (Joseph Conrad) *Things Fall Apart* (Chinua Achebe)
Womanist Fiction	*Their Eyes Were Watching God* (Zora Neale Hurston) *The Color Purple* (Alice Walker)
The Nisei Experience (Male)	*No-No Boy* (John Okada) *All I Asking for Is My Body* (Milton Murayama)
The Nisei Experience (Female)	*Obasan* (Joy Kogawa) *Nisei Daughter* (Monica Soné)

Theme/Genre	Texts
Native American Ritual	*Ceremony* (Leslie Marmon Silko) *House Made of Dawn* (N. Scott Momaday)
Native American Contemporary	*The Lone Ranger and Tonto Fistfight in Heaven* (Sherman Alexie) *There There* (Tommy Orange)
Afrofuturism	"The Space Traders" (Derrick Bell) *Parable of the Sower* (Octavia Butler)
Othering/Alienation	*The Other Americans* (Laila Lalami) *Pachinko* (Min Jin Lee)
Sudden Death	"Bullet in the Brain" (Tobias Wolff) "Without Inspection" (Edwidge Danticat)
Sexual Abuse/Domestic Violence	*The Bluest Eye* (Toni Morrison) *The Color Purple* (Alice Walker)

References

Abbott, H. P. (2015). *The Cambridge introduction to narrative* (2nd ed.). Cambridge University Press.

Achebe, C. (1996). *Things fall apart*. Heinemann Educational Publishers.

Adichie, C. N. (2014). *Americanah*. Anchor Books.

Adichie, C. N. (2018). The danger of the single story. In S. S. Oliver (Ed.), *Black ink: Literary legends on the peril, power, and pleasure of reading and writing* (pp. 215–223). Simon and Schuster.

Adjei-Brenyah, N. K. (2018). The Finkelstein 5. In *Friday black* (pp. 1–26). Houghton Mifflin.

Alexie, S. (1993a). This is what it means to say Phoenix, Arizona. In *The lone ranger and tonto fistfight in heaven* (pp. 59–75). HarperPerennial.

Alexie, S. (1993b). *Smoke signals*. Hyperion.

Alexie, S. (2009). American literature: Interview with Sherman.

Alvarez, J. (1994). *In the time of the butterflies*. Algonquin Books.

Anaya, R. (1999). Introduction. In *Bless me, ultima*. Grand Central Publishing.

Ards, A. (2005). In the twinkling of an eye. *Black Issues Book Review*, July/Aug., 21–23.

Arnold, M. (2001). *Culture and anarchy*. Blackmask Online. http://public-library.uk/ebooks/25/79.pdf

Ashcroft, B., Griffiths, G., & Tiffin, H. (2002). *The empire writes back* (2nd ed.) Routledge.

Badaracco, J. L., Jr. (2006). *Questions of character: Illuminating the heart of leadership through literature*. Harvard Business School Press.

Baldick, C. (2015). *Oxford dictionary of literary terms* (4th ed.). Oxford University Press.

Baldwin, J. (1983). *Notes of a native son*. Beacon Press.

Baldwin, J. (1985a). If Black English isn't a language, then tell me, what is? In *The price of the ticket: Collected nonfiction 1948–1985* (pp. 649–652). St. Martin's Press.

Baldwin, J. (1985b). The Harlem ghetto. In *The price of the ticket: Collected nonfiction 1948–1985* (pp. 1–11). St. Martin's Press.

Baldwin, J. (1985c). A talk to teachers. In *The price of the ticket: Collected nonfiction 1948–1985* (pp. 325–332). St. Martin's Press.

Baldwin, J. (1995). Sonny's blues. In *Going to meet the man* (pp. 101–142). Vintage Books.

Baldwin, J. (1996). *Conversations with James Baldwin*. University of Mississippi.

Banks, J. A. (1998). Multiculturalism's five dimensions. An interview with Michelle Tucker for *NEA Today Online*. https://www.learner.org/wp-content/uploads/2019/02/3.Multiculturalism.pdf

Baraka, A. (2007). *Black fire: An anthology of Afro-American writing*. Black Classic Press.

Bautista, D. (2010). Comic book realism: Form and genre in Junot Díaz's *The brief wondrous life of Oscar Wao*. *Journal of the Fantastic in the Arts, 21*, 41–53.

Bell, D. (1992). The space traders. In *Faces at the bottom of the well: The permanence of racism* (pp. 158–194). HarperCollins.

Bhabha, H. (1994). *The location of culture*. Routledge.

Bigsby, C., Ed. (2007). *The Cambridge companion to August Wilson*. Cambridge University Press.

Birkenstein, J., & Hauhart, R. (Eds.). (2017). *Critical insights: Social justice and American literature*. Grey House Publishing.

Bloom, H. (1998). *Shakespeare: The invention of the human*. Riverhead Books.

Borsheim-Black, C., & Sarigianides, S. (2019). *Letting go of literary whiteness: Antiracist literature instruction for White students*. Teachers College Press

Bosmajian, H. A. (1983). *The language of oppression*. University Press of America.

Brooks, G. (1993). *Maud Martha*. Third World Press.

Browne, N. M., & Keeley, S. (2000). *Asking the right questions: A guide to critical thinking* (6th ed.). Prentice Hall.

Broyard, A. (1950, July). Portrait of the inauthentic negro: How prejudice distorts the victim's personality. *Commentary*. https://www.commentary.org/articles/commentary-bk/portrait-of-the-inauthentic-negrohow-prejudice-distorts-the-victims-personality/

Broyard, A. (1993). *Kafka was the rage*. Vintage Books.

Bryer, J. C., & Hartig, M. C., Eds. (2006). *Conversations with August Wilson*. University Press of Mississippi.

Bures, F. (2007, September/October). Chasing the whale. *Poets & Writers, 35*(5), 52–57.

Burrelle's Transcripts. (1996, Nov. 18). How'd they do that? *The Oprah Winfrey Show*. Harpo Productions.

Butler, O. (2019). *Parable of the sower*. Grand Central Publishing.

Campbell, B. M. (1982, Sept.). What to wear to the revolution. [Originally appeared in *Ms.* magazine].

Campbell, J. (1972). *The hero with a thousand faces*. MJF Books.

Carroll, R. (1995). August Wilson. In *Swing low: Black men writing*, pp. 245–266. Crown Trade Paperbacks.

Céspedes, D., & Torres-Saillant, S. (2000). Fiction is the poor man's cinema: An interview with Junot Díaz. *Callalo: A journal of African-American and African arts and letters, 23*(3), 892–907. www.jstor.org/stable/3299679

Chamoiseau, P. (1997). *Texaco*. Random House.

Charters, A. (2003). *A story and its writer: An introduction to short fiction*. Bedford/St. Martin's.

Childress, A. (1986). *Like one of the family: Conversations from a domestic's life*. Beacon Press.

Chin, M. (2018). *A portrait of the self as nation: New and selected poems* (p. 25). W. W. Norton & Co.

Christian, B. T., Ed. (1994). *Everyday use, Alice Walker*. Rutgers University Press.

Cisneros, S. (1991). *The house on mango street*. Vintage.

Cisneros, S. (2002). Becoming a Latina writer. In R. DiYanni (Ed.), *Literature: Reading fiction, poetry, and drama* (5th ed.) (pp. 246–248). McGraw-Hill.

Clarke, J. H., Ed. (1997). *The second crucifixion of Nat Turner*. Black Classic Press.

Cleage, P. (1993). Hairpeace. *African American Review*, 27(1), 37–41.

Coleman, J. W. (2001). *Black male fiction and the legacy of Caliban*. University of Kentucky Press.

Collins, B. (2001). *Poetry 180: A poem a day for American high schools*. www.loc.gov /programs/poetry-and-literature/poet-laureate/poet-laureate-projects/poetry -180/

Collins, B. (2003). *Poetry 180: A turning back to poetry*. Random House.

Collins, B. (2005). The lanyard. In *The trouble with poetry* (pp. 45–46). Random House.

Comparison between Mexican-American and Anglo-American belief systems. (n.d.) Handout.

Connolly, J. (2005, June). Course handout. *Global mythologies*. Faculty Resource Network Seminar. New York University.

Conrad, J. (2006). *Heart of darkness*. W. W. Norton.

Cope, K. (2016). *The sympathizer: A guide for book clubs*. https://www.amazon.com /Sympathizer-Guide-Clubs-Reading-Group-ebook/dp/B01FT38LSA

Cullen, C. (2020). Incident. In Kevin Young (Ed.), *African American poetry: 250 years of struggle and song* (p. 160). Library of America.

Cummins, J. (2020). *American dirt*. Flatiron Books.

Danticat, E. (1996). Nineteen thirty-seven. In *Krik? krak!* (pp. 31–49). Random House.

Danticat, E. (1998). *The farming of bones*. Penguin.

Danticat, E. (2011). *Create dangerously: The immigrant artist at work*. Vintage.

Danticat, E. (2020). Hot air balloons. In *Everything inside* (pp. 109–130). Vintage.

Delbanco, A. (1997). *Required reading: Why our American classics matter now*. Farrar, Straus, and Giroux.

Díaz, J. (1996). *Drown*. Riverhead Books.

Díaz, J. (2007a). *The brief wondrous life of Oscar Wao*. Penguin.

Díaz, J. (2007b, June 11 & 18). Wildwood. *The New Yorker*, 74–87.

Díaz, J. (2008, March-April). In darkness we meet: A conversation with Junot Díaz. Interview by Armando Celayo and David Shook. *World Literature Today*, 82(2), 12–17. www.jstor.org/stable/40159661

Díaz, J. (2012a, September 30). Junot Díaz hates writing short stories. Interview by Sam Anderson. *New York Times Magazine*, 26–29. https://www.nytimes.com /2012/09/30/magazine/junot-diaz-hates-writing-short-stories.html

Díaz, J. (2012b, December 28). Junot Díaz on rewriting the story of America. Interview by Bill Moyers. Transcript. *The Bill Moyers Show*. https://billmoyers.com /episode/rewriting-the-story-of-america/

Díaz, J. (2012c, June 4 & 11). Monstro. *The New Yorker*. www.newyorker.com /books/page-turner/this-week-in-fiction-junot-daz-2

Díaz, J. (2012d). *This is how you lose her*. Riverhead Books.

Díaz, J. (2013a). An interview with Junot Díaz. *Bookbrowse*. https://www.bookbrowse .com/author_interviews/full/index.cfm/author_number/1496/junot-diaz

Díaz, J. (2013b, December 13). *Conversation with Toni Morrison at the New York Public Library*. https://www.nypl.org/audiovideo/toni-morrison-junot-d%C3%ADaz

Díaz, J., Ed. (2016). Introduction. In *The best American short stories 2016* (pp. xii-xx). Mariner Books.

Díaz, J. (2018a). *Islandborn*. Penguin.

Díaz, J. (2018b). MFA vs. POC. In S. S. Oliver (Ed.), *Black ink: Literary legends on the peril, power, and pleasure of reading and writing* (pp. 163–172). Simon & Schuster, Inc.

Díaz, J. (2018c, April 16). The silence: The legacy of childhood trauma. *The New Yorker*. https://www.newyorker.com/magazine/2018/04/16/the-silence-the-legacy -of-childhood-trauma

"Did You Know?" (2022, Spring). In *Learning for Justice*, 2, 12.

Dove, R. (1993). Parsley. In *Selected poems* (pp. 133–136). Vintage.

Dove, R. (2003). Either I'm nobody, or I'm a nation. In H. Bloom, *Derek Walcott (Bloom's modern critical views)* (pp. 53–78). Chelsea House.

DuBois, W. E. B. (1995). *The souls of Black folk*. Signet. (Original work published 1903)

Dunbar, P. L. (2020). We wear the mask. In K. Young (Ed.), *African American poetry: 250 years of struggle and song* (p. 83). Library of America. (From *Lyrics of Lowly Life*, published in 1896)

Edmundson, M. (2004). *Why read?* Bloomsbury.

Eady, C. (2001). *Brutal imagination*. G. P. Putnam & Sons.

Ellison, R. (1994). *Shadow and act*. Quality Paperback Publishers.

Ellison, R. (1995a). *Going to the territory*. Vintage.

Ellison, R. (1995b). *Invisible man*. Vintage. (Original work published 1952)

Ervin, H. A. (1999). *African American literary criticism: 1773 to 2000*. Twayne Publishers.

Espaillat, R. P. (1998). Bilingual/bilingue. In *Where horizons go*. New Odyssey Books. www.poetryfoundation.org

Fershleiser, R., & Smith, L., Eds. (2008). *Six-word memoirs by writers famous and obscure*. HarperCollins.

Flood, A. (2013, March 22). Junot Díaz wins world's richest short story prize. *The Guardian*. https://www.theguardian.com/books/2013/mar/22/junot-diaz-wins-short -story-prize

Flood, A. (2018, Nov. 19). After 'exhaustive' independent review, the prize has re-stored the author's position as chairman of the board. *The Guardian*. https:// www.theguardian.com/books/2018/nov/19/junot-diaz-welcomed-back-by -pulitzer-prize-after-review-into-sexual-misconduct-claims

Flournoy, K. (2008). The annotated *Oscar Wao*: Notes and translations for *The Brief Wondrous Life of Oscar Wao*. www.annotated-oscar-wao.com

Forster, E. M. (1955). *Aspects of the novel*. Harcourt Brace and Company.

Foster, T. C. (2003). *How to read literature like a professor*. HarperCollins.

Francini, A. (2003). Sonnet vs. sonnet: The fourteen lines in African American poetry. *Royal Society of Arts (RSA) Journal*. www.aisna.net/wp-content/uploads/2019 /09/14francini.pdf

Freire, P. (1970). *Pedagogy of the oppressed*. Continuum.

Fulbeck, K. (2001). *Paper bullets*. University of Washington Press.

Gaines, E. J. (1993a). *A lesson before dying*. Random House.

Gaines, E. J. (1993b). A southern road to freedom. *Washington Post*. www.washing tonpost.com/archive/lifestyle/1993/07/20/a-southern-road-to-freedom/1f56f206 -39d5-4c23-aca7-e26b58e8139f/

Gaines, E. J. (1995a, April). Interview with Bernard Magnier. *UNESCO Courier*. XLVII(4), 5–7. https://unesdoc.unesco.org/ark:/48223/pf0000099844

Gaines, E. (1995b). This Louisiana thing that drives me: An interview with Ernest J. Gaines by Charles Rowell. In J. Lowe (Ed.), *Conversations with Ernest Gaines* (pp. 87–98). University Press of Mississippi.

Gaines, E. J. (2005). *Writing A Lesson Before Dying*. In M. Gaudet & R. Young (Eds.), *Mozart and Leadbelly: Stories and essays* (pp. 52–62). Alfred A. Knopf.

Garber, M. (2012). *The use and abuse of literature*. Anchor Books.

Gates, H. L., Jr. (1988). *The signifying monkey: A theory of Afro-American literary criticism*. Oxford University Press.

Gates, H. L., Jr. (1994). *Colored people*. Vintage Books.

Gates, H. L., Jr. (1998). The passing of Anatole Broyard. In *Thirteen ways of looking at a black man* (pp. 180–214). Vintage.

Gates, H. L., Jr. (2018). What is an African American classic? In S. S. Oliver (Ed.), *Black ink: Literary legends on the peril, power, and pleasure of reading and writing* (pp. 143–154). 37INK.

Gay, G. (2018). *Culturally responsive teaching* (3rd ed.). Teachers College Press.

Ginsberg, E. K., Ed. (1996). Introduction: The politics of passing. In *Passing and the fictions of identity* (p. 1). Duke University Press.

Giovanni, N. (1996). Nikki-Rosa. In *Selected poems of Nikki Giovanni* (p. 42). William Morrow and Company, Inc.

Glover, M. (1993, Sept/Oct). To kill a hog. Review of Ernest Gaines's *A Lesson Before Dying*. *The Angolite: The Prison News Magazine* 18(5), 38–39.

Goldberg, N. (2000). Moving out beyond yourself. In *Thunder and lightning: Cracking open the writer's craft* (pp. 110–115). Bantam.

Gonzales, R. (1967). Yo soy Joaquin/I am Joaquin. https://www.ginatxsboe1.com /uploads/1/2/5/5/12552697/i_am_joaquin_pdf.pdf

Graff, G. (1992). *Beyond the culture wars: How teaching the conflicts can revitalize American education*. W. W. Norton & Co.

Griffin, F. J. (2021). *Read until you understand: The profound wisdom of black life and literature*. W. W. Norton & Co.

Guerin, W. L., Labor, E., Morgan, L., Reesman, J. C., & Willingham, J. R. (2005). *A handbook of critical approaches to literature* (5th ed.) Oxford University Press.

Hagedorn, J. (1993). *Charlie Chan is dead: An anthology of contemporary Asian American fiction*. Penguin.

Hall, D. E. (2001). Race, ethnicity, and post-colonial analysis. In *Literary and cultural theory: From basic principles to advanced applications* (pp. 265–276). Houghton Mifflin Company.

Hamid, M. (2008). *The reluctant fundamentalist*. Mariner Books.

Hamilton, V. (1985). The people could fly. In *The people could fly: American Black folktales* (pp. 166–173). Alfred A. Knopf.

Hanna, M., Vargas, J. H., & Saldívar, J.D. (2016). *Junot Díaz and the Decolonial Imagination*. Duke University Press.

Hansberry, L. (1994). *A raisin in the sun*. Signet.

Harjo, J., & Bird, G. (1997). *Reinventing the enemy's language*. Norton.

Harris, M., Levitt, M., Furman, R., & Smith, E. (1974). *The Black Book*. Random House.

Harris Poll. (2014, April 29). The Bible remains America's favorite book. https://www .prnewswire.com/news-releases/the-bible-remains-americas-favorite-book-2571 14671.html

Hemingway, E. (2003). *A farewell to arms*. Scribner.

Hinton, R. H. (2018). *The sun does shine: How I found life and freedom on death row*. St. Martin's Press.

History.com. (2010). *Manifest destiny*. www.history.com/topics/westward-expansion/manifest-destiny

Hoffman, E. (1989). *Lost in translation: A new life in a new language*. Penguin.

hooks, b. (1994). *Teaching to transgress: Education as the practice of freedom*. Routledge.

Hosseini, K. (2003). *The kite runner*. Riverhead Books.

Hosseini, K. (2021, August 21). Interview with Khaled Hosseini by H. Kaur. The author of *The Kite Runner* has a message for anyone worried about Afghanistan. CNN. www.cnn.com/2021/08/21/world/khaled-hosseini-afghanistan-taliban-qa-trnd/index.html

Howard, G. R. (2016). *We can't teach what we don't know: White teachers, multiracial schools*. Teachers College.

Hoyt, A. (2011, June 27). First drafts: Gary Soto's "Talking to myself" and "Sunday without clouds." *The Atlantic*. https://www.theatlantic.com/entertainment/archive/2011/06/first-drafts-gary-sotos-talking-to-myself-and-sunday-without-clouds/241077/

Hsu, J. (2008, Aug/Sept.). The secrets of storytelling. *Scientific American Mind*, 19(4), 46–51

Hubbard, D. (1994). *The sermon and the African American literary imagination*. University of Missouri Press.

Hughes, L. (1995a). Ask your mama: 12 moods for jazz. In A. Rampersad (Ed.), *The collected poems of Langston Hughes* (pp. 472–531). Vintage Classics.

Hughes, L. (1995b). Harlem. In A. Rampersad (Ed.), *The collected poems of Langston Hughes* (p. 426). Vintage Classics.

Hughes, L. (1995c). The Negro artist and the racial mountain. In D. L. Lewis (Ed.), *The Portable Harlem Renaissance Reader* (pp. 91–95). Penguin.

Hughes, L. (1995d). There ought to be a law. In *The best of Simple* (pp. 61–63). Hill and Wang.

Hughes, L. (1995e). When the Negro was in vogue. In D. L. Lewis (Ed.), *The Portable Harlem Renaissance Reader* (pp. 77–80). Penguin.

Hurston, Z. N. (1979). How it feels to be colored me. In A. Walker (Ed.), *I love myself when I am laughing* (pp. 152–155). The Feminist Press.

Hynes, A. M., & Hynes-Berry, M. (2012). *Biblio/poetry therapy: The interactive process*. North Star Press.

Ishiguro, K. (2006). *Never let me go*. Vintage.

Jefferson, T. (2004). Notes on the state of Virginia, 1785. In G. Colombo, R. Cullen, & B. Lisle (Eds.), *Rereading America: Cultural contexts for critical reading* (pp. 551–556). Bedford/St. Martin's. (Original work published 1785.)

Jeffrey, C. (2017). *Modern India: A very short introduction*. Oxford University Press.

Johnson, J. W. (1927). *God's trombones: Seven negro sermons in verse*. Penguin.

Johnson, J. W. (2000). *Along this way: The autobiography of James Weldon Johnson*. Da Capo Press.

Kafka, F. (1972). *The metamorphosis* (Corngold, S., Trans.) Bantam Classics. (Original work published 1915)

Kakutani, M. (2012, September 20). Acclimating to America, and to women. *New York Times*. https://www.nytimes.com/2012/09/21/books/this-is-how-you-lose-her-by-junot-diaz.html

Kawabata, Y. (2006). *Palm-of-the-hand stories* (L. Dunlop & J. M. Holman, Trans.). Farrar, Straus and Giroux.

Kennedy, X. J. (2013). *Handbook of literary terms*. Pearson.

Khan, S. R. (2009, March 7). A BMW date with SRK. *The Telegraph*. https://web .archive.org/web/20091221081259/www.telegraphindia.com/1090307/jsp/enter tainment/story_10636722.jsp

Khan, S. R. (2010, Feb. 13). My name is Khan. Interview by M. Lee for *Screen Daily*. www.screendaily.com/reviews

Kick, R., Ed. (2012–2013). *The graphic canon* (Vol. 1–3). Seven Stories Press.

Klein, M. (1986). A question of identity. In H. Bloom (Ed.), *Modern critical views: James Baldwin* (pp. 17–36). Chelsea House.

Krise, T. (1999, April 14). Response to cadet email, U.S. Air Force Academy, Colorado Springs, Colorado.

Lahiri, J. (2003). *The namesake*. Mariner Books.

Lalami, L. (2018, May/June). Laila Lalami of *The Nation*. Interview with Michael Taeckens in *Poets & Writers* (pp. 73–75).

Lalami, L. (2020). *The other Americans*. Vintage Books.

Langston Hughes Project. (n.d.). http://langstonhughesproject.org

Laskin, D., & Hughes, H. (1995). *The reading group book: The complete guide to starting and sustaining a reading group*. Plume.

LeClair, T. (1994). The language must not sweat: A conversation with Toni Morrison. In D. Taylor-Guthrie (Ed.), *Conversations with Toni Morrison* (pp. 119–128). University of Mississippi Press, 1994. (Original work published 1981)

Lee, M. J. (2017). *Pachinko*. Grand Central Publishing.

Lester, J. (1987, June 14). A truly bad rabbit. *The New York Times*. www.nytimes .com/1987/06/14/books/l-a-truly-bad-rabbit-466587.html

Lester, J. (1992). *Black folktales*. Grove Press.

Locke, A. (1995). The new negro. In D. L. Lewis (Ed.), *The portable Harlem renaissance reader* (pp. 46–51). Penguin.

Loewen, J. W. (1995). Handicapped by history: The process of hero-making. In *Lies my teacher told me* (pp. 18–36). Touchstone.

Major, C. (1968). A Black criterion. In A. Chapman (Ed.), *Black voices: An anthology of Afro-American literature*. Penguin.

Makeba, M. (1991). Spirit. In D. W. Riley (Ed.), *My soul looks back, 'less I forget: A collection of quotations by people of color* (p. 380). HarperCollins.

Mandela, N. (1994). *Long walk to freedom: The autobiography of Nelson Mandela*. Little, Brown and Company.

McIntosh, P. (1989). *White privilege: Unpacking the invisible knapsack*. The National SEED project–Wellesley Centers for Women. Wellesley College. https:// nationalseedproject.org/Key-SEED-Texts/white-privilege-unpacking-the-invisible -knapsack

McKay, C. (2020). If we must die. In K. Young (Ed.), *African American poetry: 250 years of struggle and song* (p. 228). Library of America.

McKay, N. (1998). Jean Toomer in his time: An introduction. In T. B. O'Daniel (Ed.), *Jean Toomer: A critical evaluation* (pp. 3–13). Howard University Press.

McLaughlin, E. C. (2022, June 4). Book banning in the US: These are the authors of color who censors are trying to silence. CNN. www.cnn.com/2022/06/04/us /banned-book-authors/index.html

Meyer, M. (2011). A study of Billy Collins: The author reflects on five poems. In *Literature to go* (pp. 525–549). Bedford/St. Martin's.

Micucci, D. (1994). An inspired life: Toni Morrison writes and a generation listens. In D. Taylor-Guthrie (Ed.), *Conversations with Toni Morrison* (pp. 275–279). University Press of Mississippi.

Miller, B., & Paola, S. (2004). *Tell it slant: Writing and shaping creative nonfiction.* McGraw-Hill.

Momaday, N. S. (1989). *House made of dawn.* Harper and Row.

Momaday, N. S. (1998). *The man made of words.* St. Martin's.

Moore, A. (1987). *Watchmen #12: A stronger loving world.* DC Comics.

Morrison, T. (1977). *Song of Solomon.* Penguin.

Morrison, T. (1984). Rootedness: The ancestor as foundation. In M. Evans (Ed.), *Black women writers (1950–1980): A Critical Evaluation* (pp. 339–345). Anchor Books.

Morrison, T. (1990). Unspeakable things unspoken: The Afro-American presence in American literature. In H. Bloom (Ed)., *Modern critical views: Toni Morrison* (pp. 201–230). Chelsea House Publishers.

Morrison, T. (1992). *Playing in the dark: Whiteness and the literary imagination.* Vintage.

Morrison, T. (1993). The art of fiction. *The Paris Review.* https://www.theparisreview .org/interviews/1888/the-art-of-fiction-no-134-toni-morrison.

Morrison, T. (1994a). *The bluest eye.* Plume. (Original work published 1970)

Morrison, T. (1994b). *The Nobel lecture in literature, 1993.* Alfred A. Knopf.

Morrison, T. (1998). The site of memory. In W. Zinsser (Ed.), *Inventing the truth: The art and craft of memoir* (pp. 185–200). Houghton Mifflin Co.

Morrison, T. (1999). This amazing, troubling book. In M. Twain, *The adventures of Huckleberry Finn* (pp. 385–392). Norton Critical Edition. W.W. Norton & Co.

Morrison, T. (2000, April 27). *How can values be taught in the university?* Paper presented at the Center for Human Values, Princeton University.

Morrison, T. (2004). *Beloved.* Vintage. (Original work published in 1987).

Morrison, T. (2017). *The origin of others.* Harvard University Press.

Mura, D. (2018). *A stranger's journey: Race, identity, and narrative craft in writing.* University of Georgia Press.

Murayama, M. (1988). *All I asking for is my body.* University of Hawaii Press. (Original work published 1959)

Myers, W. D. (2008). *Monster.* HarperCollins.

Nabokov, V. (1991). *The annotated Lolita.* Vintage.

Nafisi, A. (2008). *Reading Lolita in Tehran.* Random House.

Nafisi, A. (2022). *Read dangerously: The subversive power of literature in troubled times.* HarperCollins.

Naylor, G. (1995). The love of books. In D. Osen, *The writing life* (pp. 167–175). Random House.

NDN Collective. (2022). *Dedicated to building indigenous power.* https://ndncollec tive.org

Nguyen, V. T. (2015). *The sympathizer.* Grove Press.

Noah, T. (2020, Feb. 3). Tackling on-screen Asian representation with "Interior Chinatown." On Trevor Noah's *The Daily Show.* Interview with Charles Yu. YouTube. https://www.youtube.com/watch?v=j0afVYOb4kA

Norris, B. (2010). *Clybourne Park.* Farrar, Straus and Giroux.

Norris, M. (2010). The race card project. https://theracecardproject.com

O'Brien, T. (1998). *The things they carried*. Broadway Books.

Orange, T. (2019). *There there*. Vintage.

Owens, L. (1994). *Other destinies: Understanding the America Indian novel*. University of Oklahoma.

Ozeki, R. (n/d). *A tale for the time being reader's guide*. Penguin Random House. www.penguinrandomhouse.com/books/312488/a-tale-for-the-time-being-by -ruth-ozeki/readers-guide

Ozeki, R. (2013). *A tale for the time being*. Penguin.

Pratt, D. D., & Collins, J. B. (2000). *The teaching perspectives nventory (TPI)*. Adult Education Research Conference. http://newprairiepress.org.aerc/2000/papers/68

Prejean, H. (1994). *Dead man walking*. Vintage.

Prose, F. (2006). *Reading like a writer*. HarperPerennial.

Proust, M. (2004). *Swann's way*. Vol. 1 of *Remembrance of Things Past* (Lydia Davis, Trans.). Penguin.

Ramdas, A. (1998). Introduction to *Madame Bovary*. *Callalo: A journal of African American arts and letters, 21*(3), 523–528.

Reed, I. (1989). *Flight to Canada*. Atheneum.

Rich, A. (1986). *Blood, bread, and poetry: Selected prose 1979–1986*. Penguin.

Richter, D. H. (Ed.). (2000). *Falling into theory: Conflicting views on reading literature* (2nd ed.). Bedford/St. Martin's

Rodriguez, R. (1982). *Hunger of memory*. Bantam Books.

Rushdie, S. (2006, October 27). Salman Rushdie—Secular values, human rights and Islamism. [Speech, audio recording]. *Point of Inquiry*. https://pointofinquiry.org /2006/10/salman_rushdie_secular_values_human_rights_and_islamism/

Said, E. W. (1979). *Orientalism*. Vintage Books.

Said, E. (1980, January 1). Islam through Western eyes. *Genius*. https://genius.com /Edward-said-islam-through-western-eyes-annotated

Said, E. (2001, January). Globalizing literary study. *Publications of the Modern Language Association, 116*(1), 64–68. Cambridge University.

Sartre, J. P. (1994). *Literature and existentialism* (B. Frechtman, Trans.). Carol Publishing Group.

Satrapi, M. (2004). *Persepolis*. Pantheon.

Schutz, M. (2011, July 3). Upcoming New South "Huck Finn" eliminates the "N" word. *Publishers Weekly*. https://www.publishersweekly.com/pw/by-topic/industry-news /publisher-news/article/45645-upcoming-newsouth-huck-finn-eliminates-the-n -word.html

Schuyler, G. S. (1999). *Black no more*. Modern Library. (Original work published 1931)

Sembène, O. (1992). *Niiwam and Taaw*. Heinemann.

Shange, N. (1980). *For colored girls who have considered suicide when the rainbow is enuf*. Bantam.

Shannon, S. G. (Ed.). (2016). *August Wilson's Pittsburgh cycle: Critical perspectives on the plays*. McFarland & Company, Inc.

Shannon, S. G., & Richards, S. L. (Eds.). (2016). *Approaches to teaching the plays of August Wilson*. Modern Language Association.

Silko, L. M. (1977). *Ceremony*. Penguin.

Smiley, J. (2006). *Thirteen ways of looking at the novel*. Anchor Books.

Smitherman, G. (1985). *Talkin and testifyin: The language of Black America*. Wayne State University Press.

Smitherman, G. (2000). *Black talk: Words and phrases from the hood to the amen corner*. Houghton Mifflin Company.

Somé, M. P. (1994). *Of water and the spirit*. Penguin.

Sontag, S. (1966). Against interpretation. In *Against interpretation* (pp. 3–14). Farrar, Strauss and Giroux.

Soto, G. (1995). Mexicans begin jogging. In *Gary Soto: New and selected poems* (p. 51). Chronicle Books.

Soto, G. (2022). Gary Soto official website. https://garysoto.com

Spiegelman, A. (1986). *Maus*. Pantheon.

Stanford Encyclopedia of Philosophy. (2007). Identity politics. http://plato.stanford.edu/entries/identity-politics

Staples, B. (2000). Black men and public space. In X. J. Kennedy, D. M. Kennedy, & J. E. Aaron (Eds.), *The Bedford reader* (7th ed.) (pp. 168–173). Bedford/St. Martin's.

Stepto, R. B. (1979). Teaching Afro-American literature: Survey or tradition. In D. Fisher & R. B. Stepto (Eds.), *Afro-American literature: The reconstruction of instruction* (pp. 8–23). Modern Language Association of America.

Stepto, R. B. (2010). *A home elsewhere: Reading African American classics in the age of Obama*. Harvard University.

Sutherland, J. (2006). *How to read a novel*. St. Martin's Griffin.

Tan, A. (n.d). *The joy luck club reader's guide*. Penguin Random House. www.penguinrandomhouse.com/books/300526/the-joy-luck-club-by-amy-tan/9780143038092/readers-guide/

Tan, A. (1989). *The joy luck club*. Ivy Books.

Tan, A. (1996, December). In the canon, for all the wrong reasons. *Harper's Magazine*. From Required reading and other dangerous subjects (Fall issue). *The Threepenny Review*. https://harpers.org/archive/1996/12/in-the-canon-for-all-the-wrong-reasons/

Tolstoy, L. (2008). A few words apropos of the book *War and Peace*. In *War and peace*, R. Pevear & L. Volokhonsky (Trans.) (p. 1217). Vintage Classics. (Original work published in 1865).

Toomer, J. (1982). The blue meridian. In D. T. Turner (Ed.), *The Wayward and the Seeking: A Collection of Writings by Jean Toomer* (pp. 214–234). Howard University Press.

Toomer, J. (1988). *Cane*. W.W. Norton & Co.

Trask, H-K. (1994). Comin home. In *Light in the Crevice Never Seen* (p. 19–22). Calyx Books.

United Nations. (1948). *Universal declaration of human rights*. www.un.org/en/about-us/universal-declaration-of-human-rights

Vuong, O. (2019). *On earth we're briefly gorgeous*. Penguin.

Wade-Gayles, G. (1997). *No crystal stair: Visions of race and gender in Black women's fiction*. Pilgrim Press.

Walcott, D. (2014). The schooner *Flight*. In *The poetry of Derek Walcott 1948–2013* (pp. 237–252). Farrar, Straus and Giroux.

Walker, A. (1973). Everyday use. In *In love & trouble: Stories of black women* (pp. 47–59). Harcourt Brace & Co.

Walker, A. (1981). Nineteen fifty-five. In *You can't keep a good woman down* (pp. 3–20). Harcourt Brace & Company.

Walker, A. (1983). In search of our mothers' gardens. In *In search of our mothers' gardens* (pp. 231–243). Harcourt Brace Jovanovich.

Walker, M. (2019). *For my people.* Yale University Press.

Washington, D. A. (2007). Teaching *Song of Solomon*: Exploring the LIST paradigm. In J. L. Carlacio (Ed.), *The fiction of Toni Morrison: Reading and writing on race, culture, and identity.* National Council of Teachers of English.

Washington, D. A. (2008, Summer). Teaching Ernest Gaines's *A lesson before dying. Academic Exchange Quarterly* 12(2). 238–244.

Washington, D. A. (2015). Exploring the LIST paradigm: Reading and teaching *beloved.* In M. N. Eke (Ed.), *Critical insights: Beloved.* Grey House Publishing.

Watkins-Goffman, L. (2006). *Understanding cultural narratives: Exploring identity and the multicultural experience.* University of Michigan Press.

Watson, D., Hagopian, J., & Au, W. (Eds.) (2018). *Teaching for Black lives.* Rethinking Schools.

Waxman, O. B. (2022, Jan. 31). Why Toni Morrison's books are so often the target of book bans. *Time Magazine.* https://time.com/6143127/toni-morrison-book-bans/

Wideman, J. E. (2006). Stories. In J. Thomas & R. Shapard (Eds.), *Flash fiction forward* (pp. 9–10). W. W. Norton and Co.

Wilson, A. (1985). *Ma Rainey's black bottom.* Plume.

Wilson, A. (1986). *Fences.* Plume.

Wilson, A. (1988). *Joe Turner's come and gone.* Plume.

Wilson, A. (1990). *The piano lesson.* Plume.

Wilson, A. (2005). Preface. *King Hedley II.* Theatre Communications Group.

Wolfe, G. (1987). The last mama-on-the-couch play. In *The colored museum.* Broadway Play Publishing, Inc.

Womack, Y. L. (2013). *Afrofuturism: The world of black sci-fi and fantasy culture.* Lawrence Hill Books.

Woodson, C. G. (1933). *The mis-education of the negro.* Associated Publishers.

Wright, R. (1995a). Blueprint for Negro writing. In D. L. Lewis (Ed.), *The Portable Harlem Renaissance Reader* (pp. 194–205). Penguin.

Wright, R. (1996). The man who lived underground. In *Eight men* (pp. 19–84). HarperPerennial.

Wright, R. (1998a). *Black boy (American hunger).* Perennial Classics.

Wright, R. (1998b). *Native son.* Perennial Classics.

Wright, R. (2020). Between the world and me. In K. Young (Ed.), *African American poetry: 250 years of struggle and song* (p. 377). Library of America.

Young, K. (2016). Blacker than thou. In Jesmyn Ward (Ed.), *The fire this time: A new generation speaks about race.* Scribner.

Young, P. (2000). *Ernest Hemingway: A reconsideration.* Penn State University Press.

Young, V. A., Barrett, R., Young-Rivera, Y., & Lovejoy, K. B. (2014). *Other people's English: Code-meshing, code-switching, and African American literacy.* Teachers College Press.

Yousif, N. (2002, July 28). *Pop Francis: The pontiff's 'pilgrimage of penance' to Canada.* Preda Foundation: People's Recovery, Empowerment and Development Assistance. https://www.preda.org/2002/pope-francis-the-pontiffs-pilgrimage-of-penance-to-canada

Yu, C. (2020). *Interior chinatown.* Vintage.

Index

About the Author

Durthy A. Washington—a former English professor, technical writer, and writing center director—has taught graduate, undergraduate, and adult education courses at numerous colleges and universities, including Colorado College, The University of Colorado at Colorado Springs (UCCS), and the U.S. Air Force Academy, where she received the Outstanding Academy Educator Award. Durthy is the founder of *LitUnlocked*, which provides workshops and seminars on the art of mindful, culturally responsive reading. Each course centers on the **LIST Paradigm**, a unique, guided approach to literary analysis that can help readers "unlock" a text with four *keys to culture*: Language, Identity, Space, and Time.

Durthy has developed four Literary Study Guides (*Cliffs Notes*) on the works of African American authors: Toni Morrison, Harriet Jacobs, Ralph Ellison, and Ernest Gaines. Her writings include numerous critical essays, book reviews, and book chapters. She has twice served as Visiting Scholar for Language Matters Teaching Initiative, a series of faculty development workshops for high school teachers on teaching the works of Toni Morrison, sponsored by the Toni Morrison Society and funded by the National Endowment for the Humanities (NEH). Her commitment to culturally responsive reading and teaching has taken her to Tokyo, Japan; Senegal, West Africa; and St. Petersburg, Russia.

She lives in Colorado Springs, Colorado, with her books, her plants, and her MacBook Air.

Durthy A. Washington is available for select speaking engagements. To inquire about a possible appearance, please contact durthy@gmail.com.

Printed and bound by CPI Group (UK) Ltd, Croydon, CR0 4YY

09/06/2025

14685976-0001